The Future of
American Strategy

David C. Hendrickson

The Future of
American Strategy

Holmes & Meier
New York   London

355.033
H49f

First published in the United States of America 1987 by
Holmes & Meier Publishers, Inc.
30 Irving Place
New York, N.Y. 10003

Great Britain:
Pindar Road, Hoddesdon
Hertfordshire, EN11 0HF England

Book design by Gloria Tso

Library of Congress Cataloging-in-Publication Data

Hendrickson, David C.
    The future of American strategy.

    Bibliography: p.
    Includes index.
    1. United States—Military policy.   2. Strategy.
I. Title.
UA 23.H447   1987   355'.0335'73   86-25665
ISBN 0-8419-1104-5
ISBN 0-8419-1105-3 (pbk.)

Manufactured in the United States of America

Contents

v

List of Exhibits

List of Abbreviations

ASEAN	Association of South East Asian Nations
CENTCOM	Central Command
GDP	Gross Domestic Product
ICBM	Intercontinental ballistic missile
mbd	millions of barrels a day
RDJTF	Rapid Deployment Joint Task Force
SDI	
SLCM	Sea-launched cruise missile(s)
SSBN	Ballistic missile nuclear submarine(s)

Acknowledgments

I began this study in the "original position" described by the philosopher John Rawls—that is, behind a "veil of ignorance." Most of the ideas of the study were conceived in a seventeen-month period from April 1982 to August 1983 during which my wife and I lived along Deep Creek Lake in western Maryland. This time of reading and reflection was indispensable in the formation of the book. For making the enterprise possible, I owe a great debt of gratitude to the Institute for Educational Affairs and to the family members—Calvin and Frances, Christy and Richard—who helped support the undertaking. I remain grateful to Roger Kaplan and Ken Jensen for giving the project encouragement at an early stage. For serious discussions in the midst of fishing expeditions, and for innumerable ideas that wound their way into the manuscript, thanks are due to Seth Carus, Paul Dyster, David Mapel, and Walter Nelson. And I would also like to express my gratitude to the staff of the Ruth Enlow Library in Oakland, Maryland, for its valuable assistance in procuring materials on inter-library loan.

Early versions of the work were presented in three seminars at the Lehrman Institute in New York from January 1984 to April 1985. Nicholas X. Rizopoulos, Michael Mandelbaum, and Linda Wrigley of the Institute's staff have been more than generous in their advice and encouragement. Among the some forty-five individuals who participated in the seminars at the Institute, I would particularly like to thank James Chace, David Gompert, Josef Joffe, Donald Kagan, Paul Kennedy, Thomas McNaugher, Steven Miller, Daniel Pipes, Barry Posen, Jack Snyder, and Richard Ullman for comments that—though often quite critical—were invaluable in revising the manuscript.

Thanks are due to The Colorado College for making available a period of time to complete the manuscript, and for defraying various expenses associated with it. A number of my colleagues in the Political Science Department and in the Faculty Seminar on War and Peace in the Nuclear Age gave generously of their time in criticizing various parts of the book, for which I am most grateful. The detailed comments of Curtis Cook were particularly valuable, as were those of an outside reader, Benson Adams.

My two greatest debts are to Robert W. Tucker and to my wife, Clelia deMoraes. The support and generosity of Dr. Tucker reach back almost a decade, to the time when I first became his graduate assistant. Throughout our long and happy association, his political insight and intellectual honesty have remained a source of steady inspiration. To my wife I owe all the usual superlatives. She not only improved the manuscript; she improved its author. This was and remains a difficult task, which she has always gone about with wit and understanding. It is to her that this book is affectionately dedicated.

One may go wrong in many
different ways (because, as the
Pythagoreans expressed it, evil is of
the class of the infinite, good of the
finite), but right only in one; and so
the former is easy, the latter difficult;
easy to miss the mark, but hard to
hit it: and for these reasons,
therefore, both the excess and defect
belong to Vice, and the mean state
to Virtue.
> —Aristotle, *Ethics*

One must be a fox to recognize
traps, and a lion to frighten wolves.
Those who wish to be only lions do
not understand this.
> —Machiavelli,
> *The Prince*

**The Future of
American Strategy**

Introduction

The Nature of Strategic Thought

Strategy, as the British military strategist Sir Basil Liddell Hart had it, is "the art of distributing and applying military means to fulfill the ends of policy."[1] For Helmuth von Moltke, the head of the German General Staff, it consisted of "the practical adaptation of the means at hand to the ends in view."[2] Both of these views, in turn, are simply variations on the theme of Clausewitz that "war is an instrument of policy"—strategic thought being concerned with reconciling the two fundamental data in Clausewitz's formulation.

For our purposes Moltke's succinct definition is perhaps the best point of departure, though it should not be forgotten that the ends in view may themselves be affected by the means at hand—that policy, in Raymond Aron's phrase, "must know the instrument it is to employ."[3] Still, Moltke's definition has the merit of not restricting the field of investigation to military considerations as such, even though Moltke himself might be fairly charged with having done so. No such restricted field of vision can take in the infinite variety of political, economic, social, and moral considerations that—in addition to operational, logistical, and technological factors—have in past wars so often proven decisive.[4] All these factors the strategist must register and examine. It was not "for want of a nail" that America's war in Vietnam was lost; the cause of defeat was social and moral, an inevitable outcome of the strategy we chose in pursuit of victory.[5] It was not for want of dedication and competence in the admirals of the Royal Navy that Great Britain lost in the twentieth century the command of the seas. The fall of the Second British Empire had as its root cause the incessant erosion of British economic strength.[6] That its power was dissipated in a just and necessary cause and that its collapse was the outcome of

1

an antagonism from which it could not safely disengage makes the lesson no less disturbing and sobering. Over time, economic considerations are basic to strategic calculation, as all great and enduring empires have shown by their constant attention to and prudent use of the means at their disposal. War, Clausewitz declared, has its own grammar but not its own logic. In the search for that logic we are forced to go beyond the narrowly military, recognizing that the factors comprising strategy constitute a seamless web, and always keeping in mind the lesson that the most common mistakes in strategic analysis stem from the failure to widen the focus.

Breadth of focus, however, ought not to be confused with a lack of direction. If light is cast from many directions, the strategist nevertheless refracts it through a single prism. The nature of that prism was best characterized by Walter Lippmann in a little book published in 1943. Seeking to identify the "fundamental principle of a foreign policy," Lippmann gave currency to the term "solvency" for describing the condition to which American policy should aspire—a point of departure that has been adopted by many subsequent writers.[7] He meant by it an objective that seeks to bring commitments and power into balance, and he rightly averred that "without the controlling principle that the nation must maintain its objectives and its power in equilibrium, its purposes within its means and its means equal to its purposes, its commitments related to its resources and its resources adequate to its commitments, it is impossible to think at all about foreign affairs."[8] Without this controlling principle it is equally impossible to think about strategy.

Lippmann wrote at a time, in 1943, when the fully awakened armed might of the United States was leading it, in conjunction with the Soviet Union, to total victory over Nazi Germany and Imperial Japan. That victory led to an extension of the American strategic frontier so great as to be virtually beyond the imagination of those whose intellectual world was shaped by the debates of the 1930s. In 1943 the outlines of that future world were as yet dim. The mistakes of previous policy, by contrast, stood forth vividly. The central mistake, according to Lippmann, had been a failure to match military capabilities with political commitments. In Asia that failure was most vividly demonstrated, Lippmann believed, by the Washington Naval Conference in 1921–22, in which the United States acquiesced in a distribution of naval power in the Pacific that left the Philippines defenseless and disabled the United States from vindicating interests in China that it deemed vital. In Europe, that failure was dramatized by the unwillingness of the American people to assist France and Britain in the preservation of their independence until France had fallen and Britain faced its moment of supreme peril. In neither the Pacific nor the Atlantic did we maintain a sufficient degree of power to vindicate commitments that had been ours since the turn of the century. Nor did we look upon our permanent allies with an attitude commensurate with their importance in preserving our own interests from danger.

Only a few years later, in 1947, Lippmann wrote as a critic of the opposite danger.[9] Whereas before he had criticized the failure of the policy of American isolationism, he now warned of the dangers of intervention. Whereas before he had seen the insolvency of policy in terms of an inadequacy of American military power, he now saw it in terms of an excess of political commitment. This was particularly true of American policy in Asia and in what came to be known as the Third World, and it was here, indeed, that Lippmann's views were most prescient. He warned of the dangers of committing the United States to the resistance of communist aggression wherever it might occur and irrespective of the national interests it might endanger. His criticism of the Truman Doctrine and of the 1947 "X" article in *Foreign Affairs* that he took—fairly or not—as the justification of this doctrine thus summed up at the outset of the Cold War what would become the dominant theme of the liberal-realist critique of postwar American foreign policy.

Lippmann's approach to the problem of solvency in these two seminal essays of the 1940s was that the key to its resolution lay in finding the appropriate balance between military power and political commitment. That remains our task today. In seeking to resolve the American strategic predicament, we must not divorce, as Lippmann said we once did,

the discussion of our war aims, our peace aims, our ideals, our interests, our commitments, from the discussion of our armaments, our strategic position, our potential allies and our probable enemies. No policy could emerge from such a discussion. For what settles practical controversy is the knowledge that ends and means have to be balanced: an agreement has eventually to be reached when men admit that they must pay for what they want and that they must want only what they are willing to pay for.[10]

The Subject of This Book

The practical controversy this book addresses is the direction that ought to be taken by American defense policy and strategy. The central questions it investigates include:

—the identification and assessment of military threats, and the attempt to strike a balance between those that are least likely but most serious, on the one hand, and those that are most likely yet least dangerous, on the other;[11]

—the division of our attention, in force planning, between Europe and the rest of the world;

—the character of our interest in the Persian Gulf, and the economic and military means best calculated to secure it;

—the extent of our reliance on nuclear as opposed to conventional weapons in Europe, the Persian Gulf, and Korea;

—the proper mix of offensive and defensive forces in nuclear strategy;

—reflection on the object of military action, whether the forcible disarmament of the enemy's military power (annihilation) or the disruption of his morale through exhaustion or shock (attrition);

—the determination of "the circumstances under which and how American forces would be used in combat: for example, offensively or defensively, in long wars or short wars, unilaterally or in conjunction with allies, in gradual increments or in a massive initial commitment";[12]

—the apportionment of resources among air, naval, and ground forces, and the corresponding choice among continental or maritime strategies;

—the choice between modernization and readiness, active and reserve forces, forward deployments and strategic mobility, a volunteer or a conscripted military force;

—above all, the reconciliation of political commitment and military power, which in turn rests upon an assessment of the real character of our interests in the world—vital and otherwise—and an appreciation of the uses and limitations of military force in vindicating those interests.

These have long been the primary conundrums of American defense strategy, and they promise to remain so for many years to come. How they might best be resolved is the subject of this book. Because my focus is on defense policy as such, the inquiry falls well short of *grand strategy,* which Edward Mead Earle once defined as "the art of controlling and utilizing the resources of a nation—or a coalition of nations—including its armed forces, to the end that its vital interests shall be effectively promoted and secured against enemies, actual, potential, or merely presumed."[13] There are some questions in foreign and economic policy, to be sure, that are so inextricably tied to the purposes of our military establishment and the resources made available to it that they must be addressed. Of these, the most important are:

—the appropriate level of military expenditures in relation to competing social and economic purposes;

—the shape of American energy policy;

—the objectives of arms control negotiations with the Soviet Union; and

—a host of diplomatic questions associated with the two areas of the world, Europe and the Persian Gulf, that have recently placed the most extensive prospective demands on American military power.

I examine these issues because the consideration of defense policy would not be coherent without detailed attention to them. But other questions in American foreign and economic policy, although perhaps equally important in the grand scheme of things (and therefore of concern to the grand strategist), are neglected or given only the most cursory attention here.

This book was written under the conviction that the United States must learn to discriminate among competing strategic concepts with far greater care than was customary in the 1980s. The crisis in the nation's fiscal accounts, which will almost certainly outlast the Reagan presidency, will make for continual pressures on the defense budget, and there is the clear and present danger that the cuts will fall equally on the good and the bad, undermining the progress the Reagan administration has made in overcoming the "hollowness" of American forces. For the late 1980s and early 1990s, a retrenchment appears to be inevitable, and it is desirable that it be undertaken on the basis of strategic—as opposed to haphazard or last-minute—criteria. We therefore require the contemporary equivalent of Eisenhower's New Look and Nixon's Doctrine, both of which enjoyed an extraordinary degree of success in choosing among priorities at times of fiscal stringency. In seeking that equivalent, we will have to overcome a persistent tendency to exaggerate our interests and depreciate our power. The interests most often exaggerated, I argue, lie in the Third World; the power most often depreciated resides in our air and naval forces, both conventional and nuclear.

Little attention is given in this work to the domestic and bureaucratic milieu in which military policy necessarily functions. And I have tried to avoid the detailed discussion of particular weapons systems, confining my observations to a level of generality consistent with the responsibility of civilians in the making of national stategy. The significance of organizational and bureaucratic factors in the determination of American military policy, and the question of how responsibility over strategy, operations, and administration should best be allocated between civilians and the military, are among the problems that I take up in a companion work to be published in 1987, entitled *Reforming Defense: An Inquiry into the State of American Civil-Military Relations.* Two themes that run throughout that work deserve mention here. One is that the president and his principal civilian advisers enjoy more latitude in the making of national strategy than it has become customary to believe. Although their ability to chart new directions is limited by an array of bureaucratic and political interests, they can make a real difference at the margin, and, if they are bold, undertake changes of far-reaching significance. We in any case depend upon the president to rise above the fray and to adopt a perspective appropriate to the national character of the office. In defense policy, at least, and under our system of governance, there is literally no one else to do it.

Perhaps the most striking feature of the defense debate in the 1980s has been the extraordinary amount of interest in military reform. Many have proposed far-reaching changes in the organization of the military establishment and in the procedures by which weapons are procured, all of which I consider in *Reforming Defense*. But such reforms, valuable though some of them may be, are no substitute for strategic vision, and we delude ourselves if we come to believe that the American strategic predicament can be rendered much less acute, or our strategic choices much less painful, by organizational or institutional change. Nor is this all. The true grounds of strategic choice lie in the realm of high policy, and on this basis alone the call for the reformation of American strategy made herein ought to be sharply distinguished from the enterprise that now goes by the name of "military reform." The thoroughgoing change in the tactics, doctrines, and weapons systems of the military services called for by the military reformers is, I believe, a misguided project. Although the reformers differ in many respects from one another, they share the belief that the understanding of warfare displayed by our military men is almost wholly mistaken, and therefore they seek to reform the services from the ground up. Yet by focusing attention on the details of weapons systems and tactics, the enterprise deflects attention from the fundamental problems of national strategy with which civilian statesmen and strategists ought properly to concern themselves. Of even greater importance, the reform project is incompatible with the institutional considerations that ought to govern the direction and control of the military establishment. Civilians must know not only how to direct but also how to delegate, rendering "unto the civilians the things that are civilian, and unto the brass the things that are brass." A failure to respect this basic principle of military policy will yield not coherence but institutional confusion and strategic disarray.

Notes

1. B. H. Liddell Hart, *Strategy: The Indirect Approach* (New York, 1954), 335.
2. Ibid., 100.
3. Raymond Aron, *Peace and War: A Theory of International Relations* (New York, 1967), 40.
4. See Michael Howard, "The Forgotten Dimensions of Strategy," in *The Causes of War and Other Essays* (Cambridge, Mass., 1983).
5. Cf. Bernard Brodie, *War and Politics* (New York, 1973), 146.
6. See Paul M. Kennedy, *The Rise and Fall of British Navy Mastery* (New York, 1976), xv–xvi.
7. Walter Lippmann, *U.S. Foreign Policy: Shield of the Republic* (Boston, 1943).

See also Robert W. Tucker, *The Purposes of American Power: An Essay on National Security* (New York, 1981), and James Chace, *Solvency: The Price of Survival* (New York, 1981).

8. Lippmann, *U.S. Foreign Policy*, 7.

9. Walter Lippmann, *The Cold War: A Study in U.S. Foreign Policy* (New York, 1972).

10. Lippmann, *U.S. Foreign Policy*, 7–8.

11. Cf. Michael Howard, *The Continental Commitment: The Dilemma of British Defence Policy in the Era of the Two World Wars* (London, 1972), 10.

12. Samuel P. Huntington, "Defense Organization and Military Strategy," *The Public Interest* (Spring 1984), 26.

13. See "Introduction," *Makers of Modern Strategy: Military Thought from Machiavelli to Hitler,* ed. Edward Mead Earle with the collaboration of Gordon A. Craig and Felix Gilbert (Princeton, 1943), viii.

Part I
The Problem and Its Modes

1— The American Strategic Predicament

As he sat in a grove of young pines overlooking a ruined motel, the protagonist of Walker Percy's *Love in the Ruins* ruminated on the causes of the catastrophe that he believed was imminent and wondered whether

God has at last removed his blessing from the U.S.A. and what we feel now is just the clank of the old historical machinery, the sudden jerking ahead of the roller-coaster cars as the chain catches hold and carries us back into history with its ordinary catastrophes, carries us out and up toward the brink from that felicitous and privileged siding where even unbelievers admitted that if it was not God who blessed the U.S.A., then at least some great good luck had befallen us, and that now the blessing or the luck is over, the machinery clanks, the chain catches hold, and the cars jerk forward.*

The anxiety and dread reflected in this passage have been felt by many others as well over the past generation. Daniel Bell identified our condition as "the end of American exceptionalism." He saw it, like Percy, as a loss of America's customary exemption from history's ordinary catastrophes. There are many measures of such a fall from grace, and it may in the end be more revealing to render the fall from the heights in spiritual and moral terms—as Percy and Bell have done—than according to the dry statistical measures of national power.† To render it strategically is nevertheless the purpose of the following reflections.

---

*Walker Percy, *Love in the Ruins: The Adventures of a Bad Catholic at a Time Near the End of the World* (New York: Farrar, Straus & Giroux, 1971), pp. 3–4.

†See Daniel Bell, "The End of American Exceptionalism," *The American Commonwealth—1976*, Irving Kristol and Nathan Glazer, eds. (New York, 1976), 193–224; and Bell, *The Cultural Contradictions of Capitalism* (New York, 1976). And see also the fascinating work of Robert M. Adams, *Decadent Societies* (San Francisco: North Point Press, 1983).

The American *Imperium* under Challenge

The rise of the Pax Americana was one of the swiftest ascents there
has ever been in the history of the world. Favored by geography
and an equilibrium among the Great Powers at the center of world
politics, the United States grew in the nineteenth century unen-
cumbered by threats to its security from external rivals. Its situation
was such that Abraham Lincoln could boast, in 1838, that "All the
armies of Europe, Asia and Africa combined, with all the treasure
of the earth (our own excepted) in their military chest; with a
Bonaparte for a commander, could not by force, take a drink from
the Ohio, or make a track on the Blue Ridge, in a trial of a thousand
years."[1] Once the Civil War had settled the great political question
of the preceding century and determined that the resources of the
American continent were to be placed at the disposal of the Union
itself and not divided up among its contending and separate regions, it was foreordained that the United States would one day
play a great role in the politics of the world, as Tocqueville had
foreseen even before the internal question was settled.[2] The armies
that were demobilized after Lee handed Grant his sword at Ap-
pomattox Court House were larger than those of any of the continental powers of Europe; and just as the American Civil War
prefigured the coming shape of warfare, it too revealed the tremen-
dous resources that lay waiting to be tapped among the land,
industry, and peoples of the American continent. The sword, however, was laid down; the armies were disbanded. American power
was then further deepened by a single-minded concentration on
things material for the remainder of the century and beyond. In all
the indices of national power save one, we began to eclipse every
other nation in the world.

It was not until the Second World War that the true dimensions of
this power were revealed; and not until then that the United States
radically overturned and rejected the "great rule of conduct" that
George Washington had set out at the beginning of the nation's
history in his Farewell Address: in extending our commercial relations to foreign nations "to have with them as little *political* connection as possible."[3] The isolationists of the 1930s who warned, as
Washington had done, of entangling "our peace and prosperity in
the toils of European ambition, rivalship, interest, humour, or

caprice" and so subjecting ourselves to history's ordinary catastrophes were no longer heeded.[4] Nor was their advice any longer appropriate to America's new station. The two great wars of the twentieth century, so destructive of the life and civilization of Europe, were for the United States the means by which it discovered its latent strength; the latter war put an end to the Great Depression of the 1930s with a success that Roosevelt's New Deal had never achieved.

The responsibilities thrust upon the United States by its power were borne ably by the generation that conducted the Second World War and that set into policy its design for the postwar world. The political order created by American power in the aftermath of the Second World War was, as these things go, a most beneficent one. Under its aegis the peoples of Europe and Asia gave play to the creative and constructive impulses that had decayed under the shadow of war. The economic miracle was accompanied by a political miracle as Europe and Japan purged their internal demons and built constitutional democracies that offered their citizens just and stable frameworks of government unknown to the lost generation.[5] It was in this accomplishment that the real greatness of the postwar American *imperium* lay.

In the early 1960s, observers could still look forward to the perpetuation of this order for as far as the eye could see. It came under severe challenge in the 1970s. The challenge first became apparent in the 1960s, in Vietnam. But whereas the challenge of the 1960s largely revolved around the fate of the Third World, with the United States defining its interest in the emerging nations in the extraordinarily ambitious terms of a rising power, the challenge that arose in the 1970s was of a different character altogether. That challenge to the American position went to the core of the postwar order. It had three basic dimensions.

One stemmed from the growth of Soviet military power from the time of the Cuban missile crisis; another from the emergence of a security crisis in the Persian Gulf; and the third from the relative decline of the American economy. In different ways, each posed a profound threat to the ability of the United States to maintain the essentials of the postwar order. In combination, they formed the core elements of the American strategic predicament in the late 1970s. In what follows I shall consider the shape of that predicament at the end of the Carter administration. Then I hope to show why, in spite of all the efforts of the Reagan administration, that predicament remains with us still.

The Growth of Soviet Military Power

In the 1960s the Soviet Union began the long drive to achieve numerical equality with the United States in land- and sea-based ballistic missiles, an accomplishment ratified in the 1972 SALT I agreements. In the 1970s the Soviets went further, developing a fourth generation of ICBMs with greatly improved accuracy over their predecessors. This development had the effect of placing in jeopardy the survivability of American land-based ICBMs. Also undergoing modernization were a wide range of theater nuclear systems, including most prominently the SS–20 intermediate range ballistic missile and the Backfire bomber. The meaning of these developments in nuclear weaponry was the subject of prolonged debate in the United States during the 1970s, but on one point the debaters were agreed. The Soviet nuclear buildup, it appeared, put at least a temporary end to whatever thoughts most American strategists might have had of exerting "escalation dominance" in a strategic nuclear war, and it therefore further emphasized the neutralization of the American strategic arsenal. The arsenal, it was now widely believed, was only good for deterring attacks upon itself.

The apparent neutralization of the American strategic nuclear reserve occurred at a time when the balance in conventional forces was moving increasingly in the West's disfavor. The growth of Soviet naval power placed in serious question the ability of the West to retain the use of the seas in the initial stages of a conventional conflict. The Soviet Union enhanced its already formidable conventional forces in Europe, partially through an increase in their number but primarily through an extraordinarily thorough modernization effort. The introduction of the T–64 and T–72 tanks, which were the equal of the American M–60 and the German Leopard I, was only one among many elements of this change. The Soviets also introduced a new infantry fighting vehicle—the BMP—that was reputed among military experts to be one of the best in the world; they introduced new self-propelled artillery systems, which, so long as their supply trains were not disrupted, would give their artillery a greatly improved capacity for maneuver; they added to their broad range of surface-to-air missiles and air defense guns, whose effectiveness had been demonstrated in the 1973 Yom Kippur War; and they greatly improved the reach and firepower of their tactical airpower through the introduction of a new generation of fighter and attack planes. As Exhibit 1 shows, they did all of these things on a scale that dwarfed the rate prevailing in the West.[6]

EXHIBIT 1—*Production of Selected Weapons for NATO and Warsaw Pact Forces, 1974–83*

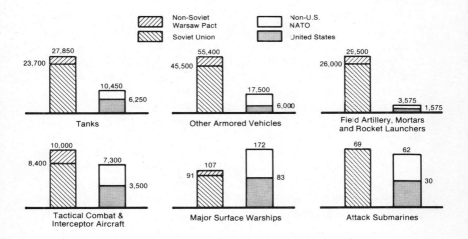

Source:—Report of the Secretary of Defense Caspar W. Weinberger to the Congress (Washington, D.C.: GPO, February 1, 1984), 23.

The expansion of Soviet conventional power was given added significance because it occurred against the background of a significant erosion in the conventional capabilities of the NATO forces. This erosion did not occur across the board. The German army was a more capable fighting force at the end of the seventies than it had been at the beginning. The American army, however, was a dif-

ferent story altogether. The promise of the McNamara years—of a
significant upgrading of American conventional capabilities in Europe—was not realized. "McNamara's policy, intended as a more
secure adjustment to changing European conditions, was made
operational just in time to sink us irreparably in the morass of
Vietnam. . . . (T)he European 'shield' had suddenly to be recon-
sidered as a Third World sword."[7] Vietnam deprived the Army not
only of the modernization of equipment suitable for European
warfare—much of which in the late 1970s dated from the 1950s—
but also of an assured source of manpower at least partly representative of a broad cross section of American life. The result, by
1980, was a "hollow Army," whose standards of tank gunnery were
the worst among the NATO armies and whose soldiers were
ridiculed by our allies. It was ironic, to say the least, that the efforts
of the Carter administration should have ended in this fashion, for
Carter's Secretary of Defense, Harold Brown, had continued and
intensified the effort begun after Vietnam to refocus the energies of
the Pentagon on the problem of fighting a conventional war with
the Soviet Union in Europe. There remains little question, however, that the effort did fail, primarily though certainly not exclusively because of the Carter administration's failure to come to
terms with the inadequacies of the All Volunteer Force.

There were many things notable about this buildup of Soviet
military power. Even though it was partially explainable by the
emergence of the Sino-Soviet rivalry, it was nevertheless concentrated in Europe. It was only possible by virtue of immense sacrifices, a fact that tells us a great deal about the significance vested in
it by the Soviet leadership. Indeed, it appeared to represent a tacit
acknowledgment on the part of the Soviet leadership that their
country had no chance of winning a race with the West in a contest
over the respective standards of living that each system afforded the
peoples under its sway, a conclusion that was very different from
that drawn by Khrushchev. It occurred against the background of
political tensions in Europe, symbolized by the four-power treaty
over Berlin and the formal recognition by the West of the territorial
changes that the Soviets had made unilaterally at the close of the
Second World War. It thus occurred precisely at the time when the
West signalled in countless ways its complete unwillingness to use
force to challenge the Soviet domination of Eastern Europe. These
signals were seen in Moscow as a demonstration of weakness. The
Soviets had not learned the lessons of Vietnam in Czechoslovakia.

In the end, the issue raised by the Soviet military buildup was not what motivation underlay it, but what the West might do to ensure that it did not lead to a permanent shift in the distribution of power. For Soviet motivations, even if defensive, could change once the results to which the buildup led were acknowledged as having come about by both sides. Those in the West who maintained that the buildup owed its scale mostly to the domestic power of the Soviet military and to the institutional momentum of its weapons programs carried a message that, in the end, failed to reassure. The great lesson taught by the history of statecraft was that such disparities in the distribution of power—whatever factors may have given rise to them—were virtually certain to issue in consequences unfavorable to the weak. The strong, to be sure, had not always profited from their strength; but the weak never profited from their weakness. To ensure that the opportunity created by the growth of Soviet military power did not transform itself at some point in the future into a motive for changing the postwar order was thus a great challenge for western security policy at the end of the 1970s. It constituted the first element of the American strategic predicament.

Energy Security and the Persian Gulf

Throughout the 1970s the growth of Soviet military capability found expression not in Europe but in the Third World. It was there, in a series of crises beginning with the 1973 Yom Kippur War and extending to the invasion of Afghanistan at the end of the decade, that the hopes of the Soviet-American détente foundered. The inclination in America to dismiss Soviet involvement in attempts to alter the status quo by force as being inherently counterproductive and involving no fundamental challenge to American interests—an analysis heavily influenced by the memory of Vietnam—steadily eroded as the Russians increased their activities in the Middle East and the Persian Gulf. The emergence of the crisis in the Gulf in effect cancelled out the strategic advantages that had been gained as a result of the Sino-Soviet split and the opening to China. The Great Game, it increasingly appeared, was being played in earnest by the Russians; and the salience of the game was underlined by the emergence of an extraordinary degree of western dependence on the oil of the Persian Gulf.

It was this increased dependence that lay at the heart of the crisis in the Persian Gulf, and which gave the Soviet Union's successes in Ethiopia and Yemen and ultimately to its invasion of Afghanistan a significance they would not otherwise have had. In 1977 Japan received 77 percent of its oil from the Persian Gulf, Western Europe 62 percent, and the United States 14 percent. Direct American dependence on the Gulf was thus still rather small, but it had grown sharply since the beginning of the decade, and it seemed to most experts that only the Persian Gulf had the reserves to increase productive capacity substantially in the decade ahead.[8] Of these nations, Saudi Arabia was clearly the most critical, and Amerian officials sought to prevail upon the Saudis to increase their productive capacity from ten to up to fourteen or even sixteen million barrels per day (mbd). Yet the Saudis seemed clearly reluctant to do so.

The fall of the shah of Iran dramatized the terrible consequences that might befall the economies of the West as a consequence of this dependence, while it underlined the inability of the West to respond to the challenge in a serious fashion. A new government arose in Iran, bitterly hostile to the United States. While this government proclaimed its defiance of the United States, the actions of our other "ally in the Gulf," Saudi Arabia, showed equally the precariousness of our situation. The great test of Saudi "moderation" came in the spring of 1979, when oil markets were deeply unsettled by the loss of Iranian production in the winter as a consequence of strikes in the oil fields and the probable future reduction of Iranian oil exports as a consequence of the new regime's oil policy. But instead of increasing their production, the Saudis reduced it, as production fell from 10.4 mbd in December of 1978 to 8.8 mbd in April of 1979. These actions by the Saudis were instrumental in driving the price increases of 1979, as prices on the spot market rose from $12.98 in October 1978 to $41.00 at the end of 1979.[9]

The conviction that lay at the heart of the crisis in the Persian Gulf was that there was no way to eliminate the critical exposure of the economies of the West to the upheavals for which the region seemed clearly destined. This conviction took a variety of forms. Within the Gulf itself, there was a pervasive conviction that the region's states were producing at levels far higher than was desirable. This conviction was felt most deeply by those who had assumed power in Iran, but it was shared in increasing degree elsewhere in the Gulf as well.[10] The character of the world oil market in 1979, moreover, seemed to demonstrate that no penalties would be incurred by a state withdrawing its production and keeping its oil in the ground, for the value of the oil so withheld, it was assumed, would appreciate, whereas the paper money received in return for it was sure to depreciate. There was no limit, on this reasoning, to the economic pressure that could be applied against the economies of the West, because there was no limit to the West's dependence on the oil of the Gulf.

The sense of crisis caused by this growing dependence was exacerbated by the balance of military power in the region. The two most powerful regional states—Iran and Iraq—were both bitterly hostile to the United States. Neither had, it appeared, an interest in preserving the Saudi oil fields from danger, and it was easily possible to imagine circumstances in which one or the other might attempt either to seize or to destroy the Saudi fields. The Soviet Union not only had an advantage over the United States by virtue of its geographic proximity to the Gulf but it also stood to profit from the multiple military, economic, and political crises that further turbulence in the Gulf would bring upon the western world. Against this array of threats, the United States was able to bring to bear very little relevant military power at all.

At the outset of the 1980s, then, the outlook in the Persian Gulf was grim. The most pessimistic forecast of the future was one made by Walter Levy, who saw no way by which the West's dependence on the oil of the Gulf could be meaningfully reduced, yet no expedient—military or political—by which it might be secured. He concluded an influential piece in the Summer 1980 issue of *Foreign Affairs* by predicting that "the world, as we know it now, will probably not be able to maintain its cohesion, nor be able to provide for the continued economic progress of its people against the onslaught of future oil shocks—with all that this might imply for the political stability of the West, its free institutions, and its internal and external security."[11]

The Specter of Economic Decline

The two great security crises that loomed as the 1970s came to a close—one arising from the growth of Soviet military power, the other stemming from the West's critical dependence for oil on the

Persian Gulf—were exacerbated by economic crisis at home. Like the preceding two problems, this crisis too had not arisen overnight. It had multiple causes. But there was little question that it posed a long-term challenge to the capacity of the United States to maintain the position of primacy in the world that it had won with the Second World War.

The general features of the declining American economic position in the 1970s are illustrated in Exhibits 2 and 3. U.S. manufacturing production as a percentage of world production fell steeply from its postwar high and was destined, most observers agreed, to fall even more as we approached the end of the century. Real GNP growth fell from its postwar high of 4.5 percent in the 1960–66 period to only 2.4 percent from 1974 to 1981. The productivity of the American economy decreased even more steeply and even began to decline by the late 1970s. The great postwar boom from 1948 to 1965 had been accompanied by annual increases in productivity of 3.2 percent, a rate that had fallen to −0.8 percent during the 1978–80 period. This rate of productivity growth was among the lowest in the industrialized world. Because increases in the American standard of living are closely tied to improvements in productivity, this decline was perhaps the most serious of all the economic problems facing the country at the close of the 1970s. It was given added significance because it occurred simultaneously with a profound structural change in the American position in the world economy. The share of GNP taken by imports and exports doubled from 1970 to 1980, greatly increasing the exposure of the American economy to international competition. By 1980, it has been estimated, over 70 percent of American goods were in active competition with foreign-made products.[12]

There remains a considerable amount of disagreement among economists over the reasons for this decline in American productivity. Among the contributing factors in the 1970s were the growth of a less experienced workforce, the explosion of energy prices, and the proliferation of regulatory controls. There is considerable evidence for the view, however, that the decline in productivity was closely linked to the low rates of capital formation the United States sustained in the 1970s. The share of gross domestic product (GDP) devoted to net fixed investment in the 1970s was over three times larger in Japan than in the United States, a fact whose significance is shown by the close relationship between investment and productiv-

EXHIBIT 2—*U.S. Manufacturing Production as a Percentage of World Production*

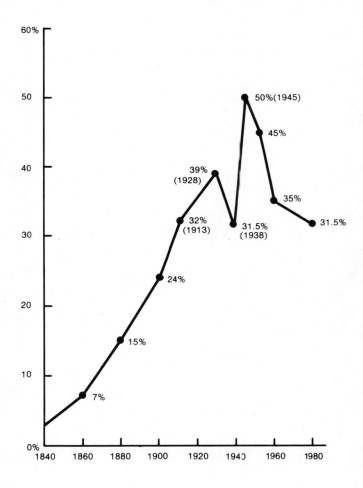

Source:—Paul Bairoch, "International Industrialization Levels from 1750 to 1980," *Journal of European Economic History* 11, no. 2 (Spring 1982); and Paul Kennedy, "The First World War and the International Power System," in *Military Strategy and the Origins of the First World War,* ed. Steven E. Miller (Princeton: Princeton University Press, 1985), 36.

EXHIBIT 3—*International Comparison of Investment and Productivity Growth, 1971–80*

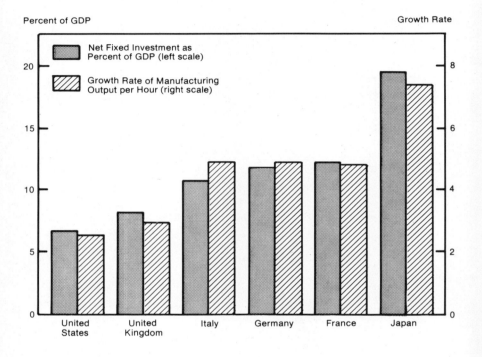

Percent of GDP

Growth Rate

Source:—The Annual Report of the Council of Economic Advisers (Washington, D.C.: GPO, February 1983).

ity growth in the 1970s (Exhibit 3). Contributing to this low rate of capital formation were two other factors. One was the lowest rate of national savings in the industrialized world. Strongly encouraged by the tax code, net savings as a percentage of GNP fell from 7.5 percent in 1966–70 to 5.8 percent in 1976–80. Net private savings in Japan, by contrast, approached 20 percent of GNP in the 1970s. The second was the explosive growth in social expenditures in the 1970s, which more than made up for the decline in military expenditures that occurred over the same period. Domestic spending (excluding interest payments) grew from 10.3 percent of GNP in 1970 to 15.1 percent in 1980, while the share of military expenditures fell from 8.4 to 5.2 percent (Exhibit 4).

EXHIBIT 4—*Budget Outlays and Receipts as Percent of GNP, Fiscal Years 1960, 1970, and 1980–85*

	1960	1970	1980	1981	1982	1983	1984	1985
Total outlays	18.5	20.2	22.4	22.8	23.8	24.3	23.0	24.0
National defense	9.7	8.4	5.2	5.5	6.1	6.3	6.2	6.4
Net interest	1.4	1.5	2.0	2.4	2.8	2.7	3.0	3.3
Domestic spending	7.5	10.3	15.1	15.0	15.0	15.3	13.9	14.3
Total receipts	18.6	19.9	20.1	20.8	20.2	18.1	18.0	18.6
Deficit	−.1	.3	2.3	2.0	3.6	6.2	5.0	5.4

Source:—Fiscal Years 1960–1982, *Annual Report of the Council of Economic Advisors 1984* (Washington, D.C.: GPO, 1983); Fiscal Years 1983–85, *Budget of the United States Government, FY 1987* (Washington, D.C.: GPO, 1986).

As the 1970s drew to a close, there was thus a visible deterioration of the American economic position. The products on which American industrial predominance had been based—steel, automobiles, textiles, electronics—were becoming increasingly uncompetitive in the new international marketplace. The newly industrializing countries of Latin America and East Asia began to copy successfully the labor and management practices that from 1920 to 1970 lay at the heart of American industrial predominance, and their wage rates were such that American products were increasingly uncompetitive.[13] Yet it was not only the older and "dying" industries that were dealt a hammer blow from abroad. The areas of industrial and commercial activity by means of which the United States would have to make up for its losses in other fields were also losing ground, primarily to the Japanese. The world economy was undergoing what Joseph Schumpeter had called the process of creative destruction, the means by which capitalist economies grow.[14] Yet while the destruction was taking place mostly in Europe and America, the creation was mostly going on in Japan and the other countries of the Pacific basin. In the 1960s the Japanese economy grew at an average annual rate of 10 to 11.2 percent, over 5 to 8 percent higher than the rate of growth prevailing in the United States. In the 1970s and early 1980s, the Japanese rate of growth fell from these extraordinary levels, but in most years it remained 2 to 3 percent above that of the United States.

The phenomenon was reminiscent of the progressive erosion of British industrial and commercial supremacy in the nineteenth century, when the British economic position was increasingly undercut by the emergence of German and American economic power.[15] Also reminiscent of the decline of the Pax Britannica was the response made to it by the United States. Ultimately the British sought refuge from their economic competitors in schemes of imperial preference, but these were no more successful in the long run in countervailing the declining competitiveness of British products than the growing American inclination to resort to protectionism is likely to be for us. Indeed, there is perhaps nothing so obvious as the fact that, far from arresting long-term economic decline, such measures make a positive contribution to it by forcing upon prosperous industries all the debilities of the old and dying.

The Predicament at the End of the 1970s

The formidable character of the challenge to the postwar order and to America's role in that order at the end of the 1970s may now be seen in its true light. Every economy and polity, whether through design or sheer inadvertence, allots shares of its national income to three competing purposes: 1) defense; 2) productive investment; and 3) public and private consumption. Without the protection provided by the first and the provision for the future provided by the second, no great nation can preserve its security, its honor, or its patrimony. It seemed in the late 1970s that we would be incapable of preserving all three, that the United States would come to resemble one of those distant Greek city-states, like Athens or Thebes, dismissed by ancient writers as unworthy objects of contemplation because "their growth was abnormal, the period of their zenith brief, and the changes they experienced unusually violent.

Their glory was a sudden and fortuitous flash," from which only negative lessons could be learned.[16]

As the 1970s drew to a close, the United States faced a military compretitor in the Soviet Union that devoted an extraordinary share of its economic surplus to military expenditures. From a much smaller economic base, the Soviet Union produced in the 1970s an absolutely much greater amount of military hardware than the United States (Exhibit 5). We faced an economic competitor in

Exhibit 5—*Comparative Economic Base (1982)*

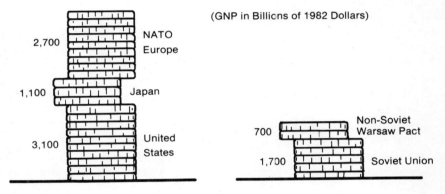

(GNP in Billions of 1982 Dollars)

2,700   NATO Europe

1,100   Japan

3,100   United States

700   Non-Soviet Warsaw Pact

1,700   Soviet Union

Source:—Report of the Secretary of Defense Caspar W. Weinberger to the Congress on the FY 1985 Budget. . . . (Washington, D.C.: GPO, February 1, 1984), 43.

Japan that devoted an extraordinary share of its economic surplus to productive investment, with the consequence that the absolute level of investment in Japan, from a much smaller economic base, approached that of the United States. These challenges became serious precisely at the time when the economic surplus that the United States might devote to military expenditures or productive investments was eaten up by the growth of the entitlements state. And American responsibilities were widened with the emergence of the crisis in the Persian Gulf, an area in which—so far as military policy is concerned—little attention had had to be paid since the emergence of the United States as a world power.

These problems were intimately related, yet in a peculiar fashion.

For while the crises caused by the growth of Soviet military power and the growth of oil dependency in the Persian Gulf posed threats to the physical security and economic well-being of our allies in Western Europe and Japan far more serious than they posed to the United States, the willingness of the United States as displayed in the last year of the Carter administration to commit its power to the resolution of these crises was far greater. This disparity was highlighted in turn by the increasing weakness of the American economy—a weakness particularly pronounced in relation to many of the very states that continued to rely on American protection to withstand the threats from the Soviet Union and to secure access to hostile oil.

The predicament of American policy as it entered the 1980s was that it would be extremely difficult for the United States to maintain its traditional role of ensuring the security of East Asia and Western Europe—as well as its additional responsibilities in the Persian Gulf—without further eroding the economic base on which its military power ultimately rested, especially if its efforts in this regard were met with no reciprocating measures on the part of America's allies. The other side of the predicament, however, was that the failure to maintain the balance of power against the Soviet Union and to maintain access to the oil of the Persian Gulf might also issue in extremely serious consequences. These opposite dangers formed the strategic setting for the Reagan administration on its advent to power in 1981.

The Reassertion of American Power

It is not an easy matter to judge the record of an administration while it remains in office, for the consequences of its actions necessarily remain obscure, and many of the facts on which an informed judgment should rest are unknown. Yet any appraisal of the first term of the Reagan administration would have to give it rather high marks in presiding over a marked easing of the American strategic predicament. Both the dangers posed by the growth of Soviet military power and the threat of hostile oil appeared far less menacing by the middle of the 1980s than they had at the beginning. This change in fortune was partly attributable to factors to which the Reagan administration made no contribution at all, but luck was only part of the story. Credit must also go to the administration's determination to rebuild American military power and to its larger conduct of foreign policy.[17]

The view frequently heard during the 1984 presidential campaign that the Reagan administration was without a single foreign policy triumph to its credit was wide of the mark. In Europe the administration successfully weathered the storms ushered in by the Euromissile crisis and thereby delivered a serious political defeat to the Soviet Union, which had staked much of its prestige on preventing the missile deployments. The fears that Mr. Reagan's old ties to Taiwan would set back Sino-American relations proved to be unfounded, as the Shanghai Communiqué of August 1982 resolved a number of outstanding differences between the United States and China and offered some hope for a further deepening of American ties with the Chinese. And the administration's use of force in Grenada provided a welcome counterweight to the widespread impression, two decades in the making, that virtually any use of American military power was destined to be counterproductive and incapable of serving any worthy end.

Perhaps the most important political development of the first half of the 1980s lay in what did not happen rather than in what did. This period witnessed no great crisis in Soviet-American relations—if we except the Euromissile crisis, which issued in an American triumph. The Soviet Union has displayed a well-founded caution in testing the United States in any substantial way. The basis for this caution no doubt lay partly in a strategic outlook averse to taking great risks, but the risks that foreign adventurism involves are of course a function of the resolve conveyed by one's adversaries; when that resolve is weak, as it appeared to the Soviet Union to be in the late 1970s, even political cultures averse to risk taking may undertake bold moves in the confident expectation that they will succeed. The reassertion of American power under President Reagan made that calculation far more dubious for Soviet leaders than it had been in the late 1970s.

There were, to be sure, other factors that contributed to the diminution of the Soviet threat. The rise of Solidarity in Poland—evident before the administration even took office—illustrated once again the precarious and unnatural character of the Soviet Union's rule over Eastern Europe. The results of the 1982 air war over Lebanon could not fail to make Soviet military planners worry about how their air forces would fare in a shooting war with the United States, a lesson reinforced by the extraordinary lapses in the Soviet air defense system revealed in the events that led to the destruction of Korean Air Lines Flight 007.

Elsewhere in the world, the Soviet Union did not advance beyond the position it had won in the 1970s. Indeed, its position came under attack in many places. Traditional Soviet allies were no longer as strong and invincible as they had once seemed, opportunities no longer knocked as regularly as they had in the 1970s. In Southeast Asia, North Vietnamese power reached a natural limit with its conquest of Indochina. Checked by China on one side and the ASEAN states on the other, the success of North Vietnam in retaining its hold over Cambodia and Laos was counterbalanced by the evident bankruptcy of its regime, which stood in striking contrast with the dynamism of the free-market states of East Asia. Deng Xiaoping's success in reorienting Chinese policy away from Maoism, which gathered steam in the early 1980s, clearly posed a formidable ideological challenge to the integrity of the Soviet system, one that may grow with each passing year. In the Persian Gulf, Soviet hopes that revolutionary turmoil in Iran would lead to an extension of their influence there were dealt a crushing blow with the imprisonment or liquidation of the pro-Soviet Tudeh party; in Afghanistan, the Soviet Union was incapable of establishing an indigenous communist government that could command popular support, and its only recourse became a brutal war against the whole of the Afghan people, in which success was measured by the number of people killed and the extent of fertile areas laid waste. These policies, though they may succeed in preserving Russian rule in Afghanistan itself, have dealt a serious blow to the prestige of the Soviet Union throughout the world, comparable to that which the United States suffered in the 1970s as a consequence of Vietnam. In Southern Africa, the Soviet-supported Angolan regime was incapable of controlling much of the countryside in its war against the insurgent forces of Jonas Savimbi; in Ethiopia, where the African regime most closely associated with Soviet power in the 1970s still ruled, there was a further confirmation of the limited ability of the Soviet Union to assist backward nations in feeding their own peoples and in bringing to them anything but war and deprivation.

A combination of skill and luck also characterized the far-reaching improvement in the West's position in the early 1980s which occurred in the Persian Gulf and with respect to the problem of energy security. Here the Reagan administration profited from the explosion of energy prices that had ruined its predecessor. The extraordinary rise in the price of oil that occurred in the 1970s brought about a far-reaching transformation of the world oil market. The salience of Persian Gulf production declined rapidly in the first half of the 1980s, falling from 21 million barrels per day (mbd) to only 9 mbd in 1985, radically decreasing the dangerous consequences that might follow from a disruption of Persian Gulf oil supplies. The two regional states that posed the most serious threat to western interests in the late 1970s—Iran and Iraq—were consuming themselves in a savage war that shows few signs of ending and from which the Soviet Union was unable to profit. The fall in the price of oil that occurred in the 1980s was also of signal importance in fueling noninflationary economic recovery in the world as a whole. The preservation of western interests in the Persian Gulf nevertheless owed something to the skill with which the Reagan administration avoided direct American military involvement in the region and increased the capability of bringing American military power to bear in a crisis, while improving diplomatic relations with both Israel and the moderate Arab states. As we shall see below, there were elements in its policy toward the Gulf—as in its policy toward the Soviet Union—that were misguided or incoherent. The fact remains that the outlook with respect to both problems underwent a far-reaching transformation for the better during the Reagan administration's first term in office.

The Insolvency of the Reagan Program

If in responding to the problems posed by the growth of Soviet military power and the crisis in the Persian Gulf the Reagan administration presided over a marked easing of the American strategic predicament, the same is not true with respect to its economic policy. On the contrary, the Reagan administration set in place economic policies that may do lasting damage to the competitive position of the United States in the world economy. In its tolerance of huge budget deficits for as far as the eye can see, the administration artificially raised the price of the dollar to unsustainable heights, severely damaged the competitive prospects of American industry and agriculture, and as a consequence presided over trade deficits of unprecedented size.

Helped greatly by the decline in world oil prices, moreover, the economic recovery of the early 1980s rested on a dubious foundation, because cheap oil will inevitably increase the salience of Persian Gulf production in the future, yielding again the security problem of the late 1970s. Because of the budget deficits, the United States became a debtor nation in 1985 for the first time since the First World War, accumulating imposing financial obligations for the next generation (already encumbered by a changing demographic profile that will require an ever-declining working class to support an ever-increasing elderly population). Unless by some good stroke of fortune we have managed to repeal the business cycle—an unlikely event, as many observers have pointed out—the accumulation of federal debt and concomitant interest payments will explode with the next economic downturn and will leave economic authorities with a set of extremely unpleasant choices. The choice facing the Federal Reserve will be between monetization of the debt (i.e. inflation) and rising interest rates that will choke off economic expansion. The choice facing political authorities will be between deficit-reducing measures that would serve to deepen the economic downturn, and measures of economic stimulus that would aggravate still further the size of the deficit.

This was not the first time in the history of postwar American foreign policy that the assumption of greatly expansible means formed the underpinning of security policy.[18] In the other two great expansions of American military power, which took place in the early 1950s and then again in the 1960s, similar assumptions were made. For the Kennedy administration, as for the Truman administration, economic growth and not an increase in the tax burden was to pay for the additional military expenditures. Kennedy believed in this proposition well before he reached the presidency, whereas Truman was a late convert to it, discovering Keynesian economics only after North Korean troops crossed the thirty-eighth parallel. He quickly accepted the argument of NSC–68, which before the Korean invasion had justified this expansion of American military power, arguing that it could be funded without sacrifice: "a buildup in the economic and military strength of the United States and the free world . . . could be accomplished without a decrease in the national standard of living because the required resources could be obtained by siphoning off a part of the annual increment in the gross national product. These are facts," the authors of the report concluded, "of fundamental importance in considering the courses of action open to the United States."[19] They were, for the Reagan administration, "facts of fundamental importance" as well.

Reviewing the objectives of the Reagan administration at the outset of its first term shows the extent to which those objectives were not realized. In the president's March 1981 Program for Economic Recovery, overall federal expenditures were supposed to decline from 23 percent of GNP in 1981 to 19 percent of GNP in 1986. Even with the implementation of its sweeping program of tax cuts, the administration expected the emergence of a balanced budget by 1984 and growing surpluses thereafter. Perhaps the most critical element of this program was the determination to bring nondefense expenditures down from their estimated level in 1981— 18 percent of GNP—to approximately 12 percent in 1986. This sharp reduction in nondefense expenditures was to have made up for both the rise in defense expenditures from 5 to over 7 percent of GNP as well as the concomitant decrease in taxation. The economic assumptions on which these budgetary projections were based were very optimistic, with sustained rates of economic growth projected to be 5 percent a year, during which both inflation and interest rates were expected to fall sharply.[20]

A number of developments derailed the Reagan program, of which the recession was perhaps the most important. The recession radically altered the budgetary picture. But even in the absence of the 1982 economic downturn, which sharply boosted spending and reduced revenues, a balanced budget would not have been realized. For one thing, the tax bill that was ultimately signed into law by the president would soon have reduced the federal tax claim to only 16.9 percent of GNP, over two percentage points below that called for in the administration's original bill. Some of this differential was made up by tax legislation in subsequent years, but the indexation of the tax code written into the 1981 law, alongside the fall in inflation, will operate to keep tax receipts as a percentage of GNP below the levels that would have existed had the president's initial program been accepted without amendment.

Of equal importance was the fate of spending on domestic programs. Nondefense spending, which was 17.4 percent of GNP in

1981, rose to 17.8 percent of GNP in 1982 and 18.2 percent in 1983 and remained stubbornly at 17.6 percent in 1985 (Exhibit 4). Part of the increase in 1982 and 1983 was due to the severity of the recession into which the American economy fell, but the primary reason for the inability to reduce such expenditures was more fundamental. Behind the social programs that constituted the driving force in the growth of nondefense expenditures—Social Security and Medicare preeminently—there existed and continues to exist a deep public consensus. In the initial formulation of the Reagan economic program in late 1980 and early 1981, its architects simply failed to appreciate the depth of that consensus in their attempts to turn back the growth of social spending and reduce it to the level contemplated in the president's Program for Economic Recovery. The earliest defeat—but one that presaged the others—was the stunning May 1981 rejection in the Republican-controlled Senate, by a vote of 96–0, of the president's initial proposals for reducing Social Security benefits. The administration, in this critical respect, misread the results of the 1980 election, which did not provide a mandate to reduce nondefense expenditures to anywhere approaching 12 percent of GNP. In effect, Reagan came to recognize this point: hence his unwillingness to specify in any detail during the 1984 presidential campaign the form that further reductions in domestic spending would take. Given this unwillingness and the persistence of public support for the domestic programs that survived the budgetary cuts of the early 1980s, it is not surprising that Congress, since the 1982 elections changed its composition, has refused to make anything more than cosmetic cuts in domestic programs. It is equally unsurprising that, with further increases in taxation ruled out and with rising payments on the debt, Congress and ultimately many within the administration would look to the defense budget as a way of curbing the growth of the deficit.

These deficits, whatever their ultimate consequences, are symptomatic of a deep disorder in the American body politic, a fundamental disequilibrium between the wants of the people and their willingness to bear the sacrifices necessary to secure those wants. The symptoms of this disorder are revealed not only in the popular resistance to cuts in the middle-class entitlement programs (such as Social Security and Medicare) but also in the unwillingness of the people to contemplate a return to conscription and in the widespread public resistance to increased taxation. In its own way, it is completely revealing of the character of our predicament and of the true mediocrity of our circumstances that the will to reassert American power in the world was not accompanied under the Reagan administration by the willingness to pay a price to do so. On the contrary, the meaning of the Reagan revolution was that the price was to be reduced. This—and not the economic theory that lay behind it—was the basic meaning of the 1981 tax bill. It was the meaning of Mr. Reagan's attack, during the 1980 presidential campaign, on President Carter's decision to reinstitute draft registration. And it is the reason why the persistence of budget deficits in the mid-1980s finally brought the defense buildup engineered by the Reagan administration to an end.[21]

In opposition to Walter Lippmann's dictum, the governing program of the Reagan administration has thus been based on a refusal to pay for what we want and an inclination to want far more than we are willing to pay for. The administration, to be sure, hardly bears exclusive responsibility for this state of affairs. The normal reflexes of the opposition Democratic Party are such that they would compound rather than ease the predicament. And in crucial respects, the Reagan administration has merely erected into policy the contradictory aspirations of the American people, for it is the people who demand lower taxes, increased entitlements, and a defense that is second to none. Ultimately, however, these considerations do not mitigate the administration's failure. "History," as George Kennan once put it, "does not forgive us our national mistakes because they are explicable in terms of our domestic politics."[22] When the voters want contradictory things, the responsibility of political leadership in representative government is to tell the people that they cannot have all the things that they desire. When it fails to do this, it discredits not only itself but the constitutional system it is charged to protect.

The Inequity of the Reagan Program

The assumption of greatly expansible means was not the only one that the administration shared with the authors of NSC–68. Another was that the economic resources of the entire Western world would need to be invested in the struggle against Soviet imperialism. This was a burden, the administration contended, which the United States should not and would not bear alone. But its initial view of alliance relations gave this conviction a particular turn: the crisis required, above all, a reassertion of American leadership. For the Reagan administration, this was so, as NSC–68 had said, because

in the absence of affirmative decision on our part, the rest of the free world is almost certain to become demoralized. Our friends will become more than a liability to us; they can eventually become a positive increment to Soviet power. In sum, the capabilities of our allies are, in an important sense, a function of our own. An affirmative decision to summon up the potential within ourselves would evoke the potential strength within others and add it to our own."[23]

A basic assumption of NSC–68 was therefore that in undertaking a massive buildup of American military power, the United States would not be making a unilateral effort. It was recognized, to be sure, that the United States had heavier responsibilities than its allies as a consequence of its greater power. Still, it was widely believed that these responsibilities would moderate as our allies grew in economic power and political maturity. It was also believed that the allies would join in and approve of this effort. And so they did.

This conception of alliance relations was remarkably similar to that of the Reagan administration. In the Reagan administration, it found expression not only in the belief that Western Europe and Japan would increase their own expenditures on defense.[24] It also formed the principal justification for the attitude the administration adopted toward commercial relations with the Soviet Union. The heart of the administration's indictment of the projected natural gas pipeline from the Soviet Union to Western Europe was that it would represent a subsidy to the Soviet Union equivalent to the earnings of hard currency—projected to be $10 to $12 billion annually—that the Soviet Union would derive from it. Such a subsidy would make a substantial, even though indirect, contribution to the Soviet military buildup.

In all these respects, the Reagan program was remarkably similar in its assumptions to the program advocated in NSC–68. There was the same emphasis on the vital importance of economic growth.

There was the common emphasis on the indispensable role that the United States must take in invigorating and giving direction to the efforts of our allies and the shared belief that such American efforts would succeed in marshalling the resources of the free world against the dangers of Soviet imperialism. Those assumptions not only gave the program of NSC–68 its inner coherence; they were largely borne out by the events of the following years. A much larger defense budget was compatible with substantial increases in the American standard of living. The efforts made by the United States to shore up the balance of military power, moreover, did have positive effects on our allies. The decision to summon up the potential within ourselves did indeed evoke the potential strength of others. Its principal accomplishment was to create the political climate that made possible the rearmament of the Federal Republic of Germany and its integration into the Western Alliance.

The assumptions underlying the Reagan program, by contrast, were defective. The expectation that our allies in Western Europe and Japan were ready to alter their economic and security relationships with the Soviet Union and needed only the impetus provided by American leadership to do so was dealt a sharp blow by the allied response to the American military buildup. It was greeted by no military buildup in Europe itself. It was met instead by a renewed emphasis on expanding European economic relations with the Soviet bloc. The profound differences between the United States and Western Europe over economic relations with the Soviet Union came to a head in the dispute over the pipeline, and when the sanctions that had been imposed in July 1982 were withdrawn in November, the administration was dealt a severe defeat. Most critics interpreted this as a partial setback, one from which the administration and indeed the Atlantic Alliance as a whole would swiftly recover. In fact, the setback was to the logic of the administration's entire approach to the world.

A comparable setback occurred with respect to military spending. As Exhibit 6 shows, defense expenditures as a percentage of Gross Domestic Product rose only slightly, if at all, among most NATO countries from 1978 to 1983. The exceptions were Britain, whose expenditures were driven upward by the Falklands war, and the United States. There has always been a disparity, to be sure, in the burdens borne by the United States and its allies in the postwar period. This disparity, however, has become less and less easy to

Exhibit 6—*Defense Expenditures for Selected NATO Countries*

	Dollars per capita		Percentage of GDP	
	1978	1983	1978	1983
Belgium	319	272	3.3	3.3
Britain	262	439	4.6	5.5
France	354	394	4.0	4.2
West Germany	438	363	4.2	3.4
Italy	110	172	2.5	2.8
Netherlands	302	300	3.3	3.3
USA	491	1,023	5.1	7.4

Source:—International Institute for Strategic Studies, *The Military Balance, 1983–84,* and *1985–86* (London: International Institute for Strategic Studies, 1983 and 1985).

justify. In the 1950s it was justifiable because European energies were concentrated on the task of economic reconstruction. In the 1960s and early 1970s it was justifiable because so much of the American defense effort was concentrated on the war in Vietnam, whose rationale the Europeans found unconvincing and of which they wanted no part. There was, however, no plausible justification for this disparity in the early 1980s, for the greater part of our extra-European defense effort was concentrated on an area in Southwest Asia that is much more important to Europe than it is to the United States.

The response of our allies to the Reagan program was thus a far cry from what the administration had anticipated it would be. It was a far cry as well from what the reaction of the allies had been in fact to the comparable buildup of military power called for in NSC–68 and undertaken by the United States in the early 1950s. Under President Reagan, the United States had assumed that it would not be making a unilateral effort to restore the balance of military power and to ensure access to the oil of the Persian Gulf. So far as tangible increases in military budgets are concerned, however, the effort proved to be unilateral in fact. And this was the case despite the fact that the interest of our allies in combating the spread of Soviet power and in ensuring access to the oil of the Gulf was greater than that of the United States.

The Restoration of Equilibrium

The unwillingness of our allies to increase, as the United States has done, their military and economic commitment to the resistance of Soviet power placed in question the Reagan administration's approach to the world. So, too, did the insolvency of our national economic accounts—an insolvency graphically illustrated by the gap between income and expenditure on the one hand, and exports and imports on the other. The beliefs that the American economy could again find the sources of rapid economic growth and that our allies were waiting only for American leadership to renew their commitments against Soviet power were what gave the Reagan program its inner coherence. For the promise of allied commitment was that no great issue of equity would arise over the respective shares devoted to defense by the free nations of the West, and that issue has arisen. The promise of economic growth was that the sacrifices entailed by the reconstruction of American military power would not in reality be sacrifices at all, for they would, in the words of NSC–68, "be obtained by siphoning off a part of the annual increment in the gross national product." Yet that promise has been fulfilled only through the accumulation of financial obligations that will one day have to be met.

Far from overcoming the American strategic predicament, then, the Reagan administration has merely delayed the day of reckoning. In supporting the buildup of American military power, the administration made a determined effort to address itself to part of the American strategic problem, but in doing so it has mortgaged the future and charted a course for the United States that is unsustainable. It remains the case, however, that the growth of Soviet military power is a real phenomenon, to which the West must make a convincing response. There is, moreover, little likelihood that the failure of the United States to meet this challenge would lead others to take our place, for that would require a fundamental change in the bases of the postwar political order, and it is apparent that the disposition to ignore the implications of the Soviet military buildup was—and remains—far stronger in Western Europe and Japan than in the United States. The predicament, then, is real. It cannot be overcome by the pretension that the maintenance of a powerful military establishment and a generous welfare state are free goods that impose no penalties on economic growth; and it cannot be overcome by the pretension that the growth in Soviet military power poses no threat to western security.

This perception of the nature of the American strategic predicament is not by any means a new one; indeed, it is very close to the one that preoccupied President Eisenhower. When Eisenhower reached the presidency, he demanded from his subordinates a program that would satisfy what he called "the great equation," a formula that would allow the United States to maintain both its economic and its military power.[25] It is a measure of the depth of our current predicament that the answer that Eisenhower gave, the main element of which was reliance on American nuclear strength, is now widely believed to be inappropriate for our own time. The growth of the entitlements state since the 1950s, moreover, has sharply reduced the size of the economic surplus available for investment in economic growth and for the maintenance of more expensive conventional forces. Still, we cannot now but marvel at the success that Eisenhower's policies enjoyed. The deficiencies in military doctrine that dissident intellectuals identified in the 1950s seem less than momentous now that we know of the uses to which the remedy was to be put. And the conservative and prudent character of the Eisenhower economic policies, widely condemned in the 1950s for their insufficiently stimulative character, seem rather more attractive after having experienced the consequences of a debauched currency.

The challenge for American security policy for the late 1980s and early 1990s is to discover the military strategy that will allow for the emergence of a more equitable relationship between the United States and its allies, and that will allow us to satisfy both of the elements that formed part of Eisenhower's "great equation." The latter requires a program that transcends security policy as such. It will require a continuing attempt to keep social expenditures in check, most particularly the middle-class entitlement programs that were virtually exempted from the budgetary cuts of the early 1980s. It will require an expansion of the federal tax claim on GNP, though this ought to be done in such a fashion that the heaviest burden falls on current consumption and not on investment for the future. And it will require, as it did under Eisenhower, restraining the projected growth in, and perhaps even reducing, military expenditures.

Whatever the prospects for tax increases and reductions in social expenditures, it is now clear in any case that the Reagan defense buildup has run its course, and that a stable level of real expenditures on defense is about all that can be expected in the near future. Yet it makes all the difference in the world how military expenditures are reined in. If the past repeats itself—as it may yet do— we will do so across the board, by stretching out weapons purchases and by freezing pay levels. Such expedients will no doubt seem attractive to many political leaders, or so one must conclude from the experience of the 1970s, when defense cutbacks often took this form. Yet from a strategic point of view such an approach suffers grave defects. The personnel problems of the services will inevitably grow worse if pay does not advance at levels commensurate to those in the civilian sector, and it must be recalled that, of all the problems afflicting the services in the late 1970s, it was the poor quality of initial recruits and the disastrous retention rates of experienced personnel that were the most serious. By the same token, stretching out weapons purchases without cancelling any major items will drive up unit costs substantially. And it will do little to alter—and may even exacerbate—the growing disproportion projected in future defense budgets between the procurement accounts and the funds required to maintain American forces in a condition of readiness.

A different approach is required. In exploring how such a different approach might be effected, we have much to learn from prior episodes in American strategy, in particular from the manner in which Presidents Eisenhower and Nixon set about restraining the growth of the defense budget when confronted with budgetary constraints similar to those we now face. We require, in other words, the contemporary equivalent of Eisenhower's New Look and Nixon's Doctrine, both of which enjoyed a remarkable degree of success in reordering American defense priorities during times of fiscal stringency. This new strategy should be less pluralistic than that embraced by the Reagan administration, discriminating with far greater care among competing strategic concepts than was customarily done in the 1980s. At the same time, it should seek to apply our own strengths against adversary weaknesses. Such an asymmetrical strategy, as John Lewis Gaddis has called it, was characterized under the Eisenhower and Nixon administrations by "a willingness to yield positions not easily defended, or to expand the confrontation to exploit positions that can be."[26] Even though the particulars will necessarily differ, we require that approach again. The delineation of this new doctrine is attempted in Part III of this work. In Part II, I examine the two areas of the world—Europe and the Persian Gulf—which place the most demanding requirements on American military forces. Only in the aftermath of this examination will the ground be prepared for a reconsideration of American strategic doctrine as such.

Notes

1. "The Perpetuation of Our Political Institutions," Address Before the Springfield Young Men's Lyceum, 1838, in *The Political Thought of Abraham Lincoln,* ed. Richard N. Current (Indianapolis, 1967), 12.

2. See the concluding passage of volume one of Alexis de Tocqueville, *Democracy in America* (New York, 1961), 521–22.

3. See "Washington's Final Manuscript of the Farewell Address, September 19, 1796," in Felix Gilbert, *To the Farewell Address: Ideas of Early American Foreign Policy* (Princeton, 1961), 145.

4. Ibid., 145.

5. See A. W. DePorte, *Europe Between the Superpowers: The Enduring Balance* (New Haven, 1979).

6. See the excellent review of W. Seth Carus, "The Evolution of Soviet Military Power Since 1965," in Edward N. Luttwak, *The Grand Strategy of the Soviet Union* (New York, 1983), 176–230.

7. George Armstrong Kelly, "The Strange Death of Liberal America," in *Beyond Containment: U.S. Foreign Policy in Transition,* ed. Robert W. Tucker and William Watts (Washington, D.C., 1973), 78.

8. See, for example, Robert Stobaugh, "After the Peak: The Threat of Hostile Oil," in *Energy Future: Report of the Energy Project at the Harvard Business School,* ed. Robert Stobaugh and Daniel Yergin (New York, 1980), 42.

9. See the analysis in William Quandt, *Saudi Arabia's Oil Policy* (Washington, D.C., 1982).

10. See particularly Walter J. Levy, "The Years that the Locust Hath Eaten: Oil Policy and OPEC Development Prospects," *Foreign Affairs* (Winter 1978/79), 287–305; and Shaul Bakhash, *The Politics of Oil and Revolution in Iran* (Washington, D.C., 1982).

11. Walter J. Levy, "Oil and the Decline of the West," *Foreign Affairs* (Summer 1980), 1015.

12. See Ira Magaziner and Robert Reich, *Minding America's Business* (New York,

1982), 31–32; *Economic Report of the President 1983* (Washington, D.C., 1983); and *Budget of the United States Government Fiscal Year 1984* (Washington, D.C., 1983).

13. An overview of the business practices that fueled the American industrial engine over the preceding century is provided in Robert B. Reich, *The Next American Frontier* (New York, 1983).

14. See Joseph A. Schumpeter, *Capitalism, Socialism and Democracy* (New York, 1942, 1976).

15. This comparison is drawn and its significance examined in Lester Thurow, "The Moral Equivalent of Defeat," *Foreign Policy*, (Spring 1981), 114–124. See also Paul M. Kennedy, "The First World War and the International Power System," in Steven E. Miller, *Military Strategy and the Origins of the First World War* (Princeton, 1985), 38–40.

16. *The Histories of Polybius* (Bloomington, 1962) 1:494–95. Quoted in Robert Gilpin, *War and Change in World Politics* (Cambridge, 1981), 98–99. See 156–59 of this stimulating work for reflections on the nature of a society's "economic surplus" and the rising demands placed on it during periods of maturation and decline.

17. See the perceptive analysis of Michael Mandelbaum, "The Luck of the President," in *Foreign Affairs: America and the World 1985*, 393–412.

18. This is one of the principal themes of John Lewis Gaddis, *Strategies of Containment: A Critical Appraisal of Postwar American National Security Policy* (New York, 1982).

19. "NSC 68: United States Objectives and Programs for National Security, 14 April 1950," in *Containment: Documents on American Policy and Strategy*, ed. Thomas H. Etzold and John Lewis Gaddis, (New York, 1978), 407–8. NSC–68 was a comprehensive study of national security policy undertaken by an ad hoc committee of State and Defense Department officials under the chairmanship of Paul H. Nitze.

20. See *America's New Beginning: A Program for Economic Recovery*, 12 and 25. The contrast between the administration's original budgetary estimates and fiscal reality is stressed in David A. Stockman, *The Triumph of Politics: Why the Reagan Revolution Failed* (New York, 1986). See also *Budget of the United States Government, Fiscal Year 1984* (Washington, D.C., 1983).

21. That this would happen was pointed out by many critics at the time. See in particular James R. Schlesinger, "Reagan's Budgetary Dunkirk," *The Washington Post*, 9 September 1981.

22. George F. Kennan, *American Diplomacy, 1900–1950* (Chicago, 1951), 73.

23. Etzold and Gaddis, *Containment*, 404.

24. See the 22 February 1981 speech by Frank Carlucci, under secretary of defense, in *The New York Times*, 23 February 1981.

25. See Glenn H. Snyder, "The 'New Look' of 1953," in Warner R. Schilling et al., *Strategy, Politics, and Defense Budgets*, (New York, 1962), 392, 413.

26. The characteristics of an "asymmetrical strategy" are described in Gaddis, *Strategies of Containment*, 352–53. Gaddis contrasts such a strategy with the "symmetrical" approach characteristic of the Truman administration after NSC–68 and Korea, the Democratic administrations of the 1960s, and the Reagan administration. See also by Gaddis, "The Rise, Fall, and Future of Detente," *Foreign Affairs* (Winter 1983/84), 354–77. "Strategic pluralism" and its opposite—strategic monism—are defined and discussed in Samuel P. Huntington, *The Soldier and the State: The Theory*

and *Politics of Civil-Military Relations* (Cambridge, Mass. 1957), 418; Huntington, *The Common Defense: Strategic Programs in National Politics* (New York, 1961), 264; and in an unpublished paper by Huntington, "The Defense Policy of the Reagan Administration," presented at the Woodrow Wilson School of Public and International Affairs, Princeton University, 23 October 1982, 1–8, 45–51. I consider the applicability of these terms to postwar American strategy in "American Strategy: Past and Future." Michael Mandelbaum, ed., *American Military Policy* (New York, 1987).

Part II
Core and Periphery

2 — American Power and European Security

Eurocentricity in American Defense Policy

It is in Europe that the debate over American strategy must first be joined, for it is Europe that drives the largest portion of the American defense budget. The extent to which this is so cannot be measured simply by adding up the cost of the ground divisions and air wings directly committed to European defense, because many of the ground and air forces stationed in the United States and forming part of the American strategic reserve are trained and equipped for a European war. The most demanding contingency our naval forces face is securing the sea lanes of communication in a protracted conflict with the Soviet Union, and thus a significant proportion of the Navy's budget must be chalked up to the European account. Perhaps most significantly, the demands of extending deterrence over the nonnuclear states of the Western Alliance—preeminently the Federal Republic of Germany—give our strategic nuclear forces tasks they would not otherwise have. In the absence of an American commitment to Western Europe and the continuing possibility that this commitment might require the first use of nuclear weapons, the problem of deterring a Soviet nuclear attack on the United States would appear in a far different light.

The Eurocentric focus of the American defense establishment, moreover, has widened over the past generation. With the end of the Vietnam War in the 1970s, the energies of the Pentagon were once again concentrated on the demands of a European war. Containment in East Asia then appeared, and still does appear, as a far less demanding enterprise than it did during the classic period of the Cold War. The emergence of China as a full-fledged rival of the Soviet Union gave to the Far Eastern state system the core foundation of an indigenous balance of power. The United States still plays a role in the maintenance of that balance of power by virtue of its commitment to Japan and South Korea. But that role has been shorn of the aspirations that marked the initial period of containment in East Asia, and the requirement for American military forces has been correspondingly reduced.

The concentration of the Pentagon in the 1970s on the demands of a European military contingency, to be sure, was soon divided. With the emergence of the crisis in the Persian Gulf, the possibility of an extra-European military contingency came once again to be taken very seriously. The military arrangements underlying the formation of the Rapid Deployment Force were in one sense competitive with our European commitment: many of the military units slated for deployment to the Gulf were also committed to the defense of Europe; in an actual shooting war, they could not be in two places at once. Still, the stakes in the Persian Gulf involved the interests of our European allies to a profound degree; in that respect, the Carter Doctrine and the Rapid Deployment Force did not lessen the Eurocentric focus of American defense policy. They deepened it.

The American role in the arrangements of European security, then, is fundamental to any appraisal of the courses open to American strategy. Any such appraisal must begin by noting the widespread view that the strategy of the past has reached the end of its tether; that it is no longer adequate for the deterrence of Soviet attack nor reassuring to the societies that continue to rely upon it. This belief that our traditional strategies have been deeply compromised—on the one hand by the growth of Soviet power, on the other by basic changes in the outlook of western societies—has sparked a wide range of proposals for fundamental change. Some want to renounce the threat to use nuclear weapons first in the event of a Soviet conventional attack on Europe; others want to alter radically the bases of NATO's conventional strategy. Still others believe that the time has finally come to begin withdrawing American forces from Europe, that Europe must now assume a military and political role commensurate with its economic power. These proposals for fundamental change are not novel. They are variations on themes that have formed part of the American strategic debate since the foundation of the Atlantic Alliance in 1949. Some reach much further back in time, calling forth a vision of American security profoundly at odds with the core assumptions of postwar American strategy.

Yet in spite of the perception of imminent collapse and the widespread calls for wholesale renovation, the edifice continues to stand. There has been no war in Central Europe since 1945, and the basic factors restraining either side from initiating one seem likely to persist for a long time to come. European deterrence rests upon many different pillars: if one or even several were removed, the edifice might totter but it would not in all probability collapse. That is no reason to set about testing the structure by placing upon it a weight it might not be able to bear. It is not a reason for kicking out from under it the supports that from time to time appear unnecessary or superfluous. Nor is it, finally, any reason for avoiding necessary repairs. It has the status merely of prosaic truth: even if we let the paint peel and the wood rot, as we did in the 1970s, the old barracks will in all probability still be able to withstand all but the harshest of storms.

The Enduring Balance

Fundamental to the stability of the postwar order in Europe has been the existence of nuclear weapons. In all likelihood, there would have been no war in Europe between the United States and the Soviet Union had these weapons never been invented—so sturdy are the other factors supporting the postwar order—but their existence on a progressively larger scale on both sides of the Iron Curtain has induced a remarkable caution in their possessors. This fact is no longer as widely appreciated as it once was; indeed, it was progressively forgotten in the midst of the alarms created by the Soviet strategic buildup of the 1960s and 1970s. For the most widely drawn lesson drawn from that buildup was that the achievement of Soviet nuclear parity had "neutralized" the American nuclear arsenal and had thereby given the Soviet lead in conventional forces a significance it had not previously had. The first use of American nuclear weapons in response to a Soviet conventional attack, on this view, had become either utterly incredible or unbelievably dangerous. As such, the critics argued, it could neither contribute to deterrence nor any longer form the underpinning of American security policy.

The denigration of the deterrent role of nuclear weapons rests upon a curious combination of assumptions. We are told, on the one hand, that nuclear weapons would never be used, that the threat to use them is sheer bluff, and therefore that it can no longer form the basis of a credible deterrent. On the other hand, we are asked to believe that any use of nuclear weapons, on however limited a scale, would rapidly lead to their unlimited use. Both analyses force the conclusion that the United States ought to move away from reliance on nuclear weapons. Yet in their estimate of the passions to which a war between the superpowers would give rise, these two analyses are inconsistent. The first analysis assumes that a conflict between the superpowers would be dominated on the American side by the fear of the consequences to which escalation would lead, that we would surrender rather than risk the suicide that a resort to nuclear weapons might bring about. The second analysis, on the other hand, assumes that a conflict would follow the course of reciprocal action—sketched by Clausewitz in the first book of *On War*—which leads combatants, in theory, to extremes: "If one side uses forces without compunction, undeterred by the bloodshed it involves, while the other side refrains, the first will gain the upper hand. That side will force the other to follow suit; each will drive its opponent toward extremes, and the only limiting factors are the counterpoises inherent in war."[1]

Each of these analyses points to an imperative—the enormous pressure to respond to the actions of the other side, the paralyzing fear of the consequences to which a nuclear response could give rise—that would no doubt have a fundamental influence on the behavior of the belligerents and thus on the outcome of the struggle. They are both implausible because they assume that one or the other of these imperatives would completely dominate the other in the event of a Soviet-American war. The dilemma of policy in the event of a Soviet attack, it is true, would be a terrible one; at the extremes, the choice is no doubt between "suicide and surrender." Since the alternatives at either extreme are so horrific, however, it is far more likely that western statesmen would seek a path of action that would somehow avoid both. Only if Soviet leaders could with confidence assure themselves that our choice would be surrender would their initial attack satisfy the minimal requirements of rationality; but they have no basis for making this assumption. On the contrary, it is apparent that, however large the initial strike—whether limited to a conventional attack on Western Europe or an unlimited attack on the nuclear retaliatory systems based in the continental United States, or something in between—the Soviet

Union would have started something that it could not finish. "Men must either be caressed or else annihilated," says Machiavelli: "they will revenge themselves for small injuries but cannot do so for great ones; the injury therefore that we do to a man must be such that we need not fear his vengeance."[2] Under the conditions existing today, in which neither side can disarm the other, this fundamental condition cannot be satisfied. Annihilation is impossible; vengeance is inevitable. That vengeance would be tempered by fear is certain; that the impulse to retaliate in some fashion deeply injurious to the other would be wholly overcome by fear is much less so. For surrender no less than escalation would carry with it profound dangers. The abyss exists on either side.*

If the United States did use nuclear weapons in the event of war, the choices then facing the Soviet leadership would all be very bad.

---

*The assumption made in the text that a war between the superpowers would not escalate to the ultimate level, it may be argued, ignores some features of the current military balance that would have a potent effect in propelling such escalation. The necessity of "using or losing" the intermediate-range missiles now being stationed in Germany would be one such factor. (See, e.g., Lawrence Freedman, "U.S. Nuclear Weapons in Europe: Symbols, Strategy and Force Structure," in Andrew J. Pierre, ed., *Nuclear Weapons in Europe* [New York, 1984], 70.) Another stems from the existence of plans in the U.S. Navy to strike at Soviet SSBNs with the American attack submarines and at Soviet naval ports with American carrier strikes. (See Barry R. Posen, "Inadvertent Nuclear War? Escalation and NATO's Northern Flank," *International Security* [Fall 1982], 28–54.) Both contain potentially escalatory features. It nevertheless remains extremely difficult to visualize the circumstances under which the leadership of either superpower would escalate a geographically limited conflict with direct nuclear attacks on the home territory of the other. The fact that plans and capabilities exist to do these things cannot be determinative of the question of whether they would in fact be done. If such "use or lose" threats seriously compromised the capacity of either side to inflict substantial damage on the other, perhaps escalation would indeed be the consequence. Precisely because of the immense nuclear arsenals possessed on either side, however—because our condition is still one of mutual vulnerability—the threat to the NATO INF forces or to Soviet SSBNs would be very unlikely to provoke such escalation. The prospect of eliminating through counterforce strikes the retaliatory capability of either side is too remote, the probability of retaliation too high. The Soviets' recognition that "war can remain localized to the contested theater should adversary forbearance permit it" is examined in Benjamin S. Lambeth, *On Thresholds in Soviet Military Thought* (Santa Monica, Calif., March 1983), 6. Cf. also Bernard Brodie, *Escalation and the Nuclear Option* (Princeton, 1966), 31: "the existence of a nuclear stalemate on the strategic level may indeed favor rather than prohibit the use of nuclear weapons on the tactical level."

It might very well be faced with a collapse of discipline within its field armies.[3] The vaunted momentum of its offensive might be completely broken, perhaps irreparably. A retaliatory strike against NATO's theater nuclear forces would not eliminate the American theater nuclear capability, much of which is not located in Europe at all. Worse, a Soviet retaliatory strike against NATO might cause enormous damage to the very prize on behalf of which the Soviets went to war. Any war that leads to the use of nuclear weapons by either side on European soil would be fundamentally contrary to the interests of the Soviet state. For this reason alone, the widespread assumption that the Soviet numerical superiority in theater nuclear forces has provided them with "escalation dominance" in a war of conquest appears fundamentally mistaken.

It may be argued that the United States would never initiate the use of nuclear weapons on European territory for fear that it could lead, by virtue of the theater response it might provoke from the Soviet Union, to the destruction of the very thing that we most desire to protect. This prospect could indeed paralyze. It is, however, of the utmost significance from the standpoint of deterrence that the Soviet leadership would have to depend upon American forbearance that was motivated by the fear of the harm that would inevitably be done to innocents and to the territory soon to be occupied by the Soviet Union rather than by the fear of the physical injury that would be done to American national territory in retaliation. Despite the Euromissile program, it is not difficult to see how the Soviets might conclude that the American nuclear arsenal had been neutralized because of the latter fear. It would be much more difficult for them to assume American forbearance on the basis of the former motive. Forbearance from motives of humanity, for states at war, is a completely unreliable guide to their conduct. In all great wars it has ultimately been cast aside.

"Escalation dominance" and "strategic superiority" are ideas that should not be considered, as they often are, apart from the political objects of a war. Under conditions of nuclear parity, they inhere in the side maintaining a vital interest, not the side bent on a course of aggrandizement. The Russians enjoy escalation dominance if we contemplate a war launched by NATO to liberate Eastern Europe from the Soviet Empire. We enjoy strategic superiority in, and can therefore deter, a war launched by the Soviet Union to conquer Western Europe. Under conditions of mutual vulnerability, everything depends on political will, and the strength of that will at a moment of deep crisis or even a war cannot be seen apart from the justice of the one cause and the injustice of the other—injustice being defined here in terms of the magnitude of the crime against the international order.

Nuclear deterrence—and the extension of deterrence to others than the self—has functioned successfully in the postwar era, and it promises to continue doing so for a very long time to come, because the will of the defender would be fortified by his knowledge that he is in the right and that he has no alternative but to resist. The potential aggressor inevitably fears this response. Because he covets what is not his own, he is drawn to the strategy of annihilation, which requires him to disarm the enemy and render him physically incapable of resistance. Under conditions of mutual vulnerability or "second strike survivability," it is precisely this that he cannot do. Put differently, there is a disjunction between Soviet strategic doctrine, with its emphasis on annihilation or forcible disarmament, and the nature of the world—between what the Soviets must do in order to win and what they can do in reality.[4] So long as that disjunction exists, deterrence will almost certainly prove to be secure. Its successful functioning in the postwar era is not a fragile phenomenon; on the contrary, it is rooted in the very composition of man, which makes him recoil in fear from enterprises that carry absolute risks and that can promise at most only relative benefits. For either of the superpowers to undertake this kind of initial assault—knowing that they could not with any assurance control the ensuing dialectic of violence—is contrary to the very geometry of human impulse.

★   ★   ★

The significance of the nuclear revolution is not limited to the balance of power between the Soviet Union and the United States. Both Great Britain and France possess extensive nuclear arsenals and are engaged in substantial nuclear modernization programs. Britain is building nuclear-capable Tornado bombers and is installing sixty-four Chevaline missiles, each with two warheads, on four submarines. It plans to purchase four new Trident submarines from the United States. Each Trident missile will probably carry eight warheads, each submarine sixteen missiles, providing Britain with

512 warheads on four submarines by the late 1990s. France also has an extensive program of nuclear modernization. It plans to install M-4 missiles (each carrying six warheads) on five submarines, with each submarine carrying sixteen missiles and therefore providing for 480 warheads at sea. France is also modernizing its bomber force with Mirage 2000 airplanes and a new air-to-surface missile, and a land mobile ballistic missile may be added to the force of eighteen ballistic missiles now existing in fixed (and vulnerable) silos. These plans will provide Britain and France with over one thousand nuclear warheads and ensure an arsenal capable of destroying every major city in the Soviet Union, as well as other targets, even after a Soviet first strike. The same logic that restrains the Soviet Union from attacking the United States restrains it also from attacking Britain and France. It therefore also serves to limit the plausible depth of a Soviet conventional attack in Central Europe to Germany and the Low Countries. It is customary to speak of a Soviet threat against "Western Europe," but the existence of the British and French nuclear arsenals would almost certainly restrict the scope of a Soviet attack to the nonnuclear powers.[5]

The existence of nuclear arsenals among two of the European NATO members is complemented by the absence of any nuclear capability among the non-Soviet members of the Warsaw Pact. The potential unreliability of non-Soviet Warsaw Pact armies in an invasion of Central Europe is often stressed by defense analysts. That unreliability has many foundations. One is that Soviet rule in Eastern Europe continues to be—forty years after its imposition—of an unnatural character. The army of Poland is utterly unreliable for the purposes of such an invasion; those of Czechoslovakia and Hungary only marginally less so; and the leaders of East Germany, as of other countries, could be warned by the American government that if they were to participate in a Soviet invasion of Western Europe, American nuclear weapons might be employed against their territories. The unreliability of the East European divisions means not only that they are to be subtracted from the Soviet side in the bean counts of forces. They are potentially agents of national liberation from the Soviet empire itself: if a Soviet attack against NATO were to go badly, the conditions would be far more favorable for an indigenous revolt in Eastern Europe than any that have existed over the whole of the postwar era—during which time the Soviet Union has always succeeded in ruling by division and by isolating the cancer of disobedience before it spread.[6]

These factors are complemented by the difficulty the Soviet Union would have in efficiently organizing the productive capacity of the territory in Central Europe it sought to conquer. It would be all but impossible to do so if nuclear weapons were employed on a substantial scale on West German territory. But even if one postulates simply a rapid conventional thrust to the Rhine, it is not easy to see how the Russians could channel the energies of the German people in a direction favorable to themselves in the aftermath of a conquest. The digestion of Eastern Europe has been difficult enough. A prudent leadership will calculate that an adventure of this character might strip from Europe the veneer of civilization it has worn since 1945 and reawaken in the peoples of Central Europe their abundant reserves of black bile. Current circumstances make these peoples very unwarlike, but a Soviet invasion would fundamentally alter those circumstances, with wholly unpredictable consequences.[7]

These factors—

1) the probability that the losing superpower would resort to nuclear weapons rather than undergo a devastating defeat in the field;

2) the existence of an independent nuclear capability in Britain and France and the consequent restriction of the plausible field of Soviet conquest;

3) the unnatural and artificial character of the Soviet Union's position in Eastern Europe, the consequent unreliability of the Warsaw Pact's Eastern European armies, and the vulnerability of the region to American nuclear retaliation; and

4) the difficulty of efficiently organizing the territory in Central Europe that the Soviet Union might conquer through military force—

have long characterized the European balance of power. They represent political and strategic considerations of the highest import. They are anterior, as it were, to assessments of the conventional balance of forces, because any conventional conflict would necessarily take place under the shadows they cast. Having distinguished the Europeans to substantially increase defense spending in have become permanent features of the strategic landscape. Their very durability points to two aspects of the post-1945 order that distinguish it sharply from the preceding half-century of war and violence.

One such aspect is the absence in Europe of the kind of standing grievances that contributed so powerfully to the outbreak of war in 1914 and 1939. There has been for the Soviet Union no equivalent of Slavic nationalism or the Polish Corridor, no standing affront to the dignity of the Soviet state. The second difference is a far greater stability in the distribution of effective power in Europe. The years from the 1890s to the 1940s, by contrast, were characterized by extraordinarily rapid changes in virtually all the indices of national power. The rise of the modern state and the stupendous growth in technological ability, both of which gathered momentum toward the end of the nineteenth century, were two striking aspects of the phenomenon. Of even greater consequence, as F. H. Hinsley has observed, was the fact that "the modern state and the technological revolution did not emerge throughout the world, or even throughout Europe, but only in some countries; and did not emerge, where they did emerge, at the same time and speed." This created, Hinsley notes, "a greater instability in the distribution of effective power, a greater political disequilibrium, than the world had ever previously known in modern times."[8]

It was this instability that underlay all the main developments in international relations from the 1890s to the end of the Second World War. It formed the central backdrop for the "new imperialism" at the end of the nineteenth century; the fears it generated contributed powerfully to war in 1914. And the disruptive instability caused by the unequal growth of power was of even greater consequence in the years that followed. "Nothing is so conducive," Hinsley writes, "to international violence as the fears and appetites that breed on inequality and instability and on the knowledge that these things exist. There never were such fears and appetites, because there never was such instability between states, as prevailed between 1918 and 1945."[9] Despite the widespread perception that we live in an age of rapid change, the historically minded observer will note that the most important features of the postwar balance of power have been distinguished by continuity and not change—a feature of the situation that seems likely to persist for a very long time to come.

★   ★   ★

This inquiry into the anatomy of deterrence should not be read as denigrating the value of conventional defenses. So long as the effort to build up such defenses is not accompanied by repeated expressions of nuclear self-denial, the prospective robustness of conventional defenses increases rather than decreases the credibility of the American nuclear guarantee and thus enhances the solidity of the postwar order. This is so because the capability of inflicting such losses by conventional means reflects the same qualities of will and determination that are relevant in Soviet assessments of the probability of nuclear escalation. If deterrence fails, moreover, the ability to repel conventional aggression through conventional means would be manifestly superior to any strategy that required the use of nuclear weapons.[10]

Whether NATO today enjoys the capacity to repel a Soviet conventional assault without recourse to nuclear weapons is a question to which there is no clear answer, for the relevant variables are large, and war, if it came, would be overwhelmed by "friction."[11] NATO has three problems that are particularly worrisome. One is its vulnerability to strategic surprise, a difficulty likely to arise not from the absence of clear warning indicators of Soviet mobilization, but rather from the unwillingness of western statemen to act upon indicators of potentially uncertain meaning for fear of actually bringing on the cataclysm they would be desperate to avoid.[12] Another stems from the advantages that precision-guided munitions would afford the Soviet Union if, as we must suppose, it were to strike first in a European war. Whereas Soviet missiles and attack planes must strike primarily stationary targets, NATO's task is both to recover from such a Soviet strike and then to hit the moving targets of a Soviet blitzkrieg, a far more difficult undertaking.[13] Finally, the line NATO must defend in Central Europe is characterized by a "disagreeable combination of frontal width and rearward constriction."[14] Its forces lack substantial operational reserves to contend with Soviet breakthrough operations, and its lines of communication—running on a North-South line from the Channel ports to Germany—are vulnerable to Soviet interdiction.

These vulnerabilities do not mean that the Soviet Union enjoys overwhelming conventional superiority. Its forces are certainly more than adequate to repel an assault by NATO against the Warsaw Pact: an offensive war against NATO, however, is quite another matter. It is doubtful that the twenty-five Soviet Category I divisions stationed in East Germany and Czechoslovakia have the numbers required for a decisive thrust to the Rhine. A successful standing-start attack would therefore require the utilization of Polish, Czechoslovakian, and East German units whose reliability under fire is very doubtful, whereas the mobilization and movement into Eastern Europe of Soviet forces, most of which are undermanned reserve divisions, would be clearly observable to western reconnaissance. In all probability, a long time would be required to bring these divisions to combat readiness—far longer than the seven to fourteen days allotted to them in many assessments. The Soviets face a clear choice, in other words, between *surprise* and *mass*. It would be difficult for them to enjoy both—despite the political obstacles NATO would face in mobilizing.[15]

The most serious weakness of Soviet forces and one that the massive investment of resources is least capable of overcoming lies in the uncertain fighting ability and morale of the ordinary soldier. If these soldiers were to fight with the kind of commitment and skill that distinguished the Soviet military toward the end of the Great Patriotic War, the hordes would in all likelihood be unstoppable. But in an offensive war against NATO there would be no time for political indoctrination, and there are in any case limits to the lies that states can tell. If the initial offensives were not successful and the Soviets faced a grinding war of attrition, the reliability of the Soviet fighting man—an increasing number of whom in coming years will be non-Russian—is by no means guaranteed. The Soviets themselves in their doctrinal writings place a great deal of emphasis on the critical significance of morale in war, and it appears likely that overt and unprovoked aggression against the West would make it difficult to maintain such morale in the event of reverses. This in part accounts for the extraordinary emphasis the Soviets place on achieving surprise and rapid victory. Moreover, Soviet forces in Eastern Europe—from the perspective of personnel management—are not well structured for a blitzkrieg-style attack against the West. The Soviet Category I divisions that would form the initial wave of an invading army are composed mostly of short-term conscripts with inadequate training and with no experience with the sort of combat they would face in a war on the central front.[16]

Estimates of the conventional balance of forces have varied widely in the postwar years. The widespread belief in the 1950s that the Soviet Union enjoyed overwhelming conventional superiority gave way in the 1960s to the more sanguine estimates of

McNamara's "whiz kids," who painted the Soviet military threat in far less ominous terms than had been customary.[17] Another period of pessimism followed in the late 1970s with the collapse of détente, the extensive qualitative modernization and numerical buildup of Soviet forces stationed in Eastern Europe, and the dissipation of American conventional fighting strength in Vietnam.[18] In the first half of the 1980s, the pendulum began to swing back again. Although it would be an exaggeration to say that a sense of optimism about NATO's conventional prospects prevails among defense analysts, there is at the least a greater appreciation of western strengths and a more pervasive sense of inherent Soviet weaknesses. Nor is the reevaluation of the conventional balance of power unrelated to events in the real world. The Polish crisis illustrated once again the precarious nature of the Soviet Union's hold over Eastern Europe; and Syria's crushing defeat by Israel in the air war over Lebanon cast doubt on the relative effectiveness of Soviet tactical airpower. Of even greater importance has been the striking improvement in American forces committed to Europe. The U.S. Seventh Army, badly afflicted in the late 1970s by the inadequacies of the All Volunteer Force, is a far more capable fighting force than it was at the outset of the decade. The readiness and overall fighting capability of U.S. air forces committed to Europe have also improved sharply. In truth, the Soviets face a formidable array of uncertainties in contemplating a war of aggression against NATO, which they cannot with confidence overcome. They might lose badly, even if nuclear weapons were not employed.[19]

*   *   *

There is, in sum, little reason to accept the judgment that NATO is wedded "to a force structure and strategy that is doomed to fail."[20] The Russians lack both the opportunity and the motive to commit the crime of military aggression against Western Europe. The lack of motive, of course, is itself to be attributed partly to the absence of opportunity, which means that NATO must continue to modernize and keep ready the military forces—nuclear and conventional—that today render wholly unattractive the prospect of a Soviet invasion. The lack of motive, however, is also to be attributed to the fact that the political order the Soviet Union would seek to change with a military invasion is one that by and large reflects its own interests. This order was not imposed on the Soviet Union, as the Treaty of Versailles was imposed upon Germany. On the contrary, it was the Soviet Union that imposed this settlement on us—an imposition bitterly opposed in the West because of its manifest injustice to the peoples of Eastern Europe. Russia's victory in the Second World War not only gave it a position in Europe unrivalled even in the days of the Czars. It also solved the security problem Russia traditionally faced on its western frontier from a united Germany—a fact of which the Soviets are aware, despite all the absurdities in their press about German revanchism. To incur the colossal risks held out by an invasion of Central Europe in order to change what has by and large been a satisfactory arrangement simply doesn't add up.

The Soviet general staff still cannot brief the Politburo, in Colin Gray's phrase, on a plausible theory of victory. It would have great difficulty doing so even if the assumption were made that the war would remain conventional. The prospect that nuclear weapons might be employed by the United States, moreover, cannot fail to make the initial use of force appear deeply unattractive to even the most adventuresome leadership. From this one may deduce two tasks for western policy: one is to recognize that the Russians wish to intimidate us; the other is not to be intimidated.

Burden Sharing and the Reconstruction of NATO

Proposals to restructure or even abolish the Atlantic Alliance are coeval with its birth in 1949. There have always been those dissatisfied with the American role in NATO, who deplore the dependence of once-proud nations on a protector across the sea, who believe that the United States committed in the postwar years a basic historical error by providing the Europeans with a security that they could and would have provided for themselves. There have always been those who have found the American future somewhere other than in Europe, whether in Asia or Latin America. There have always been those who have approved of the American commitment to Europe, but who have been deeply disturbed by the force structure and strategy on which NATO has relied. For an alliance marked by all manner of continuity, perhaps its most durable feature has been the recurrent phases of disaffection to which all parties to it have occasionally succumbed.

Even by the standards of the remarkably self-critical Atlantic Alliance, the upsurge of disaffection on both sides of the Atlantic that occurred during the crises of the early 1980s was unusual.[21] In Europe, the Reagan administration's decision to impose sanctions on European firms involved in the construction of the Siberian natural gas pipeline sharply angered European elites; the support of the administration for the 1979 NATO decision to deploy in Europe new intermediate-range missiles capable of reaching Soviet territory (Pershing IIs and GLCMs) badly disaffected much of the European mass. In the United States, anger grew with allies unwilling to do their share in combating Soviet power. There was a growing sense among many that the world had changed and that American interests had shifted away from Europe. This disposition was reflected in the growth of calls for a less Eurocentric defense policy, a view attractive all along the political spectrum. Indeed, it came to be associated with neoisolationists, military reformers, neoconservatives, global unilateralists, NATO reconstructionists, and maritime strategists. The proponents of these new approaches differ greatly among themselves as to the purposes of this newly liberated power, and among them one may find the heirs of 1930s isolationists and 1960s internationalists. They nevertheless share the desire to make less Eurocentric the foundations of American defense.

The primary sentiment that gave these calls for change increasing weight in American politics was the belief, very widely held in America, that the existing division of responsibility within the alliance was inequitable. That is a view held even by such traditional Atlanticists as Senator Sam Nunn, who sponsored in 1984 an amendment calling for progressive reductions in the American role in Europe unless the Europeans met specific goals in defense policy and spending.[22] The amendment failed, after intensive lobbying by the Reagan administration, but it expressed a point of view that is certain to persist and may even deepen. For it seems likely that European defense budgets will remain static in real terms for the remainder of the decade and beyond. The pressures on the American defense budget created by the insolvency of American economic policy, when placed alongside the past and future failure of the Europeans to substantially increase defense spending in response to the substantial American increases in 1980–85, make it likely that many Americans will continue to be deeply attracted to a policy that seeks to restore solvency and equity by substantially altering—and perhaps even eliminating—the American role in the arrangements of European security. And the attractiveness of these proposals is increased because they are often placed alongside calls for changes in NATO strategy or force structure, many of which purport to show that the "problem is not more money," that Western Europe could substantially increase its effective contribution to the common defense without sharply increasing the burdens posed by defense expenditures.

None of these changes of policy—a return to isolationism, a progressive reduction of the American role in Europe, or a radical change in NATO's force structure and strategy—offer a resolution of the American strategic predicament. Radical changes in force structure or strategy are either politically impossible or militarily unsound or both. The reversion to isolationism or the partial withdrawal of American forces from Europe, on the other hand, are inconsistent with the fundamental interest the United States continues to have in preserving the physical security of Europe. The burden of military expenditures on the United States certainly needs to be reduced, both to restore a sense of equity to the alliance relationship and to restore solvency to American economic policy. The withdrawal of American forces from Europe, however, need play no role in the restoration of solvency, and such an action would not restore equity to the Atlantic relationship. The mistake of doing more than our share will not be repaired by doing less. To expect that it might is the logic of children, despite the fact that so many of our wise men have embraced it.

*   *   *

The case for preserving the traditional elements of the American role in European security rests on many elements. The security and freedom of Western Europe is a vital American interest not primarily for reasons of economic or physical security; indeed, the burdens of maintaining American forces in Europe are large, and in some respects our physical security is endangered by our commitment to Europe, since it is by virtue of that commitment that the United States runs its greatest danger of nuclear war. The primary reasons are moral and psychological. The United States is deeply indebted to Europe, as our parent civilization, for our sense of ourselves and for the values we have inherited. The continued well-being of this civilization is not an "interest" in the conventional sense—that is, one subject to the computation of relative benefits and costs.

Most of those who call for the reduction or the elimination of the American role in Europe are aware of these considerations.[23] In calling for the alteration of American policy toward Europe, they do not by and large deny that the United States continues to have a vital interest in Europe's physical security and political freedom; they do question whether the United States must continue to play the predominant role in ensuring European security that it has played since 1945. They point to the economic resources that NATO Europe now commands, to a GNP that is larger than that enjoyed by the entirety of the Warsaw Pact; and they ask whether it has been precisely the commitment of the United States to European security that has prevented the Europeans from tapping these resources and forming a solid counterweight to Soviet power in Europe. If the American interest in Europe is largely moral and psychological, there is an important sense in which the perpetuation of European dependency on the United States—corrupting to both the protector and the protected—cannot vindicate it. Friendship, they say (and as the ancients knew), is only possible among equals.

These are powerful but ultimately unsatisfactory objections. The critics are not wrong in thinking that some form of European unification would be required in the event of an American withdrawal. As Exhibit 7 shows, the United States dominates the alliance with respect to overall defense expenditures and would do so even if the sharing of burdens within the alliance were more equitable. The Europeans would have to make up a great deal of ground in the event of an American withdrawal, and they could only enjoy the requisite political and military weight to balance the power of the Soviet Union if they were to unify their energies. Yet this prospect remains remote. The assumption of the critics appears to be that the division of Europe into sovereign states is something unnatural and artificial, but that view is very difficult to square with what we know about the continent's linguistic diversity and cultural particularity. The expectation that European unity might be brought into being by an act of American will recalls previous attempts in American statecraft that ignored reality because it was unpleasant or did not correspond with the character of our desire.

Exhibit 7—*National Shares in Defense Spending and GNP in NATO*

	Defense Spending (1982)	Gross National Product (1982)
United States	66.1%	51.0%
Britain	8.2%	7.9%
West Germany	7.5%	10.9%
France	7.4%	7.9%
Italy	3.1%	5.7%
Canada	2.1%	4.8%
Remaining nations	less than 2.0%	

Source:—The Federal Minister of Defence, Federal Republic of Germany (Bonn, Germany: The Federal Minister of Defense, 1983) *White Paper 1983: The Security of the Federal Republic of Germany.*

All such attempts in the past have issued in unforeseen and sometimes disastrous consequences, and there is little reason for thinking that an American withdrawal that sought to shock the Europeans into unified action would be any different in that respect. Yet once we see the fictitious character of the alternative proposals that advocates of American withdrawal hold out, we are drawn back to the conclusion that American power is necessary for the maintenance of the balance of power in Europe.

The most critical aspect of the American role is precisely that over which many Americans are most uneasy—and that is the contribution made by its nuclear weapons. There is no real substitute for these weapons in the arrangements of European security, and this is so regardless of the strategic doctrines that might govern their use (or non-use). The nuclear problem of the alliance revolves around Germany—around the fact that Germany is threatened by a nuclear power yet prevented by the iron law of the postwar order from acquiring nuclear weapons of its own. Were a German government to try to acquire an independent power of nuclear decision, there is little question that the remedy would be worse than the disease, for the solution would be completely unacceptable to the Russians, the French, and, not least, to a large number of the German people. To attempt to improve upon the postwar order in this manner, therefore, might very well bring it down. Yet lesser remedies are almost pathetically inadequate. The declaration by Britain or France that Germany now lies behind the shields of either nuclear power, though desirable, could not replace the American guarantee: given the past history of British and French strategic doctrine and the memory of perennial intra-European rivalry, this declaration would be much less believable—to both the Germans and the Russians—than the comparable declaration that has come from the United States over the past generation. And clever devices that would give the Germans a finger on the trigger while preserving a French or British veto are too clever by half: they would do nothing to strengthen deterrence and indeed might weaken it, since they would reduce the uncertainty induced in the aggressor by what the French strategist André Beaufre once called "multiple centers of decision."[24]

For those who believe our nuclear commitment to NATO poses the principal threat to American security, the irreplaceability of the American guarantee does not constitute a decisive objection. Even though the Europeans might suffer by an American withdrawal of this guarantee, they argue, the paramount interest we should place in our own physical security ought nevertheless to compel this measure. The argument is a plausible one: it draws attention to the striking paradox that we risk our physical security today on behalf of interests that, if lost, would not endanger that security. But ultimately the argument is unpersuasive. It requires us to neglect the compound of motives—which were partly those of physical security but also included cultural and institutional ties of deep moral and psychological significance—which led to American intervention in the two world wars of this century. Although today we are repelled from Europe because it is our very commitment to the European balance of power that seems most likely to imperil our physical security, we are also drawn back to it because our experience in the twentieth century suggests that any separation would be artificial and could not be sustained. Isolationism was discredited in this century, as Raymond Aron once put it,

because at the moment of truth the decision makers, public opinion, and events have twice brought about intervention. The question is not so much whether, if American diplomacy were governed solely by considerations of physical security, it could or should stand aside from the turmoils of history; the real question is whether nonalignment and the refusal of entangling alliances would not give rise some day to crises from which once again, however much it wished to abstain, the American republic would be incapable of standing aside.[25]

That question, in turn, suggests that the nuclear dilemma cannot be resolved by political isolation.

★   ★   ★

Most observers do not go so far as to propose the end of American participation in NATO. Many, however, would change the basis of American involvement. Some argue for the progressive withdrawal of all American ground forces—the provision of which ought to be left to the Europeans themselves—and the restriction of American involvement to providing air and naval forces. Others would withdraw only part of the American ground force contingent from the central front. Most of those who call for such reductions insist that the emergence of new threats outside Europe make imperative such a reorientation of American strategy. Their outlook is therefore sharply different from a policy of hemispheric isolation.[26] Although part of the justification for withdrawal stems from anger or disappointment with the Europeans—with allies "who want equidistance from the two superpowers, who want defense (but not too much of it), who are more afraid of American sanctions than of events in Poland, more apprehensive about American than Soviet missiles, who want to be allies and mediators at the same time"[27]—another part stems from the conviction that the world beyond Europe is becoming increasingly important to the United States. However its adherents are characterized—as interventionists, global unilateralists, or maritime strategists—all argue that our defense strategy must become less Eurocentric. All seek to begin to withdraw American ground forces from Europe.

Such proposals should be resisted. From the early 1950s to the present time, the United States has maintained some five divisions in Western Europe. The physical presence of those forces continues to be of critical importance in the arrangements of European security. They stand as a potent reminder, both to the Russians and the Europeans, that a war in Europe would inescapably engage American power. Many have argued that the continued presence of American air and naval forces could serve this function just as well, and under most circumstances they might be right. But circumstances change; American presidents come and go. What might appear as a formidable deterrent under a Richard Nixon, who combined a deep understanding of the psychology of power with the will to use it, might seem less than impressive under another president. It therefore seems best that the American commitment to Europe continue to be represented not only by airpower and thus by will but also by things in the animal and material world, like men and tanks.

If there were some compelling strategic rationale for the removal of these forces from Europe the matter might appear differently, but there is no such rationale. Of all the global interests the United States might vindicate by the use or threatened use of ground forces, none approach in importance the interest we have in maintaining the physical security of Western Europe. The Persian Gulf, to name but one of these candidates, is important because of Europe, not in spite of it. And it is Europe's economic security that is implicated there, not its physical security. American ground forces, as I will argue in chapter 3, are not necessary to secure American interests in the Persian Gulf against regional threats. If the Soviet Union were to invade the Gulf, on the other hand, this would inevitably require a reevaluation of Soviet intentions toward Europe. In these circumstances, to favor the Gulf over Europe in the distribution of American ground forces would represent a strange inversion of American priorities, for our attempt to provide a conventional defense of the Persian Gulf would inevitably come at the expense of the conventional defense of Europe. If nuclear weapons are to be used (or threatened) in a tactical role, it is far better to rely on them in the Gulf instead of in Europe.[28]

Nor could an expansion of reserve ground forces make up for the withdrawal of active U.S. forces from Europe, as some analysts have proposed.[29] Reserve formations in the ground forces, for one thing, have traditionally maintained much lower levels of readiness than active forces. Although no doubt much could be done to raise the readiness levels of existing reserve units, there is the danger that such units would still take a long time to mobilize and would be basically useless in the first stages of a Soviet-American war. Once ready, moreover, the transport of such forces overseas would require greatly expanded airlift or sealift capabilities, which is an expensive proposition. Insofar as peacetime preparation is directed toward the possibility of a Soviet-American war in Europe, it makes little sense to undermine one's prospects for winning the short war in order to marginally improve one's prospects in the long one. Scarce resources, therefore, ought to be devoted to increasing the capability of active NATO forces to prevail in the first stages of a conflict (by increasing ammunition reserves from thirty to sixty days and beyond, for instance) rather than by devoting resources to forces that could not in all probability be made ready for combat immediately. If, after the first two or three months of a war in Central Europe, NATO forces do not constitute a cohesive line but are instead broken and tattered remnants, there will be nothing for these reserve forces to reinforce. Under those circumstances, the attempt to regain a toehold in Europe would in all likelihood require years of mobilization, to which the prior efforts in the way of reserve forces would make only a minor contribution.

So long as the United States maintains anything approaching its present number of active ground divisions (seventeen plus in the Army and three in the Marine Corps), the strategic rationale for retaining at least five in forward deployed positions in Western Europe is overwhelming. To satisfy the requirements of deterrence and defense, emphasis should not be placed on forces-in-being capable of prevailing in a long war. We rather require preeminently the capability of winning the short one (and thus provoking the disruption of Soviet morale that ought to be the primary object of NATO operations, whether nuclear or conventional). Insofar as the United States maintains large ground forces in its arsenal—as it certainly will continue to do to one degree or another—the majority should have a primarily European orientation. These forces make their most important contribution to European deterrence by being instantly available for use in Europe at the outset of a conflict. Cuts in the overall size of American ground forces need to be made, but the cuts should be concentrated in the Army and Marine Corps divisions stationed elsewhere than in Europe. If they come from Europe at all, they should come from our reinforcement capability and our capacity to sustain a long war.

★   ★   ★

Proposals to begin the withdrawal of American forces from Europe are often accompanied by suggestions to change NATO's strategy on the central front. That strategy rests upon an attempt to defend against a Warsaw Pact attack as close to the inner German border as possible, and it has often been criticized for its overly defensive orientation and its vulnerability to disruption. Alternatives that offer NATO the prospect of conventional parity or even superiority, according to the critics, include:

1) the fortification of the inner German frontier;

2) the creation of a German force of territorials, capable of taking advantage of the terrain along the inner German border, which is heavily forested or dotted with stone villages;[30]

3) the restructuring of NATO forces, sharply increasing the number of armored divisions. This could be accomplished either through the dramatic reduction of tail-to-teeth (or support-to-combat) ratios in NATO armies on the model of Soviet forces or through a different use of European reserves. Steven Canby, for instance, has proposed that NATO utilize its reserves in the manner of the Dutch *Rechstreeks Instromend Mobilisable* (RIM) system. Instead of releasing conscripts into the general reserve pool, as is currently done in most continental countries, the Dutch system releases its conscripts as units with equipment that may be recalled together to active duty within fifteen months of deactivation—while the personal relationships indispensable to fighting effectiveness are still intact;[31]

4) a change in NATO operational doctrine. The two most important variations on this theme call for a defense in depth or for a strategy of conventional retaliation—what Josef Joffe has called the "Russian" and the "Prussian" solutions to the NATO defense problem:

> To escape from the curse of geography, which meant that Prussia was always better at offense than at defense, the Hohenzollerns regularly sought salvation in a lightning strike that would break the tightening ring of encirclement. Conversely, the classic Russian strategy has been to exploit territory as a trap, trading space for time in an ultimately victorious war of attrition.[32]

At first glance, these proposals are very dissimilar to one another. But the dissimilarity is in one critical respect misleading. All require basic changes in German policy. Some do so explicitly, some implicitly, some with, and some without, an appreciation of their political significance. But such an appreciation is basic to an understanding of most demands for the reconstruction of NATO, for it is the central reason why most are doomed to fail. West Germany enjoys a privileged position when it comes to questions about the size and operational requirements of forces on its national territory. It enjoys as well an effective power of veto over basic changes in NATO's strategy on the central front. Initiatives that require the Germans to challenge any of the many requirements they have come to think of as indispensable are very unlikely to succeed. They might be made to succeed only by threatening to abandon the Germans—a threat, however, that would carry unpredictable and potentially fatal consequences for Germany and the United States.

The proposals themselves are a mixed bag, quite apart from their political appeal. The least controversial from a military point of view is the fortification of the inner German frontier. As Jeffrey Record has observed,

The history of mechanized warfare since 1939 has repeatedly demonstrated that the kind of echeloned armored blitzkrieg which the Soviets are capable of launching against Europe is defeatible only by (1) a willingness on the part of the defender to trade space for time in order to identify the main axes of advance, wear down attacking forces, and form up sufficient operational reserves (assuming they are available) in rear areas to throw the enemy back, or (2) an "up front" defense along the border based on a combination of firepower superiority and extensive fortifications and such barrier defenses as minefields, tank-traps, walled terraces, water obstacles, hedgerows, and afforestation. The two are not mutually exclusive, but rather complementary.[33]

These observations are perfectly correct—and indeed cogent—as far as they go. But they do not go far enough. The Germans do not wish to construct these fortifications. Virtually every article by American defense analysts acknowledges the existence of the German objections, which are that such fortifications would stand as a permanent symbol of the division of Germany; they would meet with the objection of border residents; and they would remind the Germans of the prospect of war, a prospect that is equally unthinkable whether it is nuclear or conventional war. There is nevertheless the implication in much of this writing that the Germans require only a bit more persuasion, that they need only be presented with an argument more deftly phrased, and they will change their minds. All the evidence indicates, however, that they will not change their minds. Nor will it do to argue that the German insistence on forward defense and the German resistance to fortification is inconsistent. That is indeed the case. The fact remains that the Germans prefer some inconsistencies over others.

The proposal to create a force of German territorials—although it has aroused some interest on the political left in Germany—is suspect on military grounds. The growing constraints on German manpower (see Exhibit 8) would require a force of territorials to draw from the present force of German armored and mechanized infantry brigades—which could not therefore be maintained at current levels. Yet these divisions are the cream of NATO fighting power on the central front. Unlike these mechanized divisions, a force of territorials would be incapable of defending a forward defense line against an armored blitzkrieg. At most they might succeed in channeling an attack and disrupting its momentum. It might be argued, of course, that French, Dutch, and Belgian armored divisions might make up for the loss of the German ones. But of this two things may be said: such compensation by the other European powers is unlikely, and even if it were to happen, it is doubtful that these forces would be as competent (or as formidable to the Soviet Union) as the present German force.

Proposals to add additional armored divisions to NATO often foster the impression that the increases in combat power would be virtually cost-free, as in Steven Canby's reflection that "the problem is not more money."[34] That is not the case. Given the likelihood of stable (or even in some instances declining) defense budgets in the foreseeable future, these divisions, recently estimated to cost $97 billion over ten years, could be paid for only by eliminating some other feature of the balanced forces maintained by Britain, France, and West Germany. These three powers are the critical ones, for they have by far the largest potential supplies of reserve manpower. Yet the air and sea forces of these three powers provide the alliance with valuable auxiliaries that are duplicated nowhere else, as both the French intervention in Chad and the British victory in the Falklands have shown. The expansion of French and British nuclear forces is equally desirable. The proposal to make more effective use of European reserves seems innocuous, but what it amounts to is that the Europeans should rely on the United States to a far greater degree than they now do for their nuclear deterrent and their air and sea power. What is held out as a means of increasing the European contribution to the common defense would in fact deepen their dependence in precisely the area where such dependence is most

EXHIBIT 8—*Constraints on German Manpower*

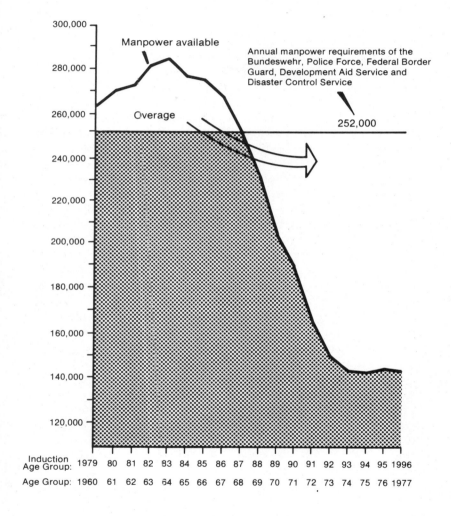

Source:—The Federal Minister of Defense, Federal Republic of Germany, *White Paper 1979: The Security of the Federal Republic of Germany and the Development of the Federal Armed Forces* (Bonn, Germany: Federal Minister of Defense, 1979).

resented. For these reasons, the proposal is not only a political *cul-de-sac;* it is strategically undesirable, and strongly reminiscent of the patronizing attitude the United States government adopted toward the French in the early 1960s. If made a central feature of a new American initiative toward Europe, it would no doubt issue in equally pernicious consequences.

The doctrinal changes (of either the rearward or forward variety) are perhaps the most suspect. Germany lacks the geographic depth to trade space for time in the classic Russian manner. The Prussian alternative, however, would inevitably exacerbate the fear that the opposing forces would collide with one another in the manner of 1914. For Germans, the ideal character of Western defense policy, as Helmut Schmidt wrote long ago, is that of "an armaments struc-ture clearly unsuited for the offensive role yet adequate beyond the shadow of a doubt to defend Germany territory."[35] A strategy of conventional retaliation—or indeed a restructuring of German forces on the Soviet model—would clearly violate this injunction. The assumption that NATO would be able to mobilize faster than the Warsaw Pact, which Canby stresses, is a dubious one, for mobilization, if it rested upon those plans, would almost certainly mean war. It has long been a commonplace among strategic ana-lysts that the most likely cause of a future European war would lie in circumstances in which the Soviet Union faced a revolt within its empire alongside the possibility of western intervention. A strategic doctrine of conventional retaliation would sharpen these fears, and indeed might inhibit mobilization in the hour of need.

The primordial reason why strategies of conventional retaliation are destined to fail in Europe is that the West Germans would be completely exposed to Soviet nuclear retaliation in the event of their launching offensive operations into the heart of the Soviet empire, and they could have little confidence at the outset either that the Soviet Union would refrain from such a nuclear attack or that the United States would respond against Soviet territory, and thus deter, a Soviet attack on West Germany. This German vul-nerability points not only to the certain failure of such an American initiative; even more, it points to the fundamental inequity of the American threat to abandon the Germans unless they do our bid-ding in this matter. In the end, there is little point for the Germans to embark on this path unless they can foresee as their destination an ability to stand equal with the Soviet Union and to confront

Soviet power in Europe in isolation from any other power. The logic of the proposal, in other words, is that the Germans acquire an extensive nuclear arsenal of their own.

And thus we come full circle. Proposals to reconstruct NATO usually begin innocuously enough, but invariably they end up by projecting a profoundly different role for Germany. Such a different role, in turn, doesn't make sense unless the question of nuclear arms for Germany is faced squarely. Yet the reasons for rejecting such a change are powerful ones, despite forty years of responsible statecraft and democratic government in the Federal Republic. The fundamental problem is not that the German state that arose out of the ashes of the Third Reich would be more reckless in its attitude toward nuclear weapons than the other nuclear powers have been; indeed, this seems wholly improbable. The central problem is that such an initiative might give rise to consequences that would leave the West more insecure than ever. No one can really say, to be sure, what the consequences of such an initiative would be in fact. It does seem clear that the Soviet Union would bitterly resist such a transformation of the postwar order, and since proposals to create a nuclear Germany most often appear in the context of arguments for a disengagement from Europe by the United States, a diplomatic initiative that reflected both of these attitudes would open up some very interesting possibilities for the Soviet Union. The effect of a sharply renewed East-West crisis on German public opinion is difficult to judge, but it requires a very optimistic outlook to believe that such opinion, under the pressures generated from all sides, would continue to be anchored in prudence and sobriety. What seems most likely, on the contrary, is that a powerful current of German opinion—perhaps even a majority of the electorate— would again become deeply attracted to nuclear pacifism and neutralism.[36]

★   ★   ★

None of the alternatives examined thus far—a return to isolationism, the adoption of a policy of global unilateralism, or the reform of NATO's force structure and strategy on the central front—offer a realistic resolution of the American strategic predicament. Yet the issues of equity and solvency remain and must be satisfied. The common assumption is that they can only be satisfied by profoundly reconstructing the bases of the Atlantic Alliance, but that is not the case. There are changes that can be made in American strategy—detailed in chapter 4 and 5—that do not require us to utterly transform an alliance that has served our interests well since the end of the Second World War. Much of the dissatisfaction over burden-sharing in the early 1980s, moreover, has arisen from the fact that the United States has assumed responsibilities in the Persian Gulf to protect interests that are of greater consequence to Western Europe than to the United States. It was the expansion of such extra-European responsibilities that was the most inequitable feature of the transatlantic division of responsibility in the early 1980s; the contraction of such responsibilities—a contraction made possible, as I argue in chapter 3, by the revolution in world oil markets—ought to be the principal means by which we restore equity in the late 1980s.

The critics are right in believing that the responsibility for improved, high-confidence conventional defenses in Central Europe is ultimately a European one. The American people should not be asked to care more for the conventional defense of Europe than the Europeans do. For reasons of equity alone, to say nothing of the requirements of solvency, it would be inadvisable to go beyond the commitment of the late 1970s to provide ten ground divisions and sixty fighter squadrons in Europe within ten days of a mobilization. But to limit America's commitment in some respects does not require us to abandon our traditional role, nor is such a limitation at all likely to yield a force structure and strategy inconsistent with the maintenance of deterrence. On the contrary, what seems most likely to produce a breakdown of European order (assuming that it is produced by the Right and not the Left) is an American initiative that seeks to transform the Atlantic Alliance on our own terms, one which is based on the assumption that the current situation is perilous (which it is not), and which threatens an American withdrawal unless we have everything our own way.

Deterrence and Reassurance

We have reached what many will regard as a disagreeable conclusion. If, as is likely, neither Western Europe nor the United States makes a great effort in coming years to improve NATO's conventional defenses, the structure of European deterrence will continue to rest on the American threat to employ nuclear weapons first in response to a Soviet conventional attack. This is so even if we reject the pessimistic analyses of the conventional balance of forces. Even though the structure of European deterrence does not by any means rest wholly on the prospect that nuclear weapons would be employed in the resistance of a Soviet attack, it is certainly the case that the nuclear sword hangs over everything and gives the structure a solidity and permanence it would not otherwise possess. Yet it is precisely this element of western strategy, it has been argued, that can no longer play a useful role in the arrangements of western security. Many of the peoples—European and American— these weapons are designed to protect are frightened by the very thought of them; they no longer provide, Michael Howard has argued, the basis for a western strategy that simultaneously deters the Soviet Union while it reassures western publics.[37]

It would be absurd to say that what Howard called a growing disjunction between deterrence and reassurance is not a serious matter facing the alliance. Indeed, it has been a serious problem for a long time. Writing in 1960, Henry Kissinger noted that "public opinion in most allied countries has been mobilized against nuclear weapons by a variety of agents" and concluded that "in these circumstances, it will become increasingly difficult to concert a strategic and tactical doctrine that is accepted by the alliance and maintained with conviction in the face of Soviet pressure."[38] What made that task "increasingly difficult" was the appearance and subsequent growth of the Soviet Union's ability to strike the United States with nuclear weapons. The nuclear dilemma of the alliance came to consist of the fact that the use of American nuclear weapons against Soviet territory in the event of a Soviet attack on Western Europe had become increasingly incredible, whereas the "limited" use of such weapons against Soviet military forces in Europe conjured up images of Europe as the nuclear battlefield of the superpowers. The dark night of the American soul was that the American commitment to Western Europe might lead to the use of nuclear weapons against American territory; the "secret dream of every European," as Henry Kissinger put it in 1979, "was, of course, to avoid nuclear war but, secondly, if there had to be a nuclear war, to have it conducted over their heads by the strategic forces of the United States and the Soviet Union."[39]

Since the 1950s, when these rival fears emerged, there have been a large number of attempts to reconcile them. "Graduated deterrence," "flexible response," "limited nuclear options," "the countervailing strategy," and many others have all been attempts to describe a nuclear doctrine for the alliance that would be both credible to the Soviet Union and reassuring to western publics. Although they differed in particulars, each solution sought a *via media* between "massive retaliation" and "no-first-use," between suicide and surrender.[40] The most credible—a geographical restriction on the use of American nuclear weapons that respected the Soviet sanctuary in an attempt to secure a sanctuary for the United States—was also the least reassuring to European public opinion; the most reassuring—the notion that there would be no sanctuaries in the event of a Soviet-American war, that an attack on one was an attack on all—was also the least credible. The central difficulty of NATO strategy was that the prospect of unlimited nuclear war was no longer credible and thus no longer deterred, whereas the prospect of limited nuclear war was repugnant to European public opinion and thus did not reassure. Deterrence and reassurance each came to rest upon a calculus that could not be officially avowed, because to fully elaborate the one undermined the foundations of the other.

All of this was illustrated in the nuclear crises of the early 1980s. Once again European opinion revolted against the prospect of a limited nuclear war in Europe—the catalytic event being the response of President Reagan to a question about whether he believed in the possibility of a limited nuclear war between the United States and the Soviet Union: "I could see," he said, "where you could have the exchange of tactical weapons against troops in the field without it bringing either one of the major powers to pushing the button."[41] There was, to be sure, an element of the absurd about the whole situation, for the European peace demonstrators directed most of their fervor against the Euromissiles, which represented the triumph of the perspective on nuclear issues traditionally held by European elites. (Since it involved the stationing on European soil of intermediate-range missiles capable of reaching Soviet territory, it conformed to the requirement that there be no sanctuaries.) The latest American attempt to provide reassurance to European opinion that a conflict between the superpowers could not remain limited was thus greeted by a substantial portion of European

opinion as an unconscionable attempt by American leaders to ensure that it would. The Euromissile crisis apart, the deeper fears on
either side of the Atlantic persisted. The American film about the
end of the world—"The Day After"—located its superpower crisis
in a conflict over Berlin that ultimately engulfed America. In the
British film on the same subject, a Soviet-American war begun in a
distant, faraway place, Iran, soon spread and engulfed Europe. Nor
are the European fears unreasonable. There are no doctrinal developments or weapons deployments that can alter the pressures an
American president would feel at the moment of truth, and which
would press him toward both resistance and limitation, that would
push him, in the event of a conventional collapse, to the logic of
limited nuclear war in Europe. For purposes of reassurance, he can
and must say in peacetime that there would be no sanctuaries, but
in a war it is likely that he would respect the Soviet one in the hope
of preserving the United States from direct nuclear attack.

If the continued existence of the Atlantic Alliance depended on
reaching a true meeting of the minds on all the nuclear issues that
have bedeviled it, the alliance would then indeed be an "empty
shell," as Henry Kissinger described it in 1981. In fact, however,
such a meeting of the minds is not necessary to maintain both
deterrence and reassurance. The alliance's nuclear elites have resolved these dilemmas in practice through calculated ambiguities—
embodied in the 1967 formula of flexible response—seeking to
impress upon friend and foe alike the certainty of an American
commitment if Europe is attacked without specifying in detail the
form this response would take. The Soviets have been left to draw
their own conclusions. The Europeans, though appalled by the fact
that their fate rests in the hands of others, are ultimately reassured
by the certainty of the American commitment and by the knowledge that this commitment would render a Soviet attack wholly
unprofitable and therefore wholly unlikely.

To say that there is a disjunction between deterrence and reassurance is therefore true enough, but it is not the whole truth. It
does not mean that the persistence of this disjunction for the indefinite future will render increasingly untenable the essentials of the
alliance's military posture, including its nuclear posture. The pro-
pensity to draw this conclusion is not only based on the conditions
of deterrence in the nuclear age. It is also and more fundamentally
based on the assumption that there are irreconcilable differences

between the United States and Europe over the importance of preserving European security. On this view, the Americans believe in the idea of "prevailing" in a protracted nuclear war, whereas the Europeans do not. The Americans believe in the inevitability of war in Europe, whereas the Europeans do not. The Americans think that Europe is merely an instrument in the pursuit of their global rivalry with the Soviet Union, whereas the Europeans see their security as an end in itself.

There are utterances and writings of American officials that may be adduced in support of this case. The European peace demonstrators have cited them without end. But in general the preceding analysis mistakes for a permanent and unalterable feature of American opinion views that have been given a temporary and indeed even isolated expression in the Reagan administration. None of the things in which "the Americans" are supposed to believe and which European opinion finds so offensive is a necessary feature of American policy. "Naturally the Europeans don't want to be the battleground for our own quarrels with the Russians," Bernard Brodie wrote a generation ago, "but that means only that our main job of persuasion is to convince the Europeans that we will never fight the Russians in Europe except in the direct defense of Europe."[42]

That is one requirement of reassurance. Another is that the Europeans be allowed to maintain their economic ties with the Soviet Union. A strategy of economic denial is difficult enough to justify if considered at face value; it cannot be effectively implemented, and limited measures that inflict pain on the Soviet Union, as the United States discovered with the grain embargo, require that we inflict pain on ourselves as well. Nor has the experience of East-West trade been wholly favorable to the Soviet bloc: it was the growth of Polish indebtedness in the 1970s that provided the foundation for the Polish crisis of the early 1980s—a crisis that, once again, advertised the weakness of the Soviet Union's hold over Eastern Europe. Underlying all these calculations of costs and benefits, however, is the strategic calculation in Europe that the maintenance of economic intercourse between East and West in peacetime reduces whatever incentives the Soviet Union might have for going to war against the West. That this is a justification capable of abuse is clear. It offers no reason for the West to enter into agreements that provide the Soviet Union with unilateral economic advantages, nor does it mean that the prohibition against the transfer of economic goods with direct military applications should not be strictly enforced. Within these constraints, however, it does give the Russians a stake in the maintenance of a peaceful relationship with the West and for this reason the Europeans consider it a basic requirement of their security.

None of this means that a strategic posture that is reliant on the first use of nuclear weapons will ever have an easy time either reassuring or deterring. It ought to remind us, however, that there is more than one way to erode public confidence in Western Europe in the alliance's strategic posture. Indeed, we know from the history of the Atlantic relationship that a new administration could very well be indicted on charges that are the opposite of those brought against Mr. Reagan. The failure of a new administration could very well reside in its intolerable lack of mean-spiritedness. To satisfy European opinion, an American president must be minimally provocative in times of peace, while simultaneously conveying his underlying determination to commit acts of unparalleled barbarity in the event of war. This is a very demanding role, acted out before very demanding critics. There is a fundamental sense, indeed, in which the performance is destined to be unsatisfactory, recalling Bethmann Hollweg's 1914 lament over "our old dilemma at every Austrian action in the Balkans. If we encourage them, they say we pushed them into it. If we discourage them, they say we left them in the lurch."[43] There is no more fitting epitaph to the crisis over the Euromissiles. But a relationship destined to be unsatisfactory is not thereby destined to break down. Nations, like individuals, will put up with a lot for want of an acceptable alternative.

★   ★   ★

These reflections are not intended to preclude the possibility that at some point in the future Europe may discover—through some as yet unknown and unforeseeable change in the international system—the secret of providing for its own security. The discovery of this secret would be desirable on many grounds. But it must also be recognized that the reasons for Europe's inability to discover this secret over the past generation are not incidental but stem rather from the fundamental nature of the postwar order. The primary obstacle to it is the unwillingness of the major participants in this state system to change in any basic way the formula of postwar

European security—to wit, that a Great Power is needed to coun-
terbalance the threat posed by the Soviet Union in Europe and that
this power cannot be Germany, France, or Great Britain.

Since the end of the Second World War, the United States has
assumed the role that the psychologically shattered and politically
divided nations of Western Europe could not assume for themselves. The order thus created has persisted for over a generation.
When we compare it with the preceding years of unrelieved disorder from 1914 to 1945—the most awful period in the history of our
civilization—we cannot fail to appreciate that the accomplishment
has been a great one. The cause of peace is best served today by
attempts to shore up the postwar order against the rival attempts of
the Right and the Left to bring it down. That means in the first
instance that the Europeans must be allowed to pursue their détente
with the Russians. And it means as well that we must resist the
efforts currently underway either to withdraw American troops
from Europe or to eliminate from the arsenals of the West the
material and declaratory bases of the nuclear deterrent.

Notes

1. Clausewitz, *On War,* 75–76. Cf. Robert McNamara, "The Military Role of
Nuclear Weapons: Perceptions and Misperceptions," *Foreign Affairs* (Fall 1983), 71–
72. The view that a nuclear conflict might remain limited, Robert McNamara has
written, "requires the assumption that even though the initial strikes would have
inflicted large-scale casualties and damage to both sides, one or the other—feeling
disadvantaged—would give in. But under such circumstances, leaders on both sides
would be under unimaginable pressure to avenge their losses and secure the interests
being challenged. And each would fear that the opponent might launch a larger
attack at any moment. Moreover, they would both be operating with only partial
information because of the disruption to communications caused by the chaos on the
battlefield (to say nothing of possible strikes against communication facilities).
Under such conditions, it is highly likely that rather than surrender, each side would
launch a larger attack, hoping that this step would bring the action to a halt by
causing the opponent to capitulate." For a similar analysis, see McGeorge Bundy,
George F Kennan, Robert S. McNamara, and Gerald Smith, "Nuclear Weapons and
the Atlantic Alliance," *Foreign Affairs* (Spring 1982), 757.

2. Niccolò Machiavelli, *The Prince,* 9.

3. For reasons explained by Edward Luttwak, "How to Think About Nuclear
War," *Commentary,* (August 1982), 25–26.

4. On the debate over Soviet strategic doctrine, see particularly Derek Leebaert,
ed., *Soviet Military Thinking* (London, 1981): Benjamin S. Lambeth, "Soviet Strategic Conduct and the Prospects for Stability," reprinted in John F Reichart and Steve

R. Sturm, eds., *American Defense Policy,* 5th ed. (Baltimore, 1982), 188–98; Richard Pipes, "Why the Soviet Union Thinks it Could Fight and Win a Nuclear War," *Commentary,* (July 1977), 21–34; David Holloway, "Military Power and Political Purpose in Soviet Policy," *Daedalus* (Fall 1980), 13–30; Donald W. Hanson, "Is Soviet Strategic Doctrine Superior?" *International Security* (Winter 1982/83), 61–83; and Jack L. Snyder, *The Soviet Strategic Culture: Implications for Limited Nuclear Operations,* (Santa Monica, September 1977). The distinction between annihilation and attrition as strategic objectives, that is, between the disarmament of the enemy and the disruption of his morale, is explored further in chapter 4 below.

5. Plans for the French and British nuclear arsenals are detailed in George M. Seigious II and Jonathan Paul Yates, "Europe's Nuclear Superpowers," *Foreign Policy* (Summer 1984), 40–53; and Michael Gordon, "British and French Missiles Complicate Life for Moscow," *The New York Times,* 26 January 1986. See also Pierre Hassner, "France, Deterrence and Europe: Rationalizing the Irrational," *International Defense Review,* 2 (1984), 133–42. On British nuclear forces, see Lawrence Freedman, "Britain: The First Ex-Nuclear Power?" *International Security* (Fall 1981), 80–104, and "Labour and the Bomb," *The Economist,* 2 April 1983, 39–42.

6. On the political reliability of Warsaw Pact armies, see Dale R. Herspring and Ivan Volgyes, "Political Reliability in the Eastern European Warsaw Pact Armies," *Armed Forces and Society* (Winter 1980), 270–96; David Holloway and Jane M.O. Sharp, eds., *The Warsaw Pact: Alliance in Transition?* (Ithaca, 1984); and A. Ross Johnson, Robert W. Dean, and Alexander Alexiev, "The Armies of the Warsaw Pact Northern Tier," *Survival* (July–August 1981), 174–82. See also David E. Albright, "On Eastern Europe: Security Implications for the USSR," *Parameters* (Summer 1984), 24–36. The vulnerability of Eastern European countries to American nuclear strikes was stressed many years ago by Morton A. Kaplan, *A Rationale for NATO* (Washington, D.C., 1973).

7. Cf. Luigi Barzini, *The Europeans* (New York, 1983), 27: "There may still be a vast reserve of local barbarians in Europe to challenge the primacy of outside barbarians and possibly defeat them." Speculations on this matter inevitably recall the attempt by the Nazis to rule Europe by force during World War II. See George F Kennan, *Memoirs 1925–1950* (Boston, 1967), 128–30, who cites Gibbon's famous observation, published in 1776, that "there is nothing more contrary to nature than the attempt to hold in obedience distant provinces." See also Louis-François Duchêne, "The Not So Hidden Hand," in *Strategic Thought in the Nuclear Age,* ed. Laurence Martin, esp. 45–47; Irving Kristol, "Does NATO Exist?" and Michael Howard, "Social Change and the Defense of the West," in *NATO: The Next Thirty Years,* ed. Kenneth A. Myers (Boulder, Colo., 1980), 363–64, 358.

8. See F. H. Hinsley, "The Development of the European States System Since the Eighteenth Century," Royal Historical Society, *Proceedings* (1963), 78–79.

9. F. H. Hinsley, *Power and the Pursuit of Peace: Theory and Practice in the History of Relations Between States* (Cambridge, 1967), 283. The most powerful recent statement of the underlying durability of the European balance can be found in A. W. DePorte, *Europe Between the Superpowers: The Enduring Balance* (New Haven, 1979), from which the title of this section is taken. See also the penetrating reflections of Josef Joffe, "The Dreams and the Power: Europe in the Age of Yalta," *Naval War College Review* (1983), 49–60, and Robert Gilpin, *War and Change in World Politics* (Cambridge, 1981), esp. 231–44.

10. Cf. James Schlesinger, "The Eagle and the Bear," *Foreign Affairs* (Summer 1985), 951.

11. The best introduction to the conventional balance of forces is Anthony H. Cordesman, "The NATO Central Region and the Balance of Uncertainty," *Armed Forces Journal International* (July 1983), 18–58. The evolving Soviet concept of operations in Western Europe is reviewed in Phillip A. Petersen and John G. Hines, "The Conventional Offensive in Soviet Theater Strategy," *Orbis* (Fall 1983), 695–739.

12. See Richard K. Betts, *Surprise Attack: Lessons for Defense Planning* (Washington, D.C., 1982), esp. 176–77. See also by Betts, "Conventional Deterrence: Predictive Uncertainty and Policy Confidence," *World Politics* (January 1985), 153–79. The serious military consequences of a failure to mobilize quickly are stressed in Phillip A. Karber, "The Strategy: In Defense of Forward Defense," *Armed Forces Journal International* (May 1984), 37, 40.

13. In his stimulating piece on "The Changing Face of Non-nuclear War," *Survival* (September/October 1982), 213, Neville Brown notes that "both elementary logic and historical experience suggest that a basic distinction ought to be drawn in respect of firepower—that improvements in light weapons have particularly favoured men resisting cavalry and infantry from prepared positions, whereas improvements in the heavier kinds of ordnance have done more to break those positions down." On this point, see also Benjamin F. Schemmer, "Soviet Technological Parity in Europe Undermines NATO's Flexible Response Strategy," *Armed Forces Journal International* (May 1984), 86.

14. Brown, "Non-nuclear War," 214.

15. Cf. Paul Bracken, "The NATO Defense Problem," *Orbis* (Spring 1983), 83–105; William Kaufmann, "Nonnuclear Deterrence," in *Alliance Security: NATO and the No-First-Use Question,* ed. John D. Steinbruner and Leon V. Sigal (Washington, D.C., 1983), 59; Robert Shishko, "The European Conventional Balance: A Primer " (Santa Monica, November 1981); and William Durch and Peter Almquist, "East-West Military Balance," in *International Security Yearbook 1984/85,* ed. Barry M. Blechman and Edward N. Luttwak (Boulder, Colo., 1985), 73–78.

16. These weaknesses are emphasized in P. H. Vigor, "Doubts and Difficulties Confronting a Would Be Soviet Attacker," *RUSI Journal* (June 1980), 32–38. Other vulnerabilities are examined in Benjamin S. Lambeth, *Risk and Uncertainty in Soviet Deliberations About War* (Santa Monica, Calif. 1981), Joshua M. Epstein, "On Conventional Deterrence in Europe: Questions of Soviet Confidence," *Orbis* (Spring 1982), 71–86; Keith A. Dunn, "Limits Upon Soviet Military Power," *RUSI Journal* (1980–81), 38–45; and Andrew Cockburn, *The Threat: Inside the Soviet Military Machine,* rev. ed. (New York, 1984).

17. See Alain Enthoven and Wayne K. Smith, *How Much is Enough?* (New York, 1971), and William W. Kaufmann, *The McNamara Strategy* (New York, 1964).

18. Among pessimistic accounts during this period, see particularly Jeffrey Record, *Force Reductions in Europe: Starting Over* (Cambridge, Mass., 1980), 5–33; and Senators Sam Nunn and Dewey F. Bartlett, *NATO and the New Soviet Threat,* U.S. Senate, Committee on Armed Services (Washington, D.C., 1977).

19. More optimistic analyses of the conventional balance in Europe include John J. Mearsheimer, *Conventional Deterrence* (Ithaca, 1983); Joshua M. Epstein, *Measuring Military Power: The Soviet Air Threat to Europe* (Princeton, 1984); and Barry Posen, "Measuring the European Conventional Balance: Coping with Complexity in

Threat Assessment," *International Security* (Winter 1984/85), 47–88. On the improvements of U.S. forces, see Robert W. Komer, "The Rejuvenation of the Seventh Army," *Armed Forces Journal International* (May 1983), 54–59; and the interview with General Jerome F. O'Malley, Commander, USAF Tactical Air Command, in *Armed Forces Journal International* (January 1985), 71–79, who argues that "TAC today is more than 250 percent better off than it was in 1980."

20. Samuel P. Huntington, "Conventional Deterrence and Conventional Retaliation in Europe," *International Security* (Winter 1983/84), 56.

21. The best analysis of the crisis of the early 1980s are the essays in Robert W. Tucker and Linda Wrigley, eds., *The Atlantic Alliance and Its Critics* (New York, 1982).

22. The amendment is described and its effect examined in "Thank You, Sam," *The Economist,* 8 December 1984, 46. See also Henry Kissinger, "A Plan to Reshape NATO," *Time,* 5 March 1984. On the problem of equity within the alliance, see Simon Lunn, *Burden Sharing in NATO,* Chatham House Paper No. 18 (London, 1983), and James R. Golden, *NATO Burden Sharing: Risks and Opportunities,* The Washington Papers/96 (New York, 1983).

23. Among notable calls for a separation from Europe, see Earl Ravenal, "Europe Without America," *Foreign Affairs* (Summer 1985), 1020–35; Earl Ravenal, *The FY 1985 Defense Budget* (Washington, D.C., 1984); and Earl Ravenal, "The Case for Withdrawal of Our Forces," *New York Times Magazine,* 6 March 1982. See also Laurence Radway, "Let Europe be Europe," *World Policy Journal* (Fall 1983), 23–43; Irving Kristol, "What's Wrong With NATO?" *The New York Times Magazine,* 25 September 1983; and Melvyn Krauss, "Prompting Europe to Better Defend Itself," *The Wall Street Journal,* 15 March 1984.

24. See André Beaufre, *Deterrence and Strategy* (London, 1965), and the discussion in Lawrence Freedman, *The Evolution of Nuclear Strategy* (New York, 1981), 318–320. An independent nuclear deterrent is examined in Josef Joffe, "Europe's American Pacifier," *Foreign Policy* (Spring 1984), 78–80; Pierre Lellouche, "Europe and Her Defense," *Foreign Affairs* (Spring 1981), 831–32; and Hedley Bull, "European Self-Reliance and the Reform of NATO," *Foreign Affairs* (Spring 1983), 882–890. The essays by Lellouche and Bull are notable for their unwillingness to propose that Germany acquire an independent power of nuclear decision. See also Samuel P. Huntington, "Broadening the Strategic Focus: Comments on Michael Howard's Paper," in *Defence and Consensus: The Domestic Aspects of Western Security Part III* (Adelphi Paper #184) (London, 1983), 30–32. In this essay, Huntington suggests that the creation of a German nuclear force "deserves a far fuller and more serious consideration than it has received for some while," but is careful to note that he does "not now recommend it." See also the penetrating reflections of Robert J. Art, "Fixing Atlantic Bridges," *Foreign Policy* (Spring 1982), 68–69.

25. Raymond Aron, "Is Isolationism Possible?" *Commentary,* (April 1974), 43. The classic analysis of the case for a new isolationism based on the nuclear revolution was provided by Robert W. Tucker, *A New Isolationism: Threat or Promise?* (Washington, D.C., 1972), to which Aron's essay was a response. See also Tucker's analysis in *The Purposes of American Power: An Essay on National Security* (New York, 1981), 121–23. Earl Ravenal has provided an interesting variation on this argument by suggesting that the American commitment to European security has driven the United States to place increasing emphasis on counterforce weapons and damage limitation strategies. See Earl Ravenal, "Counterforce and Alliance: The Ultimate

Connection," *International Security* (Spring 1982), 26–34. That there is a connection between the two is clear: the "first use" doctrine called for in NATO strategy, for many strategists, requires "first strike" capabilities. As I argue in chapter 4, however, that connection is by no means a necessary one. In truth, such strategies are required neither for deterrence nor for reassurance. There is no "ultimate connection" between them and the American commitment to European security.

26. See Eliot A. Cohen, "The Long-Term Crisis of the Alliance," *Foreign Affairs* (Winter 1982/83), 325–43; Jeffrey Record and Robert J. Hanks, *U.S. Strategy at the Crossroads: Two Views* (Cambridge, Mass., 1982). See also by Jeffrey Record, "The Europeanization of NATO: A Restructured Commitment for the 1980s," *Air University Review* (September/October 1982), 23–29, and *Revising U.S. Military Strategy: Tailoring Means to Ends* (Washington, D.C., 1984). Among military reformers, an earlier call for the restructuring of NATO is in Robert Taft, Jr., *White Paper on Defense, 1978 Edition: A Modern Military Strategy for the United States,* the 1978 edition published in cooperation with Senator Gary Hart, prepared with the assistance of Mr. William S. Lind (Washington, D.C., 1978, mimeographed). See also Stansfield Turner and George Thibault, "Preparing for the Unexpected: The Need for a New Military Strategy," *Foreign Affairs* (Fall 1982), 122–35. On these proposals, see particularly Robert W. Tucker, "The Atlantic Alliance and Its Critics." in Tucker and Wrigley, eds., *Atlantic Alliance,* esp. 174–75.

27. The passage is Walter Laqueur's widely quoted description of the state of the alliance in the immediate aftermath of the declaration of martial law in Poland. See Walter Laqueur, "Poland and the Crisis of the Alliance," *The Wall Street Journal,* 5 January 1982.

28. See chapter 3, "The West and the Decline of Oil." Most of the proposals to reorient American forces away from their traditional emphasis on preparations for European contingencies call in effect for the application of the Nixon Doctrine to Europe—they are based, that is, on the assumption that our allies should have responsibility for providing ground forces for their own defense, whereas the Amerian role should take the form of providing air and naval power. Yet it is in the Third World where this doctrine continues to have relevance—and where it was applied, of course, by the Nixon administration itself This question is examined at much greater length (and in relation to possible Third World contingencies) in chapter 5.

29. See, in particular, Eliot A. Cohen, *Citizens and Soldiers: The Dilemmas of Military Service* (Ithaca, 1985), 186–87, who proposes a system of compulsory universal militia service, alongside a reduction from 780,000 to 600,000 in the size of the active Army (which would be reoriented primarily to "small wars" in the Third World), and the withdrawal of half of American ground forces from Europe. See also Cohen, "The Long-Term Crisis of the Alliance," 341–42; and his "Military Manpower," in *American Military Policy,* ed. Michael Mandelbaum (forthcoming).

30. Steven Canby, "Territorial Defence in Central Europe," *Armed Forces and Society* (Fall 1980), 51–67; Lt. Col. Norbert Hanning, "The Defense of Europe with Conventional Weapons," *International Defense Review* 11 (1981), 1439–1443; and Udo Philipp, "NATO Strategy Under Discussion in Bonn," *International Defense Review* 9 (1980). See also Michael Howard, "NATO and the Year of Europe", *Survival* (January/February 1974), 21–27; and Adam Roberts, *Nation in Arms: The Theory and Practice of Territorial Defense* (New York, 1976).

31. Steven Canby, "Military Reform and the Art of War," *Survival* (May/June

1983). See also Andrew Hamilton, "Redressing the Conventional Balance: NATO's Reserve Military Manpower," *International Security* (Summer 1985), 111–36.

32.   See Josef Joffe, "Stability and Its Discontent: Should NATO Go Conventional?" *The Washington Quarterly* (Fall 1984), 136–47, a superb analysis of the debate. A justification of a defense in depth is provided by Edward Luttwak, "The American Style of War and the Military Balance," *Survival* (March/April 1979), 55–58; the fullest justification of a strategy of conventional retaliation is provided by Samuel P. Huntington, "Conventional Retaliation." Two excellent analyses of these alternatives are John J. Mearsheimer, "Nuclear Weapons and Deterrence in Europe," *International Security* (Winter 1984–85), 19–46; and Richard K. Betts, "Conventional Deterrence: Predictive Uncertainty and Policy Confidence," *World Politics* (January 1985), 153–79. The proposals noted in the text, of course, do not exhaust the ways in which NATO might be strengthened. (For a comprehensive survey, see R. Levine *et al., NATO Defense Concepts* (Santa Monica, Calif., 1982) and William P. Mako, *U.S. Ground Forces and the Defense of Central Europe* (Washington, D.C., 1983). In particular, the list excludes proposals that would require the United States to assume an ever-larger financial role in European security. Proposals that do require the investment of substantial American resources (and which are therefore suspect on grounds of equity alone) include: 1) the pursuit of a damage limitation strategy (considered below in chapter 4); and 2) the "deep strike" initiatives, which rely heavily upon American technology (considered in *Reforming Defense*).

33.   "NATO's Forward Defense and Striking Deep," *Armed Forces Journal International* (November 1983), 44. On the desirability of fortifications, informed opinion is virtually unanimous. See, *inter alia,* Major J. B. A. Bailey, "The Case for Pre-Placed Field Defenses," *International Defense Review* 7 (1984), 887–92; J. C. F. Tillson, "The Forward Defense of Europe," *Military Review* (May 1981), 66–67; John H. Maurer and Gordon H. McCormick, "Surprise Attack and Conventional Defense in Europe," *Orbis* (Spring 1983), 120–21; Robert W. Komer, "Maritime Strategy vs. Coalition Defense," *Foreign Affairs* (Summer 1982), 1137–38; Richard Betts, *Surprise Attack,* 224–27; and Kaufmann, "Nonnuclear Deterrence," 65.

34.   See Canby, "Military Reform," 121–23; and Hamilton, "Redressing the Conventional Balance," 131. Hamilton estimates a cost of $97 billion in 1984 dollars—exclusive of personnel—"for adding twenty Heavy Division Equivalents to the NATO European force structure, equipped with 1980s generation equipment." Canby's suggestion that the Europeans might sacrifice the development of their tactical airpower to provide for the expansion of such ground divisions is inconsistent with his favored concept of military operations in Europe. "Airpower's full premium," he once noted, "can only be obtained in conjunction with friendly forces in the attack/counterattack." If this is so, it is difficult to see why a force structure consisting of American Air Force pilots and German or other European ground forces would be more effective than current forces. See Canby, "General Purpose Forces," *International Security Review* (Fall 1980), 319–46.

35.   Helmut Schmidt, *Defense or Retaliation?* (New York, 1962), 102.

36.   In "Extending Deterrence with German Nuclear Weapons," *International Security* (Summer 1985), 96–110, David Garnham has provided as comprehensive a justification of an independent power of German nuclear decision as one is likely to find. Garnham notes that the Soviet Union "would attempt to dissuade the Germans and could even threaten preemption. There is, unfortunately," he concedes, "no

obvious and workable way to avoid a perilous transition period during which such tactics might succeed" (108). This danger shows the bankruptcy of the whole proposal, for it means that such an initiative, whatever its theoretical attractions, would fail and would result in a political victory by the Soviet Union—to say nothing of the harm it might do to Franco-German and American-European relations.

37. Michael Howard, "Reassurance and Deterrence," *Foreign Affairs* (Winter 1982/83), 309–24.

38. Henry Kissinger, "Limited War: Conventional or Nuclear? A Reappraisal," in *Daedalus* (Fall 1960), 806–7.

39. Henry Kissinger, "The Future of NATO," in *NATO: The Next Thirty Years,* ed. Kenneth A. Myers, (Boulder, Colo., 1980), 8.

40. See Laurence Martin, "Limited Nuclear Options," in J. Holst and U. Nerlich, *Beyond Nuclear Deterrence* (New York, 1977).

41. Bernard Gwertzman, "President Says U.S. Should Not Waver in Backing Saudis," *The New York Times,* 18 October 1981.

42. Bernard Brodie, *Escalation and the Nuclear Option,* 30–31.

43. Quoted in Konrad H. Jarausch, "The Illusion of Limited War: Chancellor Bethman Hollweg's Calculated Risk, July 1914," *Central European History* II (1969), 58.

3 — The West and the Decline of Oil

> As war is dominated by the political
> object the order of that object
> determines the measure of the
> sacrifice by which it is to be
> purchased. As soon, therefore, as the
> expenditure in force becomes so
> great that the political object is no
> longer equal in value this object
> must be given up, and peace will be
> the result.
> —Clausewitz, *On War*

The emergence of a security crisis in the Persian Gulf in the late 1970s provoked one of the great transformations in American foreign and defense policy in the postwar period, comparable in its effects to the resurgence of American military power sparked by the Korean War and to the decline ushered in by the Vietnam War. The assumptions that had governed American defense policy in the 1970s—assumptions profoundly influenced by the "lessons of Vietnam"—broke down under the cumulative weight of the emergence of the three components of the crisis: the extraordinary degree of western dependence on the oil of the Persian Gulf, the collapse of the shah of Iran, and enhanced Soviet activity in the "arc of crisis," culminating in the execution of Hafizullah Amin in Afghanistan and the movement of one hundred thousand Soviet troops into that country. This latter move brought Soviet tactical airpower, operating from bases in southwestern Afghanistan, within reach of the Straits of Hormuz, through which passed in 1980 16.2 million barrels of oil a day (mbd).

The Rapid Deployment Force (CENTCOM)

The Carter administration responded to the crisis in the Gulf by establishing, in its last year, a Rapid Deployment Joint Task Force charged with planning for Persian Gulf contingencies. The administration made available to the RDJTF for planning purposes three Army divisions, one Marine Amphibious Force, five Air Force fighter wings, and three carrier task forces. The administration embarked as well on a set of agreements with regional states to provide "facilities" for American use in a crisis, prepositioned the equipment for a Marine Amphibious Brigade and other forces on floating warehouses in the Indian Ocean, and pursued a number of strategic mobility programs to move American forces to the Gulf more rapidly.

Most of these initiatives were extended and deepened by the Reagan administration. A unified command covering the Middle East and Southwest Asia area was established on 1 January 1983 under the name of CENTCOM, and the administration revealed plans to make available to the new command an additional Army division, as well as an additional five Air Force wings. (The four Army divisions that were made available to CENTCOM as of fiscal year 1986—the 82nd Airborne, the 101st Air Assault, the 24th Mechanized Infantry Division, and the 9th High Technology Motorized Division—did not include the four divisions of a new light infantry type planned by the Army that might be made available to CENTCOM in the future.) The administration also embarked upon a range of strategic mobility initiatives that went well beyond those contemplated in the Carter administration. It began to buy fifty C–5B strategic airlifters to complement the force of seventy C–5As whose procurement was begun in the 1960s with spectacular cost overruns and consequent charges of gross mismanagement. It continued preliminary studies on the C–17 strategic airlifter, capable of operating under more primitive conditions than the C–5. It also sought to procure forty-four additional tankers for aerial refueling, and speeded the refurbishment of eight fast sealift ships that would enable the 24th Mechanized Infantry Division at Fort Stewart, Georgia, to be mvoed to the Gulf in less than a month. Finally, it went ahead with plans to construct a fleet of ships that would carry prepositioned material (fuel, water, weapons, ammunition, etc.) in order to ease the extraordinary logistical difficulties involved in deploying troops to Southwest Asia.[1]

These military arrangements were made in order to cope with Soviet and regional threats to Persian Gulf oil. When the crisis in the Gulf peaked, in 1980, this oil appeared to be something of absolute and not of relative value. Reductions of even a few million barrels a day, as the Iranian Revolution showed, were capable of playing complete havoc with western economies, and the prospect of much greater losses seemed entirely within the realm of possibility. Much has changed in that respect. Yet the revolution in world oil markets that occurred in the early 1980s has not brought about a corresponding transformation of our military dispositions and our strategic outlook. That revolution, however, carries with it profound implications for American strategy in the Gulf and thus for the proper composition of the RDF.

The New Geography of World Oil Production

The suddenness with which the world oil market was transformed in the early 1980s was the most remarkable political development of those years. The price rises of the 1970s finally led to a decisive reaction among consumers that sharply reduced the salience of Persian Gulf production in the world oil market. From 1977 to 1982, Persian Gulf oil as a percentage of total energy consumed fell from 7 to 2 percent in the United States, from 35 to 19 percent in Western Europe, and from 59 to 40 percent in Japan. For the Japanese and to a lesser degree the Europeans, a substantial degree of dependence remained, but it was of an entirely different character from what had existed in the late 1970s, because of the sharp decline in OPEC market power. OPEC production fell from 30.9 mbd in 1979 to 17.4 mbd in 1984, its share of world production falling in the same period from 49.5 to 32 percent. As Exhibit 9 illustrates, the burden of this decline fell most on the Persian Gulf producers, as their production fell from 21.0 mbd in 1979 to 9.5 mbd in 1985. In August 1985, it reached its lowest point before the Saudi decision to boost production in the autumn, falling to only 8.6 mbd.

The oil outlook, moreover, improved to a far greater extent than these figures indicate, for the following reasons:

EXHIBIT 9—*The Geography of World Oil Production in Million Barrels per Day (Percent of World Production)*

Year	Saudi Arabia	Iran	Iraq	Total Persian Gulf	Total OPEC	Non-Soviet Countries Outside OPEC (Minus US)	US	USSR	World Total
1973	7.6	5.9	2.0	14.7	31.0	7.0	9.2	8.5	55.6
	(14)	(11)	(4)	(26)	(56)	(13)	(17)	(15)	
1979	9.5	3.2	3.5	21.0	30.9	11.6	8.6	11.5	62.5
	(15)	(5)	(6)	(34)	(49)	(19)	(14)	(18)	
1982	6.5	2.2	1.0	12.0	18.9	13.8	8.6	12.0	53.3
	(12)	(4)	(2)	(23)	(35)	(26)	(16)	(22)	
1985	3.4	2.2	1.5	9.5	16.0	16.6	8.9	11.8	53.3
	(6)	(4)	(3)	(18)	(30)	(31)	(17)	(22)	

Source:—U.S. Department of Energy, Energy Information Administration, *Monthly Energy Review,* (December 1985), 108–09. "Non-Soviet Countries Outside OPEC (Minus US)" reflects production totals for Canada, Mexico, United Kingdom, China, and "Others"—a calculated total derived from the difference between world production and the nations represented in the Energy Department's survey.

1) Of the 9–10 mbd produced in the Gulf in 1985, approximately 1.7 mbd was consumed indigenously, leaving 7–8 mbd for export.

2) Of this amount, not all passed through the Straits of Hormuz. The giant pipeline (the Petroline) from the Saudis' eastern oilfields to the Red Sea port of Yanbu had a capacity of approximately 1.9 mbd by the end of 1985 and was being upgraded to carry nearly 3 mbd. The capacity of the Iraqi pipeline through Turkey was expanded to carry 1.0 mbd by 1985. At the beginning of 1986, Iraq was planning to expand the capacity of its Turkish pipeline to 1.5 mbd and was considering a line across Saudi territory with a 1.6 mbd capacity. Pipeline capacity thus grew from 2.5 mbd in 1980 to 4.25 mbd in 1985, and if the Iraqi pipelines come to be completed, this capacity would grow to some 7 mbd by 1987. Traffic through the Straits of Hormuz fell from 17.5 mbd in 1975 to 6.5 mbd in 1985.[2]

3) There came to exist in the early 1980s a large amount of surplus production capacity in the world. Within the Gulf itself, the existence of large amounts of excess capacity meant that any attempt to affect production levels through air attack or sabotage would be far more difficult to accomplish. Outside the Gulf, the excess capacity—anywhere from 3 to 4 mbd in 1984—could make up a large part of the loss if shipments from the Straits of Hormuz were shut off. Most of the states with excess capacity—Canada, Indonesia, Libya, Venezuela, Mexico, and Nigeria—were afflicted with severe balance of payment problems, as indeed were many states in the Gulf itself. OPEC current account balances declined sharply from a surplus of $103 billion in 1980 to a deficit of $30.4 billion in 1983, putting a sharp limit on the capacity of nearly all producers to reduce production and creating strong incentives among others to increase production in the event of a cut-off of Gulf supplies.[3]

4) The consuming states increased their strategic petroleum reserves. Although the growth of government-held reserves was partly offset by the decline in industry discretionary stocks, the countries with the largest reserves—the United States, Japan, and Germany—were capable by 1985 of putting millions of barrels per day onto the market and thus stabilizing prices in times of uncertainty.

5) The oil export system in the Gulf showed a surprising resilience against disruption. The tanker war that Iraq has conducted intermittently since 1981, which began in earnest in March 1984, did not succeed in significantly disrupting Iranian oil exports, which remained at over 2 mbd for most of 1984 and 1985. Even the large-scale attacks on Kharg Island beginning in the late summer of 1985, although they proved severely damaging to Iranian export facilities, did not succeed in eliminating Iran's capacity to export oil. Although Iraq may yet succeed in shutting down the main Iranian export terminal at Kharg Island (thus forcing Iran to speed up work on pipelines that would place its export facilities out of reach of Iraqi airpower), Iran's ability to retaliate effectively against the oil export capacity of Iraq's principal financial backers among the Arab producers seems likely to remain quite limited.[4]

This relative immunity to disruptions in the Gulf is a very good thing. Its most obvious benefit is that it eliminated the threat of an Arab oil embargo that hung over American policy in the 1970s. It broke the link between the Palestinian problem and the question of access to the oil of the Gulf, a link that many were once persuaded required pressure on Israel to make concessions on the West Bank and Jerusalem that no Israeli government—Labor or Likud—was willing to make. Stemming as they did from fear, these calculations were always unbecoming a great power. The whole diplomatic formula that resulted from them was one of stalemate, frustration, and impotence. The American government was driven to place increasing emphasis on a settlement of the Palestinian problem because of our fear of what the Arab world would do to us if we did not. It then turned out that the American government was paralyzed by the prospect of a showdown with the Israelis. To be sure, the willingness of the Arab producers to employ the oil weapon if the United States failed to deliver the goods was never clear, but it was nevertheless significant that American policymakers, urged on by the Europeans and the Japanese, continued to think in these terms. Today they have little basis for doing so. The calculations of the 1970s—calculations that began with the inescapable reality of dependence on the Arab Gulf producers and ended in various postures of servility among the consuming nations—no longer have any foundation at all.

The implications of the new geography of world oil production reach even further than this. The character of the American national interest in the area has also undergone a transformation. Our fundamental interest in the Gulf has lain and continues to lie in assuring secure access to its oil. During the 1970s, the scale of dependence was such that a complete loss of access would have entailed catastrophic consequences. Whether it would have meant the strangulation of the industrialized world or some lesser fate we cannot know, but it certainly would have badly rent the economic, social, and political cohesion of the entire world. Today the consequences would be far less severe. Painful adjustments, to be sure, would have to be made in investment and consumption patterns in the event of such a loss of access if the world were to weather the storm, but the prospects of making our way through these troubles under today's circumstances are of a qualitatively different character from what they were at the outset of the 1980s.

It is the thesis of this chapter that this revolution allows for a substantial revision of America's political and military strategy in the area, one capable of dispensing with ground forces, and reliant on American air and naval power and economic and military aid. This revision in strategy would not only allow for a more equitable division of responsibility between the United States and its principal allies than now exists. It also indicates an area of the defense budget—our expenditures on the maintenance of active ground forces—that might be trimmed with safety. This new strategy, to be sure, is dependent on the maintenance of lessened dependence on the oil of the Persian Gulf. But there is ample reason for believing that this lessened dependence and its accompanying strategic advances can be made to persist for a substantial period of time; for there is a range of measures the United States can take—preeminently the taxation of energy consumption at home—that can sharply reduce the likelihood of a return of dependence on the Gulf, while easing the severity of our fiscal predicament at home.

Countering the Soviet Threat

It was the Soviet invasion of Afghanistan in December 1979 that, more than any other event, set in motion the elaboration of detailed plans to resist further Soviet expansionism in the Gulf. Before this pivotal event, the ponderous beast that is the American government had slumbered through a string of Soviet successes in the Third World, many of which had improved the Soviet military position in the region. With the Afghanistan operation, the Soviets appeared to confirm the observation made of them by Churchill in the aftermath of the Second World War—that they would try every door in the house, and enter all those not locked. It was entirely appropriate, therefore, that President Carter, in his 1980 State of the Union message, should make "absolutely clear" the position of the American government: that "an attempt by any outside force to gain control of the Persian Gulf region will be regarded as an assault on the vital interests of the United States of America, and such an assault will be repelled by any means necessary, including military force."[5]

This declaration was indispensable in 1980 and it will in all likelihood remain so. But it should not lead us to overestimate the threat posed by the Soviet Union. A fair number of obstacles serve to deter a Soviet attack in the region, even in the absence of the high probability of it causing a Soviet-American clash. The first and

perhaps most basic consideration is the nature of the Soviet strategic situation. The Soviets, too, have a strategic predicament. They
are encircled by slumbering giants. The human and material resources of Western Europe, the Middle East, and East Asia dwarf
those of the Soviet Union. A brazen military move to the Persian
Gulf, by provoking a profoundly different view of the imminence
of the Soviet military threat in the nations that straddle the Soviet
periphery, would have the clear potential of awakening the som-
nambulists and moving the correlation of forces decisively against
the Soviet state. If the effect produced in the United States by the
Soviet invasion of Afghanistan were extended to Western Europe,
the Middle East, and East Asia in the event of a Soviet invasion of
the Gulf, the consequences could be very serious. Such an invasion
would have to hold out the prospect of maximum benefits and
minimum costs in order to be deemed worthwhile. Yet no such
prospect exists.

In the "canonical" Persian Gulf scenario—a Soviet invasion of
Iran—the obstacles are very imposing.[6] The twenty-four to thirty
divisions in the trans-Caucasian and trans-Caspian regions of the
Soviet Union are mostly Category III divisions, with a degree of
readiness below that maintained in the most underequipped and
undermanned American reserve division. Their equipment is the
oldest in the Soviet inventory, for the great modernization of the
Soviet military that occurred in the last two decades was concentrated on the Soviet forces opposite Europe and China. The divisions near the Iranian border are manned in peacetime at around 25
percent of their wartime status, and most of the men who would
have to be called upon to upgrade these forces to wartime status are
many years away from their basic training. The military districts in
which these divisions are stationed, moreover, are heavily populated by a mixture of Asiatic peoples, who account for a large and
growing segment of the Soviet population. Their reliability in a
strange and novel setting—about which they would know very
little—would have to be considered as doubtful by any prudent
Soviet military planner.

The mere assembly of this force opposite Iran would severely tax
Soviet logistical capabilities. The move south into Iran would have
to take place across some of the most formidable terrain in the
world. To reach the southern oil fields of Khuzestan, two great
mountain barriers would have to be crossed—the continuous

stretch of mountains running opposite the Soviet border from Turkey to Afghanistan, and the Zagros range in the south, which runs on a northwest to southeast axis from southeastern Turkey to a point directly above the Straits of Hormuz. The enormous quantities of fuel, food, and water that would be required to sustain such a large force would have to be trucked across a primitive road network that winds its way through deep canyons and narrow gorges. The Soviet divisional structure is notoriously ill-suited for this kind of movement. The choice to severely limit logistical support is what gives the Soviets the capability of maintaining, with a much smaller number of men, divisions with the firepower equivalent to that of an American armored division. But the assumptions on which this choice is based—movement on a well-developed road and rail network, the availability of prepositioned material, a campaign of limited depth—do not hold for a campaign whose objective is the occupation of the southern Iranian oilfields of Khuzestan. In the absence of any opposition at all, the movement of such a large force would be an enormous logistical undertaking. And such an undertaking would be sure to meet with opposition.

The Iranians themselves would be capable of putting up a lot of resistance. It is not difficult to see how the Soviets might have underestimated, in the immediate aftermath of the Islamic Revolution, the potential scale of this resistance—this, after all, was Saddam Hussein's mistake. Today the Russians have no basis for doing so. As a consequence of the war with Iraq, the Iranians have a large reservoir of military experience to draw upon. The shortages of sophisticated equipment that have proved so debilitating to the Iranians in their offensives against entrenched Iraqi positions would be less significant in opposition to the Soviets, for the Iranians are abundantly supplied with the light weapons and explosives relevant to guerrilla operations in mountainous terrain. If the United States and others were prepared to make good on their most critical deficiencies for such operations (such as a lack of shoulder-fired surface-to-air missile systems) the resistance put up by the Iranians could gravely compromise Soviet objectives. The courage with which masses of the Iranian peasantry have sacrificed their lives in the war against Iraq is the most remarkable phenomenon of that war, recalling the great offensives against impossible odds undertaken by the combatants of the First World War. A regime that can invest such sacrifices with transcendent meaning is capable of great deeds, especially in defense of its own national territory.

At the end of this one-thousand-kilometer route lies the oil of Khuzestan. The Soviets would have a very difficult time deriving any economic benefit from the possession of this territory. The turmoil induced by the Revolution has set Iranian oil development back by a generation, and its oil fields are consequently in very poor condition. The time required to move south, moreover, would afford the Iranians ample opportunity to blow up the most critical oil-producing installations, and if the Iranians bungled the job, the United States is capable of doing it for them with long-range bombers stationed in the United States—and thus without access to any land-based air bases in the region at all. The manpower requirements for operating oil fields the size of the Iranian ones are very large. Yet for this task the Soviets could not draw on local manpower. On the contrary, they would be forced to draw upon their own oil industry, in which manpower shortages are rife—which in turn could not fail to have a deleterious impact on oil and gas production in the Soviet Union itself.

Even in the absence of the direct application of American military power, it is apparent that the Soviets would face formidable obstacles in an invasion of Iran. That does not mean that the United States should not continue to pledge to resist such an invasion were it to occur. Although the revolution in world oil markets has led to a decline in the strategic significance of the Persian Gulf—a decline that has far-reaching implications for our posture in dealing with regional threats—the United States still has a vital interest in guarding against a Soviet assault against the region. This is so not only because the Gulf countries sit on top of 56 percent of the world's proven oil reserves, which the Soviet Union cannot be allowed to control, but also because of the implications such a Soviet attack would carry for the maintenance of the American position elsewhere. No order can be preserved in the world if Soviet aggression is allowed to go unpunished. A failure to resist such aggression in the Gulf would only invite it elsewhere.

In considering the form this resistance should take, however, we are not obligated to meet Soviet aggression in a precisely symmetrical manner. The emphasis placed within and without the Reagan administration on the necessity of committing American ground forces to the Gulf in the event of a Soviet invasion is misplaced. Our strategic posture should rest instead on four other elements:

1) the capacity for extending American military and economic aid to states and peoples threatened with a Soviet invasion;

2) the ability to transfer a sufficient amount of American air-power to the region, with the capability of gaining air superiority over the Persian Gulf and its approaches, interdicting Soviet troop movements through the mountains of Iran, and destroying what-ever oil facilities the Soviets might find themselves in a position to control;

3) the threat of "horizontal escalation," meaning in this instance air and naval attacks that sought to destroy the Soviet military and commercial presence on the high seas; and

4) the threat to resort to nuclear escalation against Soviet mili-tary forces in the region if these lesser measures did not succeed in halting a Soviet sweep toward the Gulf.

The emphasis that CENTCOM and others have placed on the introduction of American ground forces into Iran is mistaken for a number of reasons. Ground forces are not necessary to signal our determination to resist a Soviet attack. Insofar as deterrence rests on the dangers of a Soviet-American military clash, it is amply satis-fied by the presence of American naval forces there and by the U.S. capability for rapidly transferring land-based airpower to the re-gion. In addition, there is no reason to think that the Iranian government would look favorably upon the presence of American troops in their country. Since the intention of the American force planners appears to be the construction of a perimeter in Khuzestan alongside delaying tactics in the Zagros, American actions to deny access to the Soviets would be virtually identical to those required to secure access for ourselves, and as such would meet with fierce Iranian resistance. The Iranians would surely calculate that an invitation to the United States to occupy their most impor-tant oil province would end by "having their allies, at last, for their masters." Given the persistence of anti-American hostility and the importance the Khomeini regime has placed on making such hos-tility the principal rallying cry of the Islamic Revolution, the United States could give no assurances that its purposes were benevolent.[7]

Nor is this all. The principal reason for avoiding the commitment of American ground forces to the Gulf in the event of a Soviet invasion is that such a commitment would inevitably be in competition with the reinforcement of Europe. A Soviet invasion of the Gulf would require a fundamental reevaluation of Soviet intentions in Europe. There could be no calculation in the Kremlin—as there was in the crises over Korea, Hungary, Czechoslovakia, and Afghanistan—that the risks of direct military confrontation with the United States were miniscule. Such an invasion would signal that we lived in a profoundly different world, that our estimate of the "cautious" and "risk-averse" character of the Soviet leadership had been badly mistaken. The choice between the reinforcement of Europe and the reinforcement of the Gulf that would inevitably arise under these circumstances would be severely circumscribed by the limited capacity of American airlift and sealift capabilities, even with the expansion of such capabilities undertaken by the Reagan administration. The aerial tanker fleet in particular would be faced with multiple demands, including the reservation of some capability to the strategic bomber fleet and for the transfer of American airpower to Europe and the Gulf. As far as ground forces are concerned, the conventional reinforcement of Europe clearly ought to have the first claim on strategic lift, for it would be a foolish ordering of American interests to exclude the use of nuclear weapons against Soviet forces in Southwest Asia while continuing to rely on such use in Europe. And to give priority to the Gulf over Europe in the rapid transfer of ground forces has precisely this implication.

To restrict in this way the American role in resisting a Soviet invasion of the Persian Gulf does not mean that we are without formidable means of resistance. Military aid to regional insurgents is one such element. The ability to move American air power to the region is another. In the early 1980s, the United States made a great deal of progress in improving the capacity of friendly states to receive such a transfusion of tactical airpower. The arrangements that were made—with Turkey, Egypt, Oman, and Saudi Arabia— do not guarantee access, but there remains a strong probability that we would enjoy the use of some of these facilities in a crisis. Even if we did not, the United States might still be capable of using Israeli bases, and in any case would have available to it a number of carrier air wings alongside the B–52s of the Strategic Projection Force, which could be based on Diego Garcia in the Indian Ocean. Considered together, these capabilities would give the United States a better than fighting chance of dominating the skies over the northern and eastern approaches to the Gulf. By contrast, the Soviets would be severely handicapped in an air war by the absence of forward bases. For the critical early stages of the conflict, the Soviets would be forced to operate from bases in the southern Soviet Union and Afghanistan. Tactical aircraft operating from these bases, however, would lack the range to contest American air dominance over Khuzestan and most of the Zagros belt. Without air superiority over Khuzestan, it would be extremely difficult, if not impossible, for the Soviets to build up the logistical capabilities required for a further push southward onto the southern shore of the Gulf.

Such American measures as these are in all likelihood amply sufficient to deter a Soviet invasion of the Gulf. This invasion, about which so many were alarmed in the early 1980s, makes little sense from the Soviet point of view and is fundamentally inconsistent with the traditional Soviet method of expansion, with its emphasis on the indirect approach. This is so even in the absence of the possibility that such actions would lead to a Soviet-American war. It is doubly the case if American air and naval power is figured into the equation.

It is, of course, always possible in estimating the requirements for American military forces to pile implausible assumption upon implausible assumption and to forecast a situation in which the Soviet Union posed a direct military threat to the oil fields of the southern shore of the Persian Gulf. If this were to happen, however, the proper response would not be the introduction of American ground forces but the resort to "horizontal" or nuclear escalation. Both of these steps would carry grave risks, but so too would any course of action under these circumstances. The danger that an American reinforcement of the Gulf would uncover Europe is the largest of these risks, but it is not the only one. If the Soviet Union is unwilling to respect our vital interests, if it stages an unprovoked and wholly unjustifiable assault on our core position, and if this assault is allowed to succeed, we are lost in any case. There are no reasonable grounds for believing that the Soviets will do this, but insofar as this wild idea enters into their heads, it is just as well that they know from the outset that they are incurring the gravest risks, and that when the dust has cleared, their prospects for securing their own position in the world will have worsened rather than improved.

Contemplation of the worst case should not be allowed to obscure the strength of the American position in the Gulf relative to that of the Soviet Union. Nor should it be allowed to obscure the point that the real character of the Soviet threat in the 1970s and early 1980s lay not so much in the prospect of a direct Soviet attack as in the encouragement the Soviets gave to radical elements in the region. The Soviet Union appeared to have little or no interest in preserving stability in the Gulf or in acting so as to ensure a regular flow of oil. On the contrary, the scale of western dependence was such that the prospect of almost any explosion—political or other-wise—appeared almost certain to gravely compromise western interests. The substantial reduction of dependence on the Gulf that occurred in the 1980s made the danger of Soviet-inspired instability far less acute than it once was. By reducing the salience of both Iraqi and Iranian production in world oil markets, moreover, the trans-formed geography of oil production in the Gulf created circumstances in which it is not necessary in the event of a Soviet invasion for American forces to physically protect Iranian or Iraqi productive facilities. Indeed, the character of the world oil market in the mid 1980s is such that we could destroy these facilities ourselves if Soviet forces sought to gain physical control over them without at the same time doing serious harm to western economic interests.

Countering the Regional Threat

It is only when we consider the changed character of the regional threat that we can begin to fully appreciate the significance of the transformed geography of world oil production. For the political power of the regional states always stemmed from their importance in the world oil market; with the decline in their market power came a commensurate decline in their political importance. As late as 1981, Sheik Yamani was warning the Reagan administration that a failure to move on the Palestinian problem would generate retalia-tion by Saudi Arabia. In 1985, this threat was not even remotely credible, for Saudi Arabia was at certain times during the year producing oil at a mere 2.3 million barrels a day, and its market power lay solely in the threat of driving prices downward by increasing production. The threats that the Saudis were accustomed to making against the western powers only a short time before were not only increasingly hollow; they were unreal.

Accompanying the collapse of Arab oil power in the 1980s was the war between Iran and Iraq. Begun in 1980 by an Iraqi move into Khuzestan, the largest Iranian oil province, this war has on the whole proven advantageous to western interests.[8] The fear that the conflict would create openings for an extension of Soviet influence in the region has thus far been misplaced.[9] The Soviets leaned first toward Iran and then toward Iraq in the first five years of fighting, but the Soviet-Iranian relationship sharply deteriorated in 1982 and Soviet influence over Iraq—despite the Soviet Union's importance as a supplier of arms to the Iraqis—is no more than marginal. Once Iran expelled the Iraqis from most of its territory in the 1982 counteroffensives, the Soviets came to fear an Iranian victory with a foreboding equal to that of the West. The prospect of a militant Islamic state sweeping all opposition aside on the southern borders of the Soviet Union was not a welcome one for Moscow. The Russians, on the contrary, came to see the Iranians as little Chinese. So too, it appears, did China: hence the importance it assumed as a supplier of arms to the Iranians.[10]

The war also consumed the energies of the two regional states that seemed most likely at the beginning of the 1980s to pose a military threat to the Arab kingdoms on the southern shore of the Gulf. So long as the regime of Saddam Hussein stands, an Iraqi threat to the Arab kingdoms of the southern shore promises to remain remote. The Iraqis themselves seem to be hoping for nothing better than the restoration of the status quo ante in their war with Iran, and even if they were to achieve this their position would remain precarious. The rulers in Baghdad would have to take leave of their senses to countenance another adventure under these circumstances, not only because of the continuing dangers to Iraq from Iran and Syria but also because of Iraq's dependence on friendly relations with states, including Egypt, Jordan, and Saudi Arabia, which would be sure to oppose any move south. The Iraqis have no need of additional oil reserves. Their compelling interest if the Iranians afforded them a respite would be to increase oil production from their own fields. Regional politics would have to change profoundly for them to constitute a threat to the Arab kingdoms of the southern shore.

The war did have the effect of energizing the Islamic Revolution in Iran, giving it a solidity and permanence it might not otherwise have had. Yet there is little reason to believe that the Iranian menace cannot be successfully contained. The divisions within Iran over the wisdom of continuing the costly frontal assaults against Iraqi positions would deepen if its offensives were to continue to fail. There is a good prospect that Iraq can hold out indefinitely against such attacks. Iran, it is true, has a population three times the size of Iraq's, around forty to thirteen million. But Iran's casualties have been three times larger than Iraq's, and the morale of the Iraqi soldiers appears to remain high. Iraq has access to chemical weapons and to sophisticated western and Soviet military equipment, whereas the Iranians are severely hampered by their international isolation and are at a decided disadvantage in the equipment they can provide their troops. Iraq still has intact an operational reserve of armored units and would be able to draw on manpower elsewhere in the Arab world in the event its position worsened. Iran's financial resources, finally, are more than counterbalanced by the subsidies Iraq receives from the Arab oil producers.

There is, in sum, little reason to suppose that the Iranians can overcome the huge obstacles that stand in the way of the realization of their ambitions. Their isolation is too complete, and the international support enjoyed by the Iraqis too extensive. The Iraqis, on the other hand, no longer constitute the kind of threat to western interests that worried many observers in the late 1970s. While thus exhausting the two regional powers, the Gulf War has not created occasions for clashes between the United States and the Soviet Union. On the contrary, the outlook of the superpowers toward the Gulf War is now more alike than different; and while each remains wary of the other, each also is committed to preventing a decisive Iranian victory.

Most observers will derive little consolation from these observations. The fact that Iranian energies now appear to be spent does not mean that these energies will not revive sometime in the future; and if the threat does not come from Iran, it could conceivably come from some other source. The Middle East, we have been told again and again over the past decade, contains within it the causes of innumerable conflicts, and it would be folly to assume that the present correlation of forces will persist into the indefinite future, that the sky will not darken once again.

Such observations are in part well taken. The future is unpredictable. Circumstances may yet change radically and in a fashion detrimental to American interests. But the unpredictability of events does not mean that we are without guidance in assessing the manner in which the United States should prepare for the unpredictable in the Persian Gulf. Apart from Israel, the United States has no permanent allies in the area, only permanent interests, and it is worthwhile to investigate in somewhat more detail the true character of those interests before examining how our military power might be able to vindicate them.

Our fundamental interest in the Gulf lies in secure access to its oil. It is therefore largely expressible in economic terms. Thus expressed, it is apparent that the economic meaning of an American military intervention, if successful, would be to provide a subsidy to importers of oil, with those states who import the most oil relative to their overall energy requirements also gaining the most, and with the peculiar result that it would confer disproportionate benefits on those states that had been most profligate in the management of their oil import balances. If the United States did not intervene and the oil importers experienced another oil shock, on the other hand, the market would distribute the burden in proportion to the degree of dependence. Whereas the benefits of an intervention would be spread far and wide, the burden of such an intervention would fall disproportionately on the United States. At the outset of the 1980s, the evident inequity of such an arrangement was overshadowed by the sheer fact of dependence and by the catastrophic consequences that might follow, for us and our allies, a loss of access. As the guarantor of the postwar order, the United States was drawn by a powerful magnet to policies that attempted to ensure that this loss of access did not take place. That inevitably meant ground forces capable of physically securing oil facilities.

The revolution in world oil markets that occurred in the early 1980s allows for a strategy toward regional threats that dispenses with ground forces and that relies instead on the instruments that were associated with the Nixon Doctrine when it was first promulgated in the early 1970s—economic and military aid, and air and naval power. In its exclusion of ground forces, it is a strategy that seeks to limit the costs of any American intervention in a manner commensurate with the interests at stake. It is based on two assumptions: that a strategy dependent on ground forces would inevitably fall victim to the argument of inequity and could not command the support of the American people; and that the tools made available by the Nixon Doctrine play to our strengths and not to our weaknesses, affording a powerful basis for vindicating the interests that we do have. And it is to be sharply distinguished from the policies that were in fact pursued by the United States in the Persian Gulf in the 1970s. At that time the Nixon Doctrine came to be identified simply and exclusively with the sale of American arms to our "surrogates," particularly Iran and Saudi Arabia. That policy was flawed in two respects: as applied in Iran, it made no allowance for the destructive effects produced by the shah's unbalanced program of rearmament, which ultimately played an important role in his fall. More importantly, the policy assumed an identity of interest between the United States and the Gulf oil producers that was belied both at the time and subsequently.

But the circumstances that made the Nixon Doctrine inapplicable in the 1970s have now changed. Perhaps the most significant change is the increased salience of American air and naval power that has been brought about by the revolution in world oil markets. In 1980 the United States was incapable of credibly threatening military action against the oil export facilities of any of the regional producers. The self-imposed wounds would have been too painful. This is no longer the case, and it is a change of fundamental significance in assessing how we might respond if Iranian power were to revive in the future. For a regime that has sustained itself by its capacity to subsidize martyrdom, the loss of its oil revenues would be a crushing blow. The Iranians surely remember the action taken by the oil companies—with the support of the western powers—against the Mossadeq government in the early 1950s. They surely remember as well the consequences to which this led. Then the dominance of the oil companies over the production and trading of oil was so complete that their refusal to handle Iranian oil left this government bereft of oil revenues and paved the way for its downfall. The means to deprive an oil-producing state of its capacity to export oil are much different today, for they rest on airpower or naval blockade. But these means exist. The threat that they will be used should be the principal guarantee of Iranian good behavior.[11]

The revolution in world oil markets has not only increased the salience of the offensive use of American air and naval power. The existence of much spare capacity among the oil exporters means that the task of defending oil facilities and export routes has also been greatly eased. Perhaps most significantly, it has placed the United States in a situation where it can insist that the primary responsibility for meeting the threats of internal upheaval or of regional aggression lies with the threatened regimes themselves and with their allies in the moderate Arab world, particularly Egypt and Jordan. Five years ago, an internal revolution in Saudi Arabia that brought radical elements to the fore might have gravely compromised western interests and justified an American occupation of the Saudi oil fields. So long as Saudi oil exports remain in the low range to which they fell in 1985—anywhere from 2.1 to 4.5 million barrels a day—such a revolution would be far less harmful. Whoever sits on top of Saudi reserves will have a compelling interest in maintaining exports near the levels the Saudis reached in the mid-1980s. This is likely to be the case regardless of the hostility a new regime might feel toward the West in general and the United States in particular. And that in turn means that the burdens of such an occupation would be far more difficult to justify.

In all likelihood these dire eventualities will never have to be faced. The Arab regimes of the Gulf have displayed a remarkable durability over the last decade, which tells us something about their skill in parrying threats to their survival. The danger that the Iranian example would lead others to follow in their path appears now to have been greatly exaggerated. This regime is a model only for disaffected Shias and other fanatics, who happily remain a minority in the Middle East and the Persian Gulf. Even if time brought about an Iranian victory over Iraq and led to the downfall of Saddam Hussein, it would be very difficult for Iran to consolidate its position. Such a victory, by itself, would not give the Iranians hegemony over the Gulf. Besides, in vindicating our interests in the Gulf, we need not ensure the survival of every regime now tied to us. Our basic interests will be secured by the maintenance of a balance of power in the region, and even if we consciously limit the scale of our military involvement in the area, there is little reason to believe that a balance of sorts cannot be maintained. The objectives of Soviet policy are expressible in similar terms: in its policy toward the Iran-Iraq war we see clearly the calculation that finds in the division of the rimlands the formula for the safety of Russia. It is very difficult to believe that any indigenous power would be capable of unifying the area—which is a kind of Lebanon writ large—despite the opposition of both super-powers. Dankwart Rustow has recently noted the tendency of both regional and outside powers to rally to the weaker side when wars erupt, and against the winner when they are decided. "While many Middle Eastern countries individually nurse expansionist or hegemonic ambitions, all of them collectively, by their preference for the weaker side and their readiness to shift alignments regardless of ideology, offer strong support for the status quo." Like the European state system of old, "the pattern of hostility, interaction and maneuver thus has its self-balancing features."[12]

Indeed, the Middle East and the Persian Gulf offer fertile ground to pursue a policy of *divide et impera*. The aim of such a policy is not different from that which Great Britain traditionally pursued toward the European continent. Its objective, as George Kennan once expressed it, is "to establish a balance among the hostile or undependable forces of the world: To set them where necessary one against the other; to see that they spend in conflict with each other the intolerance and violence and fanaticism which might otherwise be directed against us."[13] If we are to conform to the spirit of this policy, we should avoid military commitments in which our forces are threatened with substantial casualties; if military power is necessary, it should be used in a fashion that plays to our strengths and not to our weaknesses. Under current circumstances, that means a reliance on American air and naval power and economic and military aid, and a recognition that the revolution in world oil markets gives us the capacity to strike at the oil export facilities of any regional aggressor that seeks to gravely undermine our interests.

Energy Policy and Military Strategy

The reflections thus far have shown the large benefits that have flowed from a reduction of Persian Gulf oil exports from 20 to 10 million barrels per day. Whether this condition will persist, however, is quite uncertain. So long as oil remained at prices approaching $27.00 a barrel, it was very unlikely—even with sustained global economic recovery—that the Gulf would have seen anything but a very modest increase in export levels. But the collapse of world oil prices in the winter of 1985–86, if it persists, seems likely to create circumstances in which the Gulf producers can regain part of the market share they lost in the 1980s.

The return of such dependence ought to be resisted by the United States with as much vigor as possible. For the market cost of Persian Gulf oil is not its real cost. Its real cost has to be measured over the long term and must include the price of another oil shock, a likely event if dependence is allowed to grow substantially. It must include the array of political and military measures necessary to secure access over time, costs that are borne primarily and disproportionately by the United States. It must include the progressive restriction of our military freedom of action, and it must even include the costs associated with a return to the diplomatic formulae of the 1970s for a solution of the Palestinian problem. The Reagan administration has failed to give these considerations the fundamental place they deserve in American energy policy. Its attitude, on the contrary, has been schizophrenic. One part of it took for granted that the United States must assume the primary military obligation for assuring access to Persian Gulf oil. Another part held that "it is not the policy of this Administration to reduce dependence on foreign energy suppliers beyond the level determined by market forces."[14]

It is impossible to predict the role that Persian Gulf production will play in the world oil market in the 1990s and beyond. Much will depend upon Saudi market strategy, the outcome of the Iran-Iraq war, and many other factors that cannot be foreseen. What *is* predictable is that the salience of Gulf production will largely be a function of price. Because oil is the world's marginal source of fuel, and because the Gulf producers are the world's marginal suppliers of oil, a low price for oil (say, from $12–$18 per barrel) will lead to greater demand for the Gulf's oil; a higher price, conversely, will reduce demand. The Saudi-engineered reduction in the price of oil from $34.00 to $29.00 a barrel in March 1983 stemmed from the perception that oil at $34.00 a barrel held clear dangers for the maintenance of the Saudi market share, even at a production rate half that which the Saudis had sustained in the early 1980s. The comparable pressure that the Saudis began to apply in the fall of 1985 (in the form of increased production), which led to the collapse of oil prices in the winter, sprang from the same motive.

The failure to appreciate the significance of price was the reason why so many analysts badly erred, in the late 1970s and early 1980s, in their estimates of the future shape of the world oil market. The oil price revolution brought about a fundamentally new situation for all consumers with regard to the relative attractiveness of imported oil. It led to investments in coal-fired boilers, houses with much improved insulation, cars with much higher fuel efficiency, and all other manner of energy conservation. The oil price revolution also sparked a flurry of activity to bring forth new supplies of oil and other forms of energy, and new oil fields in Alaska, the North Sea, Mexico, Egypt, Columbia, Malaysia, and elsewhere were discovered and brought on line. Since the consumption and production of energy are capital-intensive, the effects of the pricing revolution only appeared gradually, but they were nevertheless relentless. As M. A. Adelman has remarked, "a shift in relative prices acts like a glacial drift—imperceptible in the short run, irresistible in the long."[15]

All these far-reaching effects, touching the lives of countless individuals, were brought about by a single factor—the high price of oil. A low price, conversely, would have equally powerful effects, and it might create circumstances in which the Persian Gulf producers would find themselves in a position to assume again the commanding role they once enjoyed in world oil markets. A low oil price would make it far more difficult to finance the hugely expensive and long-term exploration and production projects in areas like the North Sea and the Alaskan North Slope; it would make the consumption of oil more attractive in comparison with substitute fuels like coal, natural gas, and nuclear power; it would ease the burden on and increase oil consumption in developing countries, whose balance of payments position in the early 1980s prevented them in many cases from purchasing imported oil when it was priced at over $25.00 a barrel; it would increase the "energy/ GDP ratio," that is, the relationship between increases in energy consumption and economic growth, which fell from unity in the 1960–1973 period, when oil prices were low, to less than .1 from 1973 to 1981, when oil prices were high. Like the rise in prices that produced the oil glut of the early 1980s, it would take a long time for energy consumption and production to show the effects of a low oil price, and many states with pressing balance of payments problems would continue to find it advantageous to encourage the production and discourage the consumption of oil. (This is particularly the case with respect to the Soviet Union, which depends upon energy exports for most of its foreign exchange, and for many developing countries, whose financial position is likely to remain precarious and who will have difficulty paying even for cheap oil.) The effects of low oil prices, moreover, seem likely to be mitigated in part by the memory of the 1970s and the possibility that what happened then will happen again. Nevertheless, over time the effects of low oil prices would likely be as relentless as high prices once were, and there is consequently the very real long-term danger that dependence on the Persian Gulf will again grow sharply unless it is obstructed or altered by governmental action.

To swim against the tide of market forces is always a difficult task. It is nevertheless manifestly undesirable to return again to the perilous condition of the late 1970s, with its very high security costs that are not measured by the market. Perhaps the most important measure the United States should take to avoid this fate is the taxation of energy consumption. A tax of thirty cents a gallon on gasoline and twenty cents a gallon on diesel, *The Economist* has estimated, could raise approximately $37 billion a year. Because the Persian Gulf states are the world's marginal producers of oil, restraints on American consumption would have a direct impact on their export levels. Of all possible increases in taxation, those on oil consumption are by far the most desirable, for they strike at two great objectives with one blow: such taxes would restrain the pressure on world oil supplies and thereby contribute to the improved strategic situation the United States now faces in the Persian Gulf; and they can make a large contribution to lessening the size of the federal budget deficit. By themselves, such taxes can go a long way toward easing the American strategic predicament.[16]

Support for the exploration of oil in the developing world, whether it is accomplished through multilateral agencies like the World Bank or through bilateral agreements with particular states, is the single most important initiative that can be taken on the supply side. Most drilling in relation to prospective oil-bearing regions has taken place in the United States. The rest of the world is comparatively unexplored. Once the discovery of huge oil reserves in the Middle East made available apparently unlimited supplies, the economic incentive to explore for oil elsewhere was minimal, and that difficulty was in turn compounded by political instability in many developing states. Financial incentives (whether in the form of tax concessions or direct subsidies) that would increase exploratory activity in the Third World—which might otherwise decline sharply alongside the drop in oil prices—is well worth the cost and could be financed by part of the proceeds from a new gasoline levy.[17]

Consideration ought also to be given to an oil tariff that would seek to ensure self-sufficiency in oil for the Western Hemisphere and that would therefore exempt neighboring states such as Mexico, Canada, Venezuela, and Columbia from its reach. Such a measure is not, to be sure, without defects, the foremost of which is that it would raise the general price level of energy and thus contribute to inflation. That negative effect, however, is more than overcome by the positive contribution it would make to energy security (the absence of which carries with it imposing costs as well). A second negative effect of a tariff is that it would encourage the further depletion of American oil reserves, which is particularly worrisome given the historical relationship between drilling and potentially petroliferous regions.[18] By bringing selected hemispheric producers within the tariff wall, however, this negative effect would be overcome by the encouragement given to exploratory and productive activity within the hemisphere that is otherwise sure to decline sharply; by providing hemispheric producers with substantial price advantages, moreover, a tariff would tie them to the North American market. Particularly important in this scheme is the position of Mexico, whose financial position deteriorated sharply in 1986 because of the collapse of world oil prices. Some form of debt relief for Mexico is inevitable, and it is desirable that it be offered in a way that will contribute to our own energy security. The proposed plan would go a long way toward doing that.

It is apparent, of course, that the ability of the United States to influence the future salience of Persian Gulf production in the world petroleum market is limited. Whether Gulf production grows in the future is a function of the oil balances maintained by every state in the world and not merely our own. These oil balances, in turn, are critically dependent on governmental action touching every aspect of the production and consumption of energy, the most important of which are the taxes and regulations governing the oil market. Some importing states will succeed more than others in the attempt to lessen the size or restrain the growth of their oil imports from the Persian Gulf. Their success or failure will depend not only on the price of oil or luck but also on 1) their willingness to offer a sufficiently attractive environment for the international oil companies such that exploration and production activities are carried forward; and 2) their willingness to tax the consumption of oil, even though such taxes might weaken their competitive position in the world economy. Those that restrain their avarice in these two respects will find themselves in a much better position to weather any economic storm brought on by a future disruption of Persian Gulf supplies. The tariff scheme recommended here for the Western Hemisphere, it may be noted, is equally relevant for Europe and Japan. In the subsidies that Great Britain pays to the Common Market and in its own need for a higher price of oil to ensure profitable North Sea exploration and production, there are the makings of a natural trade-off. The same is true in East Asia, which has some of the most promising oil frontiers in the world. By treating oil imports from Indonesia, Malaysia, and other East Asian producers in a preferential manner, Japan could help further indigenous production and thus contribute to its own energy security.

There are thus two key considerations that should guide American energy policy in the future, which would allow us to harmonize energy policy with military strategy. First, the United States should take unilateral energy measures at home to ensure that American dependence on Gulf oil remains limited. It was the growth of American import requirements in the 1970s, we should recall, that gave OPEC much of its market power. That experience should not and need not be repeated. Second, the United States should encourage indigenous energy production and conservation in both the developed and developing worlds, emphasizing to others that there are certain limits beyond which we are not willing to go in assuring their access to Persian Gulf oil. If other oil importers cannot resist the short-term price advantages the Gulf producers began to offer them in 1986, and if they allow their dependence on this oil to grow substantially, we should make it clear that we will not underwrite their profligacy with our military power. All imperial powers face the problem of free-riders among their dependents, and at the end of the 1970s, the U.S. faced it in the Persian Gulf with an acuteness seldom displayed in the past. We may yet face it again. This feature of the American position ought not to be read as excluding the use of American power in the Persian Gulf. It does, however, reinforce the wisdom of understanding our role in accordance with a rehabilitated Nixon Doctrine, and under some circumstances it might provide persuasive justification for an American disengagement from the region, in which events were allowed to take their course.

Drift and Mastery

It was the crisis in the Persian Gulf at the end of the 1970s that, more than any other factor, led a host of observers to the pessimistic conclusion that the American strategic predicament was essentially unresolvable, that things promised to get worse rather than better, and that, as Walter Levy wrote, "the world, as we know it now, will probably not be able to maintain its cohesion, nor be able to provide for the continued economic progress of its people against the onslaught of future oil shocks—with all that this might imply for the political stability of the West, its free institutions, and its internal and external security."[19] We know now that, as these very words were being written, the tide was already beginning to recede, leading to a remarkable improvement in the West's position. Now it is the opportunities, and not the dangers, that are most striking. If seized, these opportunities would provide a key foundation for the reformation of American strategy.

The comforting notion that "the Arabs can't drink their oil" was discredited in the 1970s because the economies of the Atlantic and Pacific basins allowed themselves to become overly dependent on a few oil producers in the Persian Gulf. The maxim nevertheless contains a great deal of truth. Its corollary in the 1980s is that, along with the Iranians, they are going to have a great deal of trouble in selling it. The maintenance of this happy state of affairs ought to be the great objective of American policy. For the Gulf producers, oil for export is the source of nearly all their power. If by means of intelligent economic precautions we continue to strike at this power, the specter of catastrophe will remain a distant one. A policy that ignores these considerations and allows dependence on the Gulf to grow in the future, on the other hand, will render us a hostage to circumstances that we cannot control and will inevitably increase the threat to American security.

Notes

1. On the composition of the Rapid Deployment Force, in the context of a much broader study of rapidly deployable forces since the 1960s, see Robert P. Haffa,

Jr., *The Half War: Planning U.S. Rapid Deployment Forces to Meet a Limited Contingency, 1960–1983* (Boulder, Colo., 1984). For a comprehensive critique, see Jeffrey Record, *The Rapid Deployment Force and U.S. Military Intervention in the Persian Gulf,* 2nd ed. (Cambridge, Mass., 1983). Other useful pieces on the composition of the RDF include "Rapid Deployment Force: Will Europe help America help Europe," *The Economist,* 11 December 1982, 62–64; R. J. L. Dicker, "RDF Sealift Programs: The Long-term Maritime Pre-positioning Force Takes Shape," *International Defense Review* (July 1983), 956–958; Michael Gordon, "The Rapid Deployment Force—Too Large, Too Small or Just Right for its Task?," *National Journal,* 13 March 1982, 451–455; and Richard Halloran, "Poised for the Persian Gulf," *The New York Times Magazine,* 1 April 1984, 38–61. The case for a light armored corps is contained in Lt. Gen. James F. Hollingsworth, USA, Ret., and Maj. Gen. Allan T. Wood, USMC, Ret., "The Light Armored Corps—A Strategic Necessity," *Armed Forces Journal International* (January 1980), 20–24. See also by Hollingsworth, "The Light Division," *Armed Forces Journal International* (October 1983), 84–90. The best overview of the Carter administration's approach to the area is in chapter 8, "U.S. Security Interests in Southwest Asia," in Harold Brown, *Thinking About National Security: Defense and Foreign Policy in a Dangerous World* (Boulder, Colo., 1983), 141–59. The thinking of the Reagan administration appears to have been heavily influenced by Albert Wohlstetter, "Meeting the Threat in the Persian Gulf," *Survey* (Spring 1980), 128–88.

2. The data are from Gerald F. Seib, "Persian Gulf Declines as a Vital Highway for Mideastern Oil," *The Wall Street Journal,* 24 January 1986. The network of pipelines in the Middle East is described by E. Stanley Tucker, "Focus on Pipeline Developments," *Petroleum Economist* (August 1982), 313–15.

3. See Thomas J. Lueck, "Coping with an Oil Cutoff: Persian Gulf's Role Lessened," *New York Times,* 29 February 1984. Producing states outside the Gulf with excess capacity in 1984 included Canada (200,000 b/d), Indonesia (300,000 b/d), Libya (600,000 b/d), Mexico (300,000 b/d), Nigeria (700,000 b/d), and Venezuela (700,000 b/d). OPEC current account balances from 1980 to 1983 are included in "OPEC: Grimace and Bear It," *The Economist,* 10 December 1983.

4. On the tanker war, see Raphael Danziger, "The Persian Gulf Tanker War," *U.S. Naval Institute Proceedings* (May 1985), 160–67.

5. 23 January 1980, Weekly Compilation of Presidential Documents, 16 (28 January 1980), (Washington, D.C. 1980), 197.

6. For a detailed investigation of these obstacles, see Joshua M. Epstein, "Soviet Vulnerabilities in Iran and the RDF Deterrent," *International Security* (Fall 1981), 126–58; Thomas L. McNaugher, *Arms and Oil: U.S. Military Strategy and the Persian Gulf* (Washington, D.C. 1985); and Richard K. Betts, *Surprise Attack: Lessons for Defense Planning* (Washington, D.C. 1982), 261–73.

7. Proposals to send a large force of American light infantry to operate in hostile Iranian territory, such as those made by Steven Canby in "Military Reform and the Art of War," *Survival* (May/June 1983), 124–25, only make sense if their tactical merits are considered in isolation from the huge strategic penalties they would incur.

8. The best sources on this conflict are Mark Heller, ed., *The Middle East Military Balance,* published annually beginning in 1983 (Tel Aviv, Israel); Shahram Chubin, "The Iran-Iraq War and Persian Gulf Security," *International Defense Review* 6 (1984), 705–12; William F. Hickman, *Ravaged and Reborn: The Iranian Army* (Wash-

ington, D.C., 1982); and Anthony Cordesman, *The Gulf and the Search for Strategic Stability* (Boulder, Colo., 1984).

9. See, for instance, the comments of Eugene Rostow, then director of the Arms Control and Disarmament Agency: "The Soviet pause for appraisal of this administration is over, and we're going to be tested. I believe Iran is the place we're going to be tested." Quoted in Youssef M. Ibrahim and Karen Elliot House, "Ascendancy of Iran in Conflict with Iraq Imperils Mideast Oil," *The Wall Street Journal,* 24 February 1982.

10. The Chinese played both sides of the street. See Clarence A. Robinson, Jr., "Iraq, Iran Acquiring Chinese Built Fighters," *Aviation Week and Space Technology,* 11 April 1983, 16–18.

11. See the discussion in Mark Heller, "Turmoil in the Gulf," *The New Republic,* 23 April 1984.

12. Dankwart A. Rustow, "Realignments in the Middle East," *Foreign Affairs, America and the World: 1984,* 598.

13. George F. Kennan, *Memoirs, 1925–1950* (Boston. 1967).

14. *The Annual Report of the Council of Economic Advisers,* (Washington, D.C. 1983), 108. See also on this point the perceptive observations of Robert J. Lieber, "Energy Policy and National Security: Invisible Hand or Guiding Hand?" in Kenneth A. Oye et al., *Eagle Defiant: United States Foreign Policy in the 1980s* (Boston, 1983), 181.

15. Quoted in "The Power Savers," *The Economist,* 26 December 1981, 65. The best single introduction to the energy problem—and a model work in political economy—is Peter Odell, *Oil and World Power,* 7th ed., (New York, 1983). Others who, like Odell, saw early the significance of the pricing revolution include Arlon R. Tussing, "An OPEC Obituary," *The Public Interest* (Winter 1983), 3–21; S. Fred Singer, "An End to OPEC? Bet on the Market," *Foreign Policy* (Winter 1981/82), 115–21; and S. Fred Singer, "Saudi Arabia's Oil Crisis," *Policy Review* (Summer 1982), 87–100. Their works should be compared with the analysis in Herman T. Franssen, "World Energy Supply Trends: Implications for Energy Security," in Franssen et al., *World Energy Supply and International Security* (Cambridge, Mass. 1983), 1–27; Robert Stobaugh, "World Energy to the Year 2000," in Daniel Yergin and Martin Hillenbrand, eds., *Global Insecurity: A Strategy for Energy and Economic Renewal* (Boston, 1982); Bijan Mossavar-Rahmani, "The OPEC Multiplier," *Foreign Policy* (Fall 1983), 136–48; and Anthony H. Cordesman, "The 'Oil Glut' and the Strategic Importance of the Gulf States," *Armed Forces Journal International* (October 1983), 30–47. Despite the failure of the latter group of analysts to appreciate the full significance of the pricing revolution, the collapse in oil prices in early 1986, if it persists, may yet vindicate their pessimistic forecast that Persian Gulf production will increase in salience in the future.

16. Because energy taxes put additional downward pressure on prices, such measures in effect transfer revenue from the OPEC government to the U.S. federal treasury. The estimates for gasoline and diesel taxes are from "Curing that American Deficit," *The Economist,* 15 December 1984.

17. The debate over the probable size of ultimately recoverable oil reserves may be followed in International Energy Agency, *World Energy Outlook* (Paris, 1982), chapter 5, and Franssen, *World Energy Supply,* 12–13. The International Energy Agency's position on this issue was quite similar to that of the international oil

companies. For a comprehensive challenge to this pessimistic forecast, see Peter R. Odell and Kenneth E. Rosing, *The Future of Oil: A Simulation Study of the Inter-relationships of Resources, Reserves and Use, 1980–2080* (New York, 1980), esp. 23–45; and Peter R. Odell, "An Alternative View of the Outlook for the International Oil Market," *Petroleum Economist* (October 1983), 392–94. The World Bank's program to encourage energy production and conservation in the Third World is described in The World Bank, *The Energy Transition in Developing Countries* (Washington, D.C. 1983).

18.   On the prospects for domestic oil production, see Robert Stobaugh, "After the Peak: the Threat of Hostile Oil," in *Energy Future: Report of the Energy Project at the Harvard Business School,* 3rd ed., ed. Robert Stobaugh and Daniel Yergin, (New York, 1983), 51–57.

19.   Walter J. Levy, "Oil and the Decline of the West," *Foreign Affairs* (Summer 1980), 1015.

Part III
American Strategic Doctrine:
The Case for Change

4 — Strategic Nuclear Policy

The Significance of the Debate

Of all the defense programs sponsored by the Reagan administration, none has attracted as much controversy as its plan to "modernize" a wide range of offensive nuclear systems and its program to investigate the feasibility of strategic defenses. No other area of defense policy had a higher priority for the administration itself. Most of the programs sponsored by the administration were conceived before it took office, and in the first few years of its term it appeared that in its strategic nuclear policy it was merely following the lead marked out by the Carter administration in its last year. It has become increasingly apparent, however, that the elements of change are far more impressive than the elements of continuity; indeed, that we are witnessing with the Reagan administration a far-reaching challenge to the strategic doctrine embraced by every American administration for the past two decades.

The debate provoked by the administration's policy has thus been far-reaching. But in one critical respect, what has been most striking about this debate has not been the obvious differences that divide the administration from its critics but the degree to which they share a common assumption regarding the significance of nuclear weapons. The most striking instance of common outlook on the Right and the Left is the distrust of the arrangements of mutual deterrence and the desire to escape a world of nuclear weapons—to render them, in the President's words, "impotent and obsolete." Also notable has been the tendency, common to analysts on both sides, to assume that a first-use policy requires first-strike capabilities, that an inseparable connection exists between the two, that you can't have one without the other. For the Right, this

117

assumption has made the maintenance of extended deterrence a function of the ability to limit damage to the United States in a full-scale exchange of nuclear weapons, which in turn requires the development of offensive missiles aimed at the offensive missiles of the Soviet Union (counterforce weapons such as the MX and D-5) and defensive systems capable of protecting a full range of military and civilian targets in the United States. For the Left, this assumption has led to the conclusion that nuclear weapons have lost their utility as a deterrent, and that the first use of nuclear weapons by the United States in response to a massive Soviet attack in Eurasia is too dangerous to form any longer an underpinning of American security policy.

Both Right and Left profess a desire for mutual disarmament; that failing, the Right is drawn to strategies of forcible disarmament, the Left to unilateral disarmament. Those who are so drawn believe that, once nuclear weapons are employed, there is no logical stopping point short of a full-scale nuclear exchange; for the Right, the imperative of policy is therefore to develop military capabilities that would allow the United States to physically disarm the Soviet Union in the event of such a full-scale nuclear exchange while minimizing damage to ourselves; for the Left, the imperative of policy is to "denuclearize" international politics. Both sides believe that "extended deterrence," insofar as it rests upon the American threat to use nuclear weapons first in the event of a Soviet non-nuclear attack on our principal allies, no longer exists or at least has been gravely weakened. The Right seeks to recapture "extended deterrence" and believes that we can only do so by regaining "strategic superiority"; the Left, believing that such an aspiration is both dangerous and unrealizable, seeks to abandon altogether both "first use" and "extended deterrence."

Both of these extreme views, I believe, reflect a misunderstanding of the significance of the nuclear revolution and a failure to appreciate both the potentialities and the limitations of nuclear weapons. It is the principal thesis of the following chapter that the threatened first use of nuclear weapons must remain of central importance to American strategy *and* that the United States ought to dispense with some of the key elements of the Reagan administration's strategic modernization program, particularly those that will give the United States an impressive range of first-strike capabilities.

The Choice in Nuclear Strategy

The basic choice in nuclear strategy is whether one should seek to acquire military capabilities, whether offensive or defensive or both, that allow one to physically disarm the enemy. This choice is quite similar to the basic problem of strategy in the prenuclear age. Perhaps the most famous distinction in the history of strategic thought is that which the German military historian Hans Delbrück drew between the strategy of annihilation and the strategy of attrition. The choice between annihilation and attrition as strategic objectives, as Delbrück saw it, revolved around the question of whether one should aim to disarm the enemy (annihilation) or whether one should attempt to weaken his will through exhaustion or shock (attrition). In the former case, victory is achieved through a physical process; in the latter, through a psychological one. The basic problem of nuclear strategy revolves around the same question that preoccupied Delbrück: whether one should aim to forcibly disarm the enemy or whether one should attempt to weaken his will.[1]

Many observers, particularly on the Left, believe that this question is no longer the appropriate one; indeed, that the question itself is dangerous, since it suggests that there might be a political purpose served by the use of nuclear weapons. Instead they insist that the critical distinction in the nuclear age is between deterrence and "war-fighting."[2] But this is a misleading way of posing the nuclear dilemma. To give nuclear weapons a war-fighting role is not to abandon deterrence. It is simply to recognize that there must exist some credible theory of use, some plausible connection between the existential moment and a recognizable human motivation, for the calculations of deterrence to be persuasive. This being so, there is both self-deception (and the danger of the adversary's misperception) in the kind of advice offered in the Pastoral Letter of the U.S. Catholic bishops, with its avowal of "no use—never" and its continuing reliance on deterrence. What Machiavelli said of Hannibal's reputation for cruelty and its utility in keeping his army disciplined may justly be said of the bishops: "Thoughtless writers admire on the one hand his actions, and on the other blame the principal cause of them." The bishops seek to enjoy the effect, deterrence, while disposing of the cause—the fear induced by our conditional intention to use nuclear weapons in response to Soviet attack.[3]

American officials have always been conscious of the necessity of articulating a credible theory of nuclear use. War planning, moreover, has always placed primary emphasis on targets that were significant (whether directly or indirectly) to the enemy war effort. In the 1950s and 1960s, this emphasis on military targeting was part and parcel of a nuclear strategy that would have sought, in the event of war, to forcibly disarm Soviet military capability. As the Soviet strategic nuclear arsenal grew, it came to be realized that such a disarming strike would be unlikely to eliminate the Soviet retaliatory capability, and would therefore pose enormous risks of retaliation against American territory. This realization pushed many analysts away from strategies of forcible disarmament (annihilation) and led to the search for more limited nuclear options—designed to have a direct military effect on the battlefield or simply to show resolve in a war of nerves played for the highest stakes. Some who embarked on this path lost their nerve and went so far as to recommend policies of no-first-use—as Robert McNamara recently revealed he did in private with Presidents Kennedy and Johnson. There was, in any case, the recognition that strategies of annihilation or forcible disarmament would raise the dangers of accidental war (and hence were incompatible with "crisis stability"). There was also the recognition that such strategies would lead to steps taken by the other side to preserve its retaliatory capability, an "action-reaction" phenomenon incompatible with "arms race stability."[4]

In departing from annihilation, American officials in effect embraced the strategy of attrition. This is clearly the case with respect to James Schlesinger and Harold Brown, who did the most as secretaries of defense in the 1970s to bring the new American nuclear doctrine to public attention. Neither man sought military capabilities that would allow the United States to physically disarm the enemy in a full-scale exchange of nuclear weapons. Rather, the United States sought to make it clear to the Soviet Union, in Brown's words, "that no course of aggression by them that led to use of nuclear weapons, on any scale of attack and at any stage of conflict, could lead to victory, however they may define victory." The objective, in other words, was to impose such costs on the adversary that his will to prevail would weaken—the classic objective of the strategists of attrition. This objective, in turn, presupposed that one's own means of inflicting punishment on the enemy would be kept intact for as long as possible—hence the emphasis placed on the maintenance of survivable nuclear forces and communications facilities that would allow the United States to retaliate even if the Soviet Union were to attempt a disarming first strike against us. Both Schlesinger and Brown recognized that "reflexive, massive attacks on Soviet cities and populations," i.e., a targeting doctrine of assured destruction, was no longer credible and could no longer adequately deter. Critical to this policy was the assumption that "escalation of a limited nuclear exchange can be controlled," and that "it can be stopped short of an all-out, massive exchange." Secretary Brown, to be sure, expressed skepticism that this assumption was well-founded. Still, he was "convinced that we must do everything we can to make such escalation control possible, that opting out of this effort and consciously resigning ourselves to the inevitability of such escalation is a serious abdication of the awesome responsibilities nuclear weapons thrust upon us."[5]

Both Schlesinger and Brown recommended the acquisition of counterforce capabilities. Both made it clear that the term referred to "the full range of Soviet (and, as appropriate non-Soviet Warsaw Pact) military power, conventional as well as nuclear." It thus included, for both, "hard target, counter-silo capabilities." For Schlesinger, the development of American counter-silo capabilities was justified because the Soviet Union was acquiring such capabilities, and it was important, for psychological reasons, that the United States maintain "essential equivalence" with Soviet forces. The MX program, as conceived by Brown, was justified because "it is important—for the sake of deterrence—to be able to deny to the potential aggressor a fundamental and favorable shift in the strategic balance as a result of a nuclear exchange." These developments undoubtedly began the uncertain return to a damage-limitation strategy within the American government, but it should nevertheless be noted that both Schlesinger and Brown disavowed any intention to acquire nuclear systems capable of forcibly disarming the enemy. Other factions within and without the government who wanted counter-silo capabilities may have had their minds set on a return to strategies of forcible disarmament; for the civilian secretaries of defense, however, the limitation of damage in a nuclear war still rested on the threat of reprisal and not on the capacity to physically disarm the enemy. They did not seek to overcome the condition of mutual vulnerability.

American nuclear strategic doctrine in the 1970s—with its emphasis on deterrence through the threatened disruption of enemy morale, either through exhaustion or shock—is therefore to be distinguished from a strategic doctrine that a) seeks deterrence through military capabilities allowing for the forcible disarmament of the enemy (annihilation or damage limitation); and b) one that seeks deterrence through the threat of massive societal punishment and that eschews all "war-fighting" options (assured destruction). The term "damage limitation" is sometimes employed to signify a strategy of attrition, for such a doctrine is consistent with the use of nuclear weapons against military targets (such as concentrations of ground forces and air bases) in as discriminating a manner as possible. Nevertheless, strategists of attrition assume that damage will be limited in war not only through discriminating targeting but also through fear of reprisal. Their insistence on counter-military targeting, alongside their belief in the possibility of limiting a nuclear conflict, sets them apart from assured destructionists on the one hand; their reliance on retaliation in kind, and their renunciation of a first-strike capability, set them apart from forcible disarmers on the other.*

Understanding American nuclear strategy in this light makes it apparent that we have reached in the 1980s a fundamental turning point in the nuclear debate. The inability to attempt the disarmament of the enemy without risking the devastation of one's own national territory has been the point of departure for strategic thought since the Soviet Union acquired an intercontinental nuclear capability in the 1950s. The early reflections of Bernard Brodie, Robert Osgood, William Kaufmann, and others all had this seemingly inescapable fact as their point of departure, which in turn

---

*There is no more regrettable feature of the contemporary nuclear debate than the tendency of analysts on both the Right and the Left to ignore the existence of an alternative in the middle. Cf., for example, Fred S. Hoffman, "The SDI in U.S. Nuclear Strategy," *International Security* (Summer 1985), 14, and Spurgeon M. Keeny, Jr., and Wolfgang K. H. Panofsky, "MAD Versus NUTS: The Mutual Hostage Relationship of the Superpowers," *Foreign Affairs* (Winter 1981/82), 293–94. The former article implicitly lumps together assured destructionists with strategists of attrition, as if nothing had changed in American nuclear doctrine since McNamara made a few loose statements before congressional committees in the 1960s. The latter conflates the desire of strategists of attrition to articulate a credible theory of use with the views of those, like Colin Gray, who believe in "deterrence by anticipation of U.S. victory," through the maintenance of arsenals capable of forcible disarmament.

provoked the search for the principle of limitation that another war between the great powers might observe.[6] Many American strategists, to be sure, have long been dissatisfied with the condition of mutual vulnerability and have championed the cause of counterforce weapons and strategic defenses: the contemporary nuclear debate is therefore similar in many respects to the one over continental air defenses in the 1950s and the one over antiballistic missile systems (ABMs) in the late 1960s.[7] But a strategy of forcible disarmament, which the technical supremacy of the offense appeared to foreclose in earlier periods, has reasserted itself in the 1980s.

The reasons for the revival of such strategies are complex, but three stand out—technological, political, and spiritual. With the development of offensive weapons of ever-increasing accuracy and of defensive systems based on exotic new technologies, the technical assumptions underlying the condition of mutual vulnerability have been called increasingly into question. Of perhaps even greater moment, it became increasingly apparent during the 1970s and early 1980s that the Soviet Union was making a frantic attempt to overcome its own vulnerability, that it was pursuing the strategy of annihilation that the United States had renounced in the 1960s and 1970s. Finally, many on the Left and Right have lost their faith in deterrence. It appears to them a rickety arrangement, certain to break down in time. The condition underlying it—mutual vulnerability—is therefore seen as something we should make every effort to escape. All three of these themes are fundamental to the outlook of President Reagan and his most articulate supporters. His belief in them marks the President as a man seeking changes in national strategy even more far-reaching than those he has sought in domestic life.

Disarmament and Damage Limitation: The Trouble with Star Wars

The vision held by Mr. Reagan and his supporters is of a world freed from the fear of the apocalypse, one in which the threat of mutual destruction is replaced by the progressive reduction of offensive arsenals and the progressive build-up of defensive systems. The achievement of this objective, according to the administration, would take place in three stages: in the first stage, it would "seek a radical reduction in the number and power of exist-ing and planned offensive and defensive nuclear arms." As research on nonnuclear defenses against ballistic missiles, bombers, and cruise missiles bore fruit, the defensive systems would be deployed. In the third and final stage, "offensive nuclear weapons would be eliminated so that the only nuclear threat the defense would have to work against would be offensive nuclear weapons hidden through cheating, or attacks from nuclear-armed third countries."[8]

If we take the objective of mutual nuclear disarmament at face value, nothing seems more far removed from a strategy of forcible disarmament. Yet there are compelling reasons for dismissing the prospect of a nuclear-free world, and indeed for seeing in it a form of utopianism that is doomed to fail. The classic objection to disarmament—which applies equally to a nuclear and a nonnuclear world—is that the acquisition of arms by states is no independent phenomenon but a reflection of their conflicts with one another. To eliminate the effect, one must attend to the cause. Yet the causes of conflict, according to this old but powerful account, are inherent in the nature of man and the social setting in which he finds himself. Man is a desiring creature; the things that he desires, however, are inevitably in short supply. This is inevitably so with respect to security, a good desired by all states. Not all can enjoy it in equal measure. The attempt by one state to ensure its own security invariably compromises the security of others, and even though such attempts might be undertaken for defensive motives, the other side will inevitably be wary that this is really the case. The "abso-lute predicament and the irreducible dilemma" lie in what Herbert Butterfield once called the situation of

Hobbesian fear—that you yourself may vividly feel the terrible fear that you have of the other party, but you cannot enter into the other man's counter-fear, or even understand why he should be particularly nervous. For you know that you yourself mean him no harm, and that you want nothing from him save guarantees for your own safety; and it is never possible for you to realize or remember properly that since he cannot see the inside of your mind, he can never have the same assurance of your intentions that you have.[9]

This predicament might lead to a serious conflict, Butterfield be-lieved, even if the parties were "fairly intelligent and reasonably well-intentioned."

These considerations apply with even greater force to mutual nuclear disarmament, for nuclear arms make the fears arising from mutual want of confidence more acute than ever. The extraordinary destructive power contained in a single nuclear weapon would give disparities at a low numerical level a much greater significance than they have today, when each weapon is only one of thousands. For this reason, neither side will surrender its power of striking the national territory of the other so long as it fears that the other side retains this power for itself. No satisfactory assurances, however, may be given on this point. Even under extensive strategic defenses, a residual degree of doubt must exist about their effectiveness in an actual shooting war and their susceptibility to what Clausewitz called "friction." Unable to reassure itself that the weapons of the other would not get through the net, each side would have no incentive to surrender its power of striking the other; indeed, each is certain to make enormous sacrifices in order to retain this power. In addition, neither side could realistically hope to profit from arms control negotiations with the other (apart from a cynical attempt to score points with public opinion). They have no basis on which to compromise. The only way to split the difference between the two sides is for each to accept its vulnerability to the other; but this result is precluded by the object of the negotiation, which is to eliminate its vulnerability to the other.

The "defensive transition" on which the Reagan administration has rested its strategic nuclear policy is therefore a chimera. This does not rule out the possibility that the United States might try to do unilaterally what we cannot do mutually. The nature of this enterprise, however, ought to be clearly understood. To eliminate our vulnerability to Soviet nuclear weapons means that we would have to acquire a first-strike capability against it—a result that stems from a seemingly perverse feature of nuclear weapons systems. If they are capable of forcibly limiting the damage in a second strike, such systems would in principle be far more capable of doing so in a first strike. And although it is possible in theory to imagine a strategic nuclear policy based on the full development of strategic defenses that at the same time renounced counterforce weapons, in practice it is extremely unlikely that a defensive shield could be built that could intercept all (or nearly all) of the missiles the Soviet Union might fire at it. In practice, the aim of a damage-limitation strategy can only be satisfied by a combination of offensive counterforce weapons and strategic defenses. The offensive systems, in any case, cannot be surrendered until the defensive systems are deployed, for to do so would open a gaping window of vulnerability. [10]

In his speeches Mr. Reagan has repudiated the notion that the Strategic Defense Initiative has any offensive implications. He has also publicly renounced the desire to acquire a first-strike capability against Soviet nuclear forces. The heavy stress that has been placed by the Reagan administration on both counter-silo weapons and strategic defenses, however, makes the administration's policy explainable in these terms, and it is not surprising that the Soviet Union has so understood it. While in theory the administration has no strategy of forcible disarmament, in practice it has something very close to it, which in turn is the residue of three ostensibly unrelated facets of its strategic nuclear policy: 1) an intention to develop strategic defenses so as to make nuclear weapons "impotent and obsolete"; 2) a determination to build counter-silo weapons equivalent to those maintained by the Soviet Union; and 3) a war planning mechanism in the American military, which has been traditionally predisposed toward a damage-limitation strategy and will almost certainly in the future (as it has in the past) develop operational war plans corresponding with that predisposition.

Whether an effective damage-limitation capability can be constructed in coming years is a question to which there is no clear answer. It is now possible to build counter-silo weapons of extremely high accuracy and low explosive yield that would be capable of destroying a great many Soviet missiles and bombers on the ground, but there are a range of measures (deception, mobility, etc.) that the Soviet Union might take that would limit the effectiveness of such strikes and still leave it with a formidable retaliatory force (on its ballistic missile submarines if nothing else). Strategic defenses are therefore indispensable if such a capability is to be achieved. The reliability, effectiveness, and cost of such defensive systems are among the questions the research made possible by SDI is intended to answer; the preliminary answers given by our men of science are so various and contradictory that the layman has little ground for confident judgment. [11] If the "exchange ratio" between offensive and defensive arms turns out to favor heavily the offense, much of the current debate is moot, for under these circumstances the attempt of one side to defend its society against the nuclear weapons of the other will ultimately come to appear as a bad bargain—expensive if pursued, yet unachievable because defensive measures can be offset by cheaper offensive countermeasures. Under these circumstances, it is true, the acquisition of defensive systems might still be justifiable on lesser grounds—such as guarding against accidental or third party launches—but even with such systems, the central strategic relationship between the United States and the Soviet Union would continue to rest on mutual vulnerability.

The United States once enjoyed something close to a disarming first-strike capability against the Soviet Union—or so at least our military leaders assured us. It would be foolish to deny that this condition of superiority conferred real advantages on the United States during the classic period of the Cold War.[12] Whether the 1962 Cuban missile crisis was resolved in favor of the United States because of this superiority or for other reasons cannot be answered with any precision. Certainly it did not hurt. That American nuclear superiority did play a role in the outcome of that crisis was the conclusion drawn by the Soviet Union, which launched its own vigorous nuclear effort soon after. The loss of American strategic superiority that occurred as a consequence of the Soviet nuclear build-up, moreover, has had a debilitating effect on the maintenance of "extended deterrence." Even though the first use of American nuclear weapons in response to a massive Soviet conventional assault on the West appears to this writer to remain both credible and necessary under conditions of nuclear parity, it nevertheless is the case that this view is a minority opinion. If a consensus can be said to exist on this matter, it consists of the proposition that the achievement of Soviet nuclear parity has neutralized the American nuclear arsenal—both tactical and strategic—and made the threatened use of any of these weapons utterly unbelievable and their actual use incredibly dangerous.

The advantages that might be gained from the reacquisition of a meaningful damage-limitation capability cannot therefore be ignored in any assessment of the desirability of making the attempt to achieve one, if it were technically feasible. Still, the disadvantages appear to be more weighty than the advantages. The quest does raise some serious dangers, and even though these dangers have occasionally been exaggerated by the arms control lobby, they are real enough. In my view, five stand out:

a) Even if one accepts the objectives of the program, the willingness of American public opinion to support such a shift in strategy
over time is questionable. To be meaningful, the effort must be
sustained over the course of a generation. Given the state of the
nation's finances, it is surely reasonable to wonder where the resources for this ambitious new enterprise are to be gotten. Unless
we sharply raise taxes, abandon the safety net, or mortgage our
finances at an even deeper rate, the only reasonable speculation is
that these resources will be gotten from funds now devoted to the
modernization, readiness, and sustainability of our air, ground, and
naval forces. It is not unduly pessimistic to foresee a result that
leaves us with a penetrable shield alongside dilapidated conventional forces. This consideration is of particular importance if
the restraints that now govern the Soviet-American arms competition—primarily the 1972 ABM treaty—are renounced. Once taken
off, these restraints will be much more difficult to put back on. The
proponents of damage limitation assume that the United States will
inevitably win the ensuing arms race with the Soviet Union. That
our resources and technological ability are far greater is indisputa-
ble; that our desire for sacrifice will be equivalent to that of the
Soviet Union is much less so. The history of the Soviet-American
competition does not bear out the assumption that the United states
will emerge over the space of a generation in the dominant position
marked out by the damage limitationists.

b) It is inevitable that the Soviets will understand the pursuit of
this objective in the worst possible light. For the objective is the
acquisition of military capabilities that would allow the United
States to disarm the Soviet Union and render it impotent. Its fate, if
we were successful, would rest entirely in our hands. As such, it
would almost certainly preclude any abatement of the Soviet-
American rivalry and any composition of our (inevitable) differences. The permanent exacerbation of tensions to which it
would lead, moreover, is significant not only because it would
complicate the settlement of other issues dividing the superpowers
but also because of its impact on western public opinion. Even
those who are profoundly skeptical that the nature of the Soviet
leadership permits a normalization of relations should recognize
that public support in the West for defense spending rests on the
public's conviction that we are not pursuing an aggressive policy.
There is a clear historical relationship between the existence of

embittered Soviet-American political relations and the loss of public faith in deterrence. This loss of faith, it is true, has in the past yielded some public support for damage-limitation strategies. But it has also provoked a rise in support for policies of no-first-use and unilateral disarmament.

c) A damage-limitation strategy, often put forward as a means of overcoming the nuclear dilemmas of the Atlantic Alliance, would in fact not do so. The willingness of European governments to participate in research on "Star Wars"—largely for commercial reasons—does not reflect a receptivity to any basic change in allied strategy. Britain and France, faced with the development of counterforce systems and strategic defenses on the part of the Soviet Union, will inevitably worry about the possibility that their own national nuclear forces will no longer have the significance they now do. A Soviet defensive shield that the United States would be able to overcome might not be penetrable by the nuclear missiles of Britain and France. Neither power will lightly acquiesce in the effective loss of their nuclear status, especially if they doubt, as seems likely, the impenetrability of the defensive shield the United States might erect over them. Nor is this all. Even if a large number of technological hurdles are crossed, it is difficult to see how the vulnerability of the nonnuclear European powers, particularly Germany, can truly be eliminated. The territory controlled by the Soviet Union is too close, the means of nuclear delivery too various. The Germans will inevitably fear that they will be made a hostage by the Russians, as they were in the 1950s. This is, of course, the same fear they have today.

A reversion to a damage-limitation strategy would therefore not solve the nuclear dilemmas of the alliance, and it would in all probability compound them. At the outer reaches of allied strategy, it is true, there exists a set of dilemmas on which no real meeting of the minds is possible. But it is one thing to say, as the critics of flexible response have persuasively done, that the existing differences over nuclear strategy (which are merely theoretical and therefore bearable in peacetime) would be gravely exacerbated in war. It is quite another to maintain that if deterrence broke down, the Europeans would be reassured by a general nuclear war in which the United States sought to disarm the Soviet Union. The imminent prospect of a general nuclear war—in which each side sought to disarm the other—would be no less horrifying to Europe than the prospect of a limited nuclear war, and those who interpret the European demand that there be no sanctuaries as a plea for a damage-limitation strategy badly mistake the character of European opinion on this issue. The Europeans demand the reaffirmation of the community of fate, not strategies of forcible disarmament. The latter conjures for them visions of 1914, of war plans and military arsenals that, by virtue of their offensive character, provoke a deepening spiral of suspicion and, ultimately, a war.[13]

d) One of the claims most often made on behalf of counter-silo systems and strategic defenses is that they are far more compatible with the traditional limits on the conduct of war that moral reflection and legal rules have traditionally prescribed. The claim, however, is fundamentally misleading. It is true, as Albert Wohlstetter has persuasively argued, that there is no moral or strategic justification for conceiving of the use or threatened use of nuclear weapons in terms oblivious to the distinction between combatants and noncombatants, or in a fashion contemptuous of the principle of proportionality. There is therefore a strong case for imagining nuclear use in countermilitary terms—that is, as being directed against concentrations of ground forces, air bases, fuel depots, and communications links—while making every effort to minimize harm to innocent bystanders. The harm to innocents that the use of nuclear weapons might cause is not something that is entirely out of our control: it is possible to design weapons of low yield that can be accurately delivered on their target, causing less collateral damage and harm to innocents than would otherwise be the case. The ability to use nuclear weapons with discrimination and direct military effect, moreover, increase the likelihood that they would be used in war, and thus enhances deterrence.

But that is not the end of the matter. To insist that countermilitary targeting is necessary does not tell us what the *purpose* of such a use of nuclear weapons would be—whether the disarmament of the enemy (annihilation) or the disruption of his morale (attrition). If the former, there is little reason to believe that limits could in fact be maintained in the conduct of the war. The disarmament of the enemy is not a limited objective; on the contrary, as a war aim it is identical with "unconditional surrender." Forcible disarmament can be made to appear limited only if it is contrasted with an operational strategy of instantaneous mass murder in response to aggression of a far more limited character—but that is a caricature of what American strategic nuclear doctrine has been in the past. A strategy that seeks the disarmament of the enemy would in practice be far less compatible with the principle of proportionality than a strategy reliant on exhaustion or shock, for the reason that the former's objective is so much more ambitious than the latter's. It is precisely ambitions of this sort that carried the doctrine of necessity to terrible extremes in the two world wars of this century. Because ambitions of this sort underlie the justification of counter-silo weapons and strategic defenses, the claim of superior morality and prudence made on their behalf must be rejected.*

---

*Wohlstetter's position is set out in "Bishops, Statesmen, and Other Strategists on the Bombing of Innocents," *Commentary*, June 1983. 15–35, and "Between an Unfree World and None," *Foreign Affairs* (Summer 1985), 962–994. See also the succinct statement of his position in "Nuclear Temptations: An Exchange," *The New York Review of Books*, 31 May 1984, 44–47, and "Morality and Deterrence: Albert Wohlstetter and Critics," *Commentary*, December 1983, 13–22. Wohlstetter's treatment of these issues, though very sensible in most respects, fails to address explicitly the question of whether counterforce targeting would have as its objective the disarmament of the enemy or the disruption of his morale. Nor does he explore whether countermilitary targeting should be directed against missile silos (and if so for what purpose). It is reasonable to conclude, however, that Wohlstetter's position is a variant of the strategy of attrition and not of annihilation. Despite Wohlstetter's favorable references to the president's Star Wars program, he still apparently rests his hopes for damage limitation, as Colin Gray notes, "on a large measure of Soviet targeting restraint to be induced by Soviet fears of military-political damage that might still be suffered." (See "War Fighting for Deterrence," 21–22).

The strategy recommended by Wohlstetter thus continues to rest on the threat of reprisal, though it is reprisal directed against military assets and not cities. He argues that the prospect of such countermilitary strikes is sufficient to deter a Soviet attack. In this assertion, he is almost certainly right. There must nevertheless exist a residual degree of fear that the total renunciation of such threats against enemy innocents might confer political advantages on the side willing to threaten such measures. For this reason, it is inadvisable to renounce the threat of harming enemy civilians: *in extremis*, it is the threat of reprisal that guarantees the security of our own. For this reason as well, Wohlstetter's position does not refute the argument, set out a generation ago by Robert W. Tucker in *Force, Order, and Justice,* that "there is an irreconcilable conflict between the requirements of *bellum justum* and the requirements of deterrent strategies." This conclusion, as Tucker observed, "is not prompted in the first place by the unpersuasive character of the attempts that have been made to reconcile possible deterrent strategies with the requirements on means laid down by *bellum justum*. Even if these attempts were more persuasive than they are, they would fail in what must be their fundamental purpose, which is to show that in principle as well as in practice such reconciliation is possible. It is not enough

e) Finally, there is the question of the effect of counter-silo weapons and strategic defenses on "crisis stability." The proponents of strategic superiority argue that a situation in which the United States enjoyed a first-strike capability against the Soviet Union would not be unstable. This argument rests on the doubtful assumption that the Soviets would not resort to expedients to overcome their inferiority, like launch on warning, which would clearly raise the danger of accidental war. Yet even if this assumption is well taken, there would remain serious dangers from the "period of transition," i.e., during the time when the United States was building up its damage-limitation capability. If the deployment of offensive and defensive systems held out the prospect of conferring a disarming first-strike capability on their possessor, the power against which these capabilities were directed would be placed in a severe dilemma, which it might very well break through war. We certainly have every right to stipulate that we will never allow the Soviet Union to acquire such a capability and that we would prevent it from doing so, through peacetime deployments if possible, through war if necessary. But the same rule that gives us this right gives it also to the Soviet Union.

A rough justice exists in great power competitions, which may be summarized in a single phrase: rights of action are conferred by relative vitality of interest. The failure of statesmen to observe this precept was closely associated with the diplomatic preludes to both the First World War in 1914 and the Pacific War in 1941. Both the mobilization of the Central Powers and the Japanese attack on Pearl Harbor sprang from the soil of an agonizing dilemma. In the former case, the dilemma was exacerbated by the support Russia gave to the Serbian nationalists intent on bringing down the Dual Monarchy; in the latter case, by the American demand that Japan evacuate the whole of China as a condition for lifting the oil and

---

to demonstrate that a hypothetical deterrent strategy or an equally hypothetical strategy for waging thermonuclear war may just possibly be compatible with *bellum justum*. What must instead be shown is that the limiting conditions that may just possibly establish this compatibility can also be made, as a matter of principle and practice, politically effective yet remain self contained. No one has shown this, however, and it is altogether unlikely that anyone will be able to show this. All that can be shown is that the principal, and apparently the indispensable, sanction for the limits required of the just war, nuclear or otherwise, remains the meaningful threat of a nuclear war which clearly exceeds these limits." (318–19) See also by Tucker, *The Nuclear Debate: Deterrence and the Lapse of Faith* (New York, 1985), chapter 2.

scrap embargoes the Roosevelt administration had imposed upon it. The Russians are seldom blamed for the war of 1914 and the Americans even less so for the Pacific War of 1941, but each was deeply implicated in their origins. Each was responsible for extreme assertions of interest, which, if accepted by the other side, would have constituted profound humiliations or far worse. It was the unwillingness of the Central Powers to accept this assertion of Russian interest in the Balkans that gave them no choice but to mobilize; it was Japan's unwillingness to abandon ten years of conquest in China at the behest of the United States that led to the attack on Pearl Harbor. That both the Germans and the Japanese may fairly be charged with bringing their dilemmas on them-selves—as the Soviet Union may fairly be charged today—did not make their predicaments any less acute or any less dangerous.[14]

A similar lesson may be drawn from the 1962 Cuban missile crisis, when the superpowers drew closer to war than at any other time in postwar history. American strategic superiority may have been the thing that resolved the crisis in our favor, but it also in an important sense brought the crisis on. For it was only when Amer-ican leaders discoverd that Khrushchev had been bluffing and that the missile gap favored not the Soviet Union but the United States that Khrushchev made his gamble to place intermediate-range mis-siles in Cuba. That decision in turn provoked Kennedy to declare, in justification of the American naval quarantine, that

We no longer live in a world where only the actual firing of weapons represents a sufficient challenge to a nation's security to constitute max-imum peril. Nuclear weapons are so destructive and ballistic missiles are so swift, that any substantially increased possibility of their use or any sudden change in their deployment may well be regarded as a definite threat to peace.[15]

His words make chilling reading today, for it is on these very principles that the Soviet Union might one day stand to prevent the deployment of offensive and defensive systems capable of disarm-ing it.

All three examples—1914, 1941, and 1962—contain a simple lesson. It is that great powers require a certain measure of breathing space. When pressed on all sides, they tend to lash out, or resort to "hare-brained schemes." "Nothing is so conducive to international violence," to recall the formulation of F. H. Hinsley, "as the fears and appetites that breed on inequality and instability and on the knowledge that these things exist."[16] To close the vice around a lesser power and to "squeeze until the pips squeak" may or may not be compatible with prudence or justice, but it is frequently not a crime against international order. Indeed, to act without mercy against the weak may reinforce the order that exists among the strong. But to take these maxims as the rule of conduct toward one's principal rival is to play a deadly game, in which the very hope of victory condemns all to defeat.

"The distinguishing feature of a revolutionary power," Henry Kissinger once wrote, "is not that it feels threatened—such feeling is inherent in the nature of international relations based on sovereign states—*but that nothing can reassure it*. Only absolute security—the neutralization of the opponent—is considered a sufficient guarantee, and thus the desire of one power for absolute security means absolute insecurity for all the others."[17] The neutralization of the opponent is precisely what the damage limitationist requires if our own security is to be satisfied, and one cannot help thinking that the aspiration is incompatible with the most venerable tradition of western statecraft, in which moderation was a virtue and ambition was confined to the maintenance of equilibrium. That the Soviet Union has entertained revolutionary aspirations in its own strategic nuclear policy—as it assuredly has done—does not constitute a sufficient justification for us to do the same.

The Future of American Nuclear Policy

The direction that ought to be taken by American nuclear policy is a question that cannot be seen in isolation from the behavior of the Soviet Union over the past two decades. "Since the beginnings of the current Soviet buildup that was inaugurated by the Brezhnev regime in 1965," as two observers have put it, "almost every major feature of Soviet strategic force development has been directed toward providing a high-confidence attack capability against the strategic warfare infrastructure of the United States."[18] The military doctrine underlying this build-up was one of forcible disarmament, or annihilation. That the Soviets might have undertaken this program for defensive reasons (as the United States has been tempted to do) is irrelevant in the assessment of its significance. To demand absolute security for oneself and to remain unsatisfied until one has achieved the capability of neutralizing the adversary is the very definition of a revolutionary power. We see this proclivity not only in the Soviet Union's strategic nuclear policy. In the construction of its conventional forces opposite Western Europe it has pursued the same malignant ambition.

In considering the form that our response should take, we face an acute dilemma. Both reciprocity and stability are important in statecraft; yet no policy can be exclusively faithful to either. Reciprocity is essential because it is the means by which we convey to the Soviet Union that we have the will to defend our vital interests and that no attempt on their part to assault our position with force will succeed. Stability is important because our interests are best served by peace. There is a path by which we might satisfy the twin requirements of reciprocity and stability, but it does not consist of reciprocating the Soviet Union's own bad conduct by borrowing its own worst features and adopting them as our own (which is the road on which the damage limitationists would take us). Rather, it consists of an effort to build up those nuclear systems that are good for retaliation but not for initial attack, that can survive a first strike by the Soviet Union but are poor instruments for a disarming first strike against it. We cannot "break the sword." We must stand ready to wield it in response to a massive Soviet assault on our vital interests. But we can construct the sword in such a way as to totally frustrate the ability of the Soviet Union to achieve a damage-limitation capability itself, thus ensuring that the Soviet general staff can never brief the Politburo on a plausible theory of victory; and if we act in this way we can also quiet the voices of those in the West who fear the first-strike potential of a damage-limitation strategy. It is a path, therefore, that leads to both deterrence and reassurance.

Among U.S. strategic nuclear systems, the most important are the manned penetrating bomber, the programs for air-, sea-, and ground-launched cruise missiles, the Trident I submarine, and improvements in command and control. The long-range bomber is important not only because modernizing this leg of the strategic triad complicates the Soviet attack problem but also because the strategic bomber can be used, as in Vietnam, to carry conventional weapons. It thus can serve double duty. The cruise missile also has large possibilities as a conventional weapons carrier, and its procurement on a large scale and on a variety of platforms would severely complicate the Soviet attack and air defense problem. The large size of the Trident I submarine, often criticized, allows for extended patrols, and it remains invulnerable to attack. Finally, improvements in command and control are needed to deal with what is perhaps the most vexing aspect of the nuclear problem, that posed by "strategic decapitation." None of these programs provide a first-strike capability. Bombers and cruise missiles are too slow, the C–4 missiles on the Trident I too inaccurate. Collectively, however, they establish the principle of reciprocity. They ensure beyond even an unreasonable doubt that the Soviet Union will not achieve a first-strike capability itself.

Both the MX and the "Midgetman" are of far more dubious merit. The former poses a counter-silo threat we should renounce and in its current basing mode does not solve the vulnerability problem. The latter promises to be enormously expensive (estimates now approach $50 billion), and it would only make sense if the problem of ICBM vulnerability could be addressed in no other way. The D–5 missile, scheduled for deployment on Trident submarines in 1989, is of equally questionable merit. It too is a counter-silo weapon, and we should renounce it on the same principles that we renounce the MX.

Such decisions, it is true, would leave the Soviet Union with far more "hard-target, counter-silo capability" (operational uncertainties apart) than the United States, but that disparity is only significant in that nether-world of strategic logic in which the Russians are expected to launch an attack against our Minuteman fields so that they can improve their position on a graph showing the post-exchange disparities in counter-silo capabilities. Such an attack against strategic systems based in the United States would cause anywhere from two to twenty-five million casualties, and under certain assumptions might be difficult to distinguish from a countersocietal assault. Yet it would have failed to eliminate a substantial portion of the American strategic arsenal. The threat to retaliate against the lineaments of Soviet conventional military power or against one or several Russian cities is supposed not to matter, as if Russian communists cared only for their missiles and not for their land, their army, or their people. The only plausible justification for such counter-silo systems is the one advanced in the 1970s—that it is important, for psychological reasons, to maintain strategic nuclear forces with characteristics roughly comparable (essentially equivalent) to Soviet systems. But the psychological significance of such disparities has been exaggerated to the point of absurdity; worse, the argument has foreclosed the procurement of additional conventional and nuclear weapons carriers, like the B–1 bomber, that are usable in real live military conflicts, as opposed to those that bring about the end of the world.[19]

The Relevance (and Irrelevance) of Arms Control

It will be objected that the cancellation of U.S. counter-silo missiles would deprive the United States of the bargaining chips it requires to bring arms control negotiations with the Soviet Union to a successful end. But the objection reveals more about the futility and absurdity of the "arms control process" itself than anything else, for no agreement to limit offensive arms contributory both to arms race stability and crisis stability is in sight. The Reagan administration is often blamed for this fact, but it is not responsible for it. It is a consequence of novel technological developments and the arms control process itself. With the development of greatly improved accuracies and multiple warheads (MIRVs), the very things that are central to restrictions on offensive arms—limitations on number of launchers, verifiable through national technical means—subvert the ends that arms control negotiations ought to seek. Revolutionarily new accuracies ensure that what can be seen can be destroyed; multiple warheads ensure that this can be accomplished with only a fraction of the attacker's offensive force. Limitations on numbers of launchers ease the attacker's task by limiting the number of targets; the requirement that all systems be observable—so as to verify the numbers possessed by the other side—prevents measures that would complicate the attacker's task.

Nor is this all. Our safety depends on our ability to ride out an initial Soviet attack, on whatever scale, and retain the means of inflicting damage on them proportionate to their initial assault on us. The most useful nuclear systems are therefore those that cannot be destroyed by the Soviet Union, and which at the same time do not provide us with the capability of destroying the Soviet Union's means of retaliation in a first strike. Poseidon submarines—some of which the Reagan administration decided to dismantle to stay at least temporarily within the terms of the SALT II agreement—fit this description precisely. So, too, does the cruise missile. Though extremely accurate, it is too slow to be used in a first strike against Soviet missiles; at the same time, it is small and versatile enough to be placed on a wide variety of launchers—mobile ground-based systems, bombers, surface vessels, submarines. Yet the deployment of cruise missiles is a bad thing according to the arms control lobby. Because they are difficult to distinguish from conventional weapons and because they can be hidden so easily, they cannot be adequately counted.[20]

The pursuit of comprehensive restrictions on offensive arms has therefore reached a dead end. Restrictions on limited items—such as the testing of depressed trajectory missiles—still hold out value and still ought to be pursued. So, too, may an agreement on the Euromissiles and the SS–20s (however difficult the achievement of one may be). But the comprehensive agreements represented by SALT I and II ought to be given up, along with the bargaining chips that will not secure them and that would take us down a path we ought to renounce. Thus liberated from the tyrannies imposed by the arms control process itself, the United States would then be free to act unilaterally to solve, or at least sharply mitigate, the problem of ICBM vulnerability that has bedeviled our policy for the last decade. The threat to Minuteman vulnerability can be greatly reduced by constructing a large number of "dummy silos" within existing Minuteman fields—some of them "super-hardened," some not—employing the arcane arts of meteorology and cratology to hide from the Soviet Union the knowledge of which silos contain missiles and which do not. Each Minuteman field, moreover, could be protected by terminal or point defenses of one sort or another, a combination that would exponentially complicate the Soviet attack problem. For this kind of limited defense, the exchange ratio between offense and defense appears to favor substantially the defense. The Soviet Union could continue to add additional offensive missiles only by engaging in a resource race with us that it would be bound to lose. It would, of course, have even greater recourse than it now does to the same techniques of stealth and deception. The United States might not be able to count with great accuracy the number of warheads and launchers it had hidden in the vast reaches of Siberia. But it would not matter. Neither side could disarm the other. Neither would have an incentive to attack.

The reasons for rejecting strategic defenses if they are part and parcel of a strategy of forcible disarmament have already been reviewed at length. There do exist, however, a set of lesser justifications for defensive systems. Terminal defenses, as noted, would allow us to ensure the survivability of at least a portion of the American land-based ICBM force. Area defenses could offer a measure of protection against accidental or third party launches, or for command and control centers. The applications of defenses to conventional warfare are equally promising and might significantly retard some of the technological developments—such as the ability to knock out airfields and prepositioning sites with surface-to-surface missiles armed with conventional warheads—that have increased the value of preemption in a crisis. Terminal defenses involve little danger to the stability of the larger relationship, and if the Reagan administration made a modification of the 1972 ABM Treaty allowing for such defenses the object of its arms control negotiations with the Soviet Union, it could no doubt have an agreement along these lines. Whether thin area defenses could be introduced without disrupting the stability of the central nuclear balance is far less certain. Because of its implications for Britain and France, it may yet appear undesirable from the standpoint of the interests of the Western Alliance as a whole. These considerations are nevertheless not determinative. Much will depend upon technological possibilities and political developments, such as the rate of advance of nuclear proliferation, which are as yet uncertain. It is not a prospect to be entirely foreclosed.

The Strategic Defense Initiative is widely credited with having forced the Soviet Union to return to arms control negotiations with the United States, and there is no question but that the Soviet Union fears the consequences that might ensue were the United States to proceed with the full development of counterforce weapons and strategic defenses. Many who are otherwise opposed to SDI have suggested that this fear be turned to a beneficent end by harnessing it to a negotiation. Yet the specific proposals that have been advanced to do so, which would tie restrictions on strategic defenses to deep cuts in offensive forces, particularly in the Soviet Union's most important counterforce systems, the SS–18s, are of dubious merit. The difficulty is only that some restrictions on defence are not desirable; the central problem is that restrictions on offensive arms would be extremely difficult to agree upon and would be unlikely to yield a balance of forces more stable than what exists now. The entirely predictable consequence is that strategic defenses justified as bargaining chips would be developed and deployed in lieu of that ever-receding mirage, a comprehensive agreement on offensive nuclear arms. Once the United States signals its willingness to trade strategic defenses for offensive controls, moreover, the Soviet Union would have lost the incentive to engage in negotiations, and therefore what is held out as an indispensable preliminary to serious negotiations would in all probability condemn them to failure.

A more profitable avenue of exploration would be to seek to reaffirm the basic principles of the 1972 ABM Treaty while nevertheless allowing for the deployment of terminal defenses. Such an arms control objective would renounce the comprehensive agreements on offensive arms that have complicated the achievement of a stable nuclear balance, and it would allow for the deceptive basing and active protection of retaliatory forces. It would satisfy the public urge for arms control, and it is certainly more achievable than the proposals the Reagan administration has thus far set forth. At the same time, it would make a real contribution to both arms race stability and crisis stability. In the very nature of things, it could not end the political competition between the two states, but arms control, as distinguished from disarmament, is not designed to do so. It is designed simply to turn the rivalry in a different direction, mitigating without eliminating the reasonable and ineradicable fears generated by the unprecedented destructive power of the atom.

Deterrence and the Restoration of Faith

For technology, John von Neumann once wrote, "there is no cure." A product of human invention, it has a perpetual tendency to escape human control. The contemporary attitudes of the Right and Left toward this phenomenon are polar opposites to one another, the Right finding in technology our salvation, the Left our curse. There is a measure of truth in both perceptions, for the nuclear revolution has been both a curse and a blessing, the means of our ultimate ruination providing a critical bulwark in the maintenance of the postwar balance of power and thus providing a means of temporal salvation. Yet the truths told by Right and Left are ultimately half-truths: to freeze the procurement of nuclear arms and to resist entirely the opportunities afforded by the new technologies would both violate the principle of reciprocity, on which the continued operation of deterrence depends, and prohibit us from channeling the development of nuclear arms in a less destabilizing direction. To give free play to the technological impulse, on the other hand, is to put us on a road fraught with uncertainty and danger.

It is, of course, not only the promise—or terror—of the new technologies that has prompted many to seek a transcendence of the condition of mutual vulnerability. Parts of the nuclear priesthood, like countless numbers of ordinary souls, have lost their faith in deterrence. It is the deepest irony of the contemporary nuclear debate that this loss of faith drives both Right and Left in their programs of strategic defenses and unilateral disarmament, the fears of the one reinforcing those of the other in a deepening spiral.

This spiral must be broken, the faith in deterrence restored. To do so is the most difficult task of modern statesmanship, for fear and hope—"the two mainsprings of the political and the moral order"—must be maintained in equilibrium with one another, and we know from experience that their relationship is unstable. "Nuclear weapons deter," as Josef Joffe has observed, "precisely because they do not reassure completely. Deterrence works, paradoxically, because it might fail, and it is the never-quite-tamed terror of nuclear weapons that renders their possessors vastly more cautious than the traditional behavior patterns of great powers would lead us to expect."[21]

The task is therefore difficult, and requires the high-wire skills of the equilibrist—as every American president in the postwar era has sooner or later discovered. But it is not a hopeless undertaking. The West did recover its psychological balance after the turmoils of the late fifties and early sixties, and it appears to have done so again. In truth, the loss of faith is unwarranted. The scenarios of universal doom and destruction only appear plausible because we have invested our adversary, and sometimes ourselves, not only with demonic characteristics but with a thoroughgoing irrationality. Whatever the merit of the former charge, the latter will not bear scrutiny. It is the case, to be sure, that only faith in deterrence can relieve what would otherwise be a dark view of the human prospect. It is equally the case that our nuclear faith does not stand in irreconcilable conflict with reason or experience, but is supported and confirmed by both.

Notes

1. The distinction between annihilation and attrition as strategic objectives is examined with lucidity in Michael Howard, "The Influence of Clausewitz," in Carl Von Clausewitz, *On War,* ed. and trans. Michael Howard and Peter Paret (Princeton, 1976); Russell F. Weigley, *The American Way of War: A History of United States Military Strategy and Policy* (Bloomington, Ind., 1973), xxii; Raymond Aron, *Peace and War,* 31–36, and Raymond Aron, *Clausewitz: Philosopher of War,* trans. Christine Booker and Norman Stone (Englewood Cliffs, N.J. 1985), 9–10, 70–87, 241–64, and 410; and Gordon A. Craig, "Delbrück: The Military Historian," in Earle, *Makers of Modern Strategy,* 272. The basic features of a strategy of forcible disarmament have been set forth most fully in the writings of Colin Gray. See, *inter alia,* Colin Gray, "War Fighting For Deterrence," *Journal of Strategic Studies* (March 1984), 5–28; and Colin Gray, *Strategy and the MX* (Washington, D.C., 1980). A particularly clear and forthright exposition of this position may also be found in Stephen Peter Rosen, "Foreign Policy and Nuclear Weapons: The Case for Strategic Defense," in *The Strategic Imperative: New Policies for American Security,* ed. Samuel P. Huntington (Cambridge, Mass., 1982). I consider this question in relation to a range of historical examples in "The Influence of History Upon Strategy: Annihilation vs. Attrition" (forthcoming).

2. See Theodore Draper, "Nuclear Temptations," *The New York Review of Books,* 19 January 1984, 43; Leon Wieseltier, *Nuclear War, Nuclear Peace* (New York, 1983), 38; and Robert Jervis, *The Illogic of American Nuclear Strategy* (Ithaca, 1984), 19: "A rational strategy for the employment of nuclear weapons," in Jervis's words, "is a contradiction in terms." See also the discussion of this problem in Robert W. Tucker, "The Nuclear Debate," *Foreign Affairs* (Fall 1984), esp. 3–5 and 20–21; and Charles Krauthammer, "On Nuclear Morality," *Commentary,* (October 1983), 49.

3. Machiavelli, *The Prince,* chap. 17, "Of Cruelty and Clemency, and Whether It is Better to Be Loved or Feared." See also The Pastoral Letter of the U.S. Bishops on War and Peace, "The Challenge of Peace: God's Promise and Our Response," *Origins,* vol. 13, no. 1, 19 May 1983. Men and women can imagine anything—they have "minds that can wander beyond all limit and satiety." It is therefore possible to imagine nuclear attacks whose deterrence rests not only on the prospect of retaliation by man but also on some form of retribution by Nature, God, or History. On the prospect of the former, see the discussion in Carl Sagan, "Nuclear War and the Climatic Catastrophe," *Foreign Affairs* (Winter 1983/84), 257–92; and Albert Wohlstetter, "Between an Unfree World and None," *Foreign Affairs* (Summer 1985) 962–94.

4. On the movement away from strategies of forcible disarmament in the early 1960s, see the valuable study of Michael Mandelbaum, *The Nuclear Question: The United States and Nuclear Weapons, 1946–1976* (Cambridge, 1979). See also Desmond Ball, *Targeting for Strategic Deterrence,* Adelphi Paper 185 (London, 1983); and Henry S. Rowen, "The Evolution of Strategic Nuclear Doctrine," in *Strategic*

STRATEGIC NUCLEAR POLICY   143

Thought in the Nuclear Age, ed. Laurence Martin (Baltimore, 1979). McNamara's revelation is contained in Robert S. McNamara, "The Military Role of Nuclear Weapons," *Foreign Affairs* (Fall 1983), 79.

5. The quotations in this and the following paragraph are from *Report of Secretary of Defense Harold Brown to the Congress on the FY 1982 Budget.* . . (Washington, D.C. 1981), 38–43. On strategic doctrine in the 1970s, see Lawrence Freedman, *The Evolution of Nuclear Strategy* (New York, 1981), 375–87; Warner R. Schilling, "U.S. Strategic Nuclear Concepts in the 1970s: The Search for Sufficiently Equivalent Countervailing Parity," *International Security* (Fall 1981), 49–79; Lynn Etheridge Davis, *Limited Nuclear Options: Deterrence and the New American Doctrine,* Adelphi Paper no. 121 (London, 1976); Laurence Martin, "Changes in American Strategic Doctrine: An Initial Interpretation," *Survival* (July/August 1974), 158–64; and Walter Slocombe, "The Countervailing Strategy," *International Security* (Spring 1981), 18–27. Slocombe noted that "nothing in the countervailing concept offers the United States the prospect of eliminating Soviet ability to respond effectively to an American attack" (26).

6. See Robert E. Osgood, *Limited War: The Challenge to American Strategy* (Chicago, 1957); William Kaufmann, ed., *Military Policy and National Security* (Princeton, 1956); and Bernard Brodie, *Strategy in the Missile Age* (Princeton, 1959). The most interesting retrospective on this literature is Robert E. Osgood, "The Post-War Strategy of Limited War: Before, During and After Vietnam," in *Strategic Thought in the Nuclear Age,* ed. Martin, 93–130. See also "NSC-68: The Strategic Reassessment of 1950," in Thomas H. Etzold and John Lewis Gaddis, *Containment: Documents on American Policy and Strategy, 1945–1950* (New York, 1978), 415–416.

7. See, for example, Fred Iklé, "Can Nuclear Deterrence Last Out the Century?" *Foreign Affairs* (January 1973), 267–85; and Donald Brennan, "When the SALT Hit the Fan," *National Review,* 23 June 1972.

8. See Harold Brown, "Reagan's Risky Approach," and Kenneth L. Adelman, "Toward a Defense Strategy," *The New York Times,* 10 March 1985. See also Paul H. Nitze, "The Objective of Arms Control," *Survival* (May/June 1985), 104.

9. Herbert Butterfield, "The Tragic Element in Modern International Conflict," in *History and Human Relations* (London, 1951), 21.

10. On this point, see Colin Gray, "A Case for Strategic Defence," *Survival* (March/April 1985), 53: "it must be a mission of the strategic offensive to guard the defensive transition."

11. The possibility of effective strategic defenses is examined in Harold Brown, "The Strategic Defense Initiative: Defensive Systems and the Strategic Debate," *Survival* (March/April 1985), 55–64, and Harold Brown, "IS SDI Technically Feasible?" in *Foreign Affairs: America and the World 1985,* 435–54; James R. Schlesinger, "Rhetoric and Realities in the Star Wars Debate," *International Security* (Summer 1985), 3–12; Sidney D. Drell *et al.,* "Preserving the ABM Treaty: A Critique of the Reagan Strategic Defense Initiative," *International Security* (Fall 1984), 51–91. See also Robert Jastrow, "The War Against 'Star Wars,'" *Commentary,* (December 1984), 19–25; Robert Jastrow, "Star Wars & the Scientists: Robert Jastrow & Critics," *Commentary* (March 1985), 4–22; Lewis Lehrman and Gregory A. Fossedal, "How to Decide About Strategic Defense," *National Review,* 31 January 1986, 32–37; Ashton B. Carter and David N. Schwartz, eds., *Ballistic Missile Defense* (Washington, D.C., 1984); and Franklin A. Long, *et al., Weapons in Space* (New York, 1986).

12. See Tucker, "Nuclear Debate," 23–24.

13. See William J. Broad, "Allies in Europe Are Apprehensive About Benefits of 'Star Wars' Plan," *The New York Times,* 13 May 1985; John Newhouse, "The Diplomatic Round: Europe and Star Wars," *The New Yorker,* 22 July 1985, 37–54. Cf. Fred Iklé, "NATO's 'First Nuclear Use': A Deepening Trap?" *Strategic Review* (Winter 1980), 18–23; Fred Iklé, "Nuclear Strategy: Can There Be a Happy Ending?" *Foreign Affairs* (Spring 1985), 818–21; and Colin Gray, "War Fighting for Deterrence," 13–14. The transformation of U.S. nuclear strategy called for by both Iklé and Gray is intimately linked with the necessity of "extending deterrence" over our Western European allies.

14. See on these points the seminal though neglected works of Paul W. Schroeder, "World War I as Galloping Gertie: A Reply to Joachim Remak," *Journal of Modern History* (September 1972), 319–45; and Paul W. Schroeder, *The Axis Alliance and Japanese-American Relations, 1941* (Ithaca, 1958).

15. John F. Kennedy, "Radio and Television Report to the American People on the Soviet Arms Buildup in Cuba," 22 October 1962, *Public Papers of the Presidents, John F. Kennedy, 1962* (Washington, D.C. 1963), 807.

16. Hinsley, *Power and the Pursuit of Peace,* 283.

17. Henry A. Kissinger, *A World Restored: Metternich, Castlereagh, and the Problems of Peace, 1812–1822* (Boston, 1957), 2. See also the masterful discussion in Martin Wight, *Power Politics* (New York, 1979), 81–94.

18. See Benjamin S. Lambeth and Kevin N. Lewis, *Economic Targeting in Modern Warfare* (Santa Monica, Calif., July 1982), 64.

19. For proposals similar in spirit (if not always in letter), see Barry M. Blechman, ed., *Rethinking the U.S. Strategic Posture* (Cambridge, Mass., 1982); and Graham T. Allison, Albert Carnesale, and Joseph Nye, Jr., *Hawks, Doves, & Owls: An Agenda for Avoiding Nuclear War* (New York, 1985).

20. On these points, see Henry S. Rowen, "Potholes on the Road to Geneva," *The Wall Street Journal,* 17 December 1984; and Thomas C. Schelling, "What Went Wrong with Arms Control?" *Foreign Affairs* (Winter 1985/86), 219–33. Before entering the administration, a similar critique was made by Richard Burt. See Richard Burt, "The Relevance of Arms Control in the 1980s," *Daedalus* (Winter 1981), 159–78. Cf. also Kenneth L. Adelman, "Arms Control With and Without Agreements," *Foreign Affairs* (Winter 1984/85), 240–263; and Theodore Draper, "How Not to Think About Nuclear War," *The New York Review of Books,* 15 July 1982, 43. Many observers, it should be acknowledged, have argued against sea-launched cruise missiles (SLCMs) on the grounds that they would increase the danger of "strategic decapitation." See for instance John Steinbruner, "Arms Control: Crisis or Compromise," *Foreign Affairs* (Summer 1985), 1045–46. It is doubtful, however, that there is any way to prevent a determined effort on the part of the Soviet Union to "decapitate" America's political leadership. What deters such attacks is the knowledge that control over surviving nuclear weapons would be decentralized and would revert to the hands of military officers, who in all likelihood would exact revenge in kind.

21. Josef Joffe, "Stability and Its Discontents: Should NATO Go Conventional?" *The Washington Quarterly* (Fall 1984), 146. The preceding citation is from Charles Gravier, Comte de Vergennes, who wrote in 1774 that "Fear and hope have been and always will be the two mainsprings of the political and the moral order." See "Memoir of M. De Vergennes at the Beginning of the Reign of Louis XVI, in 1774," Wright, ed., *Balance of Power,* 84.

5—General Purpose Forces

The Reagan administration formulated ambitious new requirements for American military forces not only in the realm of strategic nuclear policy. The strategic doctrines governing the appropriate size and composition of general purpose forces also underwent a significant change under Reagan. Force structure goals edged up only slightly—with the Army planning an expansion from sixteen to eighteen divisions (with a fixed number of personnel), the Air Force from thirty-six to forty active and reserve fighter wings, and the Navy from twelve to fifteen carrier battlegroups. On the basis of this evidence, one might doubt the significance of the administration's doctrinal innovations. The new doctrines are nevertheless significant. They tell us a great deal about how the Reagan administration views the American position in the world, and they provide an interesting benchmark by which to assess the strategy that has in the past, and will in the future, govern general purpose forces. From these doctrines stem the requirements that the military services use to justify their requests before Congress. Even though the public pays the greatest attention to strategic nuclear weapons, expenditures on them in fact comprise less than 20 percent of the defense budget. The rest pours mostly into conventional forces.

Postwar Doctrine before Vietnam: Eisenhower and Kennedy

Only against the background of the past can we begin to understand the significance of the changes introduced by the Reagan administration. The relevant past, however, is fairly recent. Although the basic structure of the American position in the world has remained similar in many respects to what it was at the outset of the Cold

War, in other respects much has changed. The further back we push in postwar history, the less relevant this history appears. Though the experiences of both the Eisenhower and Kennedy administrations have much to teach us in other respects, with respect to general purpose forces the lessons are limited—the Eisenhower administration because of its near-total integration of nuclear weapons into general purpose forces, the Kennedy administration because of the ambitions it entertained in Asia and the rest of the Third World.

The Eisenhower administration's policy rested on the assumption that nuclear weapons were simply another form of firepower, more effective and less costly than conventional ordnance. In its pentomic divisions of the 1950s, the Army was constructed in such a way that conventional operations on a large scale in any theater would have been extremely difficult if not impossible—a deficiency frequently stressed by critics in the Army and in the opposition Democratic party. This near-total reliance on nuclear weapons in the Eisenhower administration was unbalanced even then and would be all the more so today. Although our general purpose forces ought to have access to tactical nuclear weapons, and though it would be a serious mistake to renounce the possibility of their "first use," these forces should nevertheless be capable of conducting sustained operations without recourse to them.[1]

The Eisenhower approach was abandoned in the 1960s under Robert McNamara. In keeping with its aversion to a primary reliance on nuclear weapons, the Kennedy administration sought to provide general purpose forces with the capability of conducting sustained conventional operations—an approach that was most successful in the most receptive service, the Army, and rather more difficult in the case of the Air Force and the Navy.[2] The number of active Army divisions was raised from eleven to sixteen, and their readiness and sustainability were greatly improved. These decisions left the United States with a force structure in the Army and the Air Force remarkably similar to what they have today. What makes the Kennedy administration's approach appear suspect is the heavy stress that it placed on the possibility of military conflicts with China and a host of lesser powers. All these contingencies were thought to require the use of American ground forces. In the 1962 General Purpose Forces Study no less than eleven possible contingencies were considered as requiring the commitment of American ground forces. The Kennedy administration finessed these requirements by assuming, as William Kaufmann has noted, that the Soviet Union would be

capable of launching no more than one major attack, with the northern, central, and southern parts of Western Europe as both the most logical targets and the theaters in which Russia and its Warsaw Pact allies could bring the largest force to bear. Similarly, China might be able to undertake a fairly large-scale campaign in Korea or Southeast Asia, but not both. It was also thought that military action would be required at the same time but on a much smaller scale against one of the lesser troublemakers such as Cuba.[3]

These assumptions lay at the core of the "two-and-a-half-war" strategy adhered to by the Democratic administrations of the 1960s. But with its assumption of a simultaneous attack by Russia and China, this strategy postulated requirements that came increasingly to be viewed as highly implausible, as the split between the two great Communist powers gathered momentum in the 1960s. Its requirements for American ground forces throughout the Third World also came to appear highly questionable with the failure of American policy in Vietnam.

One-and-a-Half-Wars and the Nixon Doctrine

Only with the advent of the Nixon administration did the doctrine governing general purpose forces begin to assume a shape relevant to the strategic problems of the 1980s. This doctrine was dominated by two great events—the Sino-Soviet split and the War in Vietnam. Both had far-reaching consequences; both made the world and the American role in it profoundly different from the period of the classic Cold War, which began in 1950 when the United States despatched forces to Korea and interposed units of the Seventh Fleet between Taiwan and the Chinese mainland and ended with the day of reckoning brought on by the Tet Offensive of 1968. As Soviet hostility to China grew and was reflected in the enormous build-up of Soviet military power along the Sino-Soviet border, China's calculations underwent a momentous shift, a shift that in its turn was aided by the retreat of American power from Southeast Asia. The intelligence and wisdom with which the Nixon administration played upon this rivalry was its most impressive accomplishment in foreign policy. Holding the balance between these two powers, the

United States improved its relations with both, and this despite the fact that the year in which these relations showed most improvement, 1972, was marked by the most blistering use of American air and naval power in the postwar era.

In military policy, the Nixon administration's response to changed conditions in Asia took two forms. The Pentagon was directed to prepare for only "one-and-a-half" conventional wars, a departure from the "two-and-a-half-war" strategy initiated under the Kennedy administration; and the strategy for the "half war" was reformulated in accordance with the Nixon Doctrine. The first change reflected the conclusion that "a simultaneous Warsaw Pact attack in Europe and Chinese conventional attack in Asia is unlikely."[4] If it were to occur, Kissinger argued in a memorandum to Nixon, it neither could nor should be met with ground forces. This change of policy, as Kissinger notes in his memoirs, was one of the more important decisions of the Nixon presidency. "First of all, it harmonized doctrine and capability. We had never generated the forces our two-and-one-half-war doctrine required; the gap between our declaratory and our actual policy was bound to create confusion in the minds of potential aggressors and to raise grave risks if we attempted to apply it." To pretend that, if faced with a joint assault by China and the Soviet Union, "we would confine our response to a conventional war in two widely separated areas would multiply our dangers."[5]

Of a significance equal to the adoption of the one-and-a-half-war strategy was the new attitude that emerged toward the use of American power in Asia—and more generally to the military forces necessary to satisfy the "half war" requirement. The Nixon Doctrine, as it was formally elaborated in the president's Vietnam speech of 3 November 1969 and in his Foreign Policy Report of 18 February 1970, contained three key points:

—The United States will keep all its treaty commitments.

—We shall provide a nuclear shield if a nuclear power threatens the freedom of a nation allied with us, or of a nation whose survival we consider vital to our security or the security of the region as a whole.

—In cases involving other types of aggression we shall furnish military and economic assistance when requested and as appropriate. But we shall look to the nation directly threatened to assume the primary responsibility of providing for its own defense.[6]

Some, but not all, of the ambiguity in these phrases was soon removed. The administration left the true character of the "nuclear shield" deliberately obscure. As applied to East Asia, the division of responsibility broached in the third section came largely to consist of the distinction between ground forces, which were to be provided by our allies, and air and naval forces, which were to remain an important American responsibility. One of the two ground divisions then stationed in South Korea was withdrawn and overall force levels in Vietnam were reduced from 542,000 servicemen in January 1969 to 45,600 in July 1972. The size of the Army as a whole fell from its Vietnam War peak of 1,570,000 troops to 811,000 in 1972 (Exhibit 10)—a reduction that was partly a consequence of the one-and-one-half-war strategy and partly a consequence of the Nixon Doctrine and "Vietnamization."[7]

The promise of the new strategic approaches of the Nixon administration was short-lived. The one-and-a-half-war strategy continued to form an underpinning of military policy throughout the 1970s, but Watergate and then Carterism consigned the Nixon Doctrine to a strange fate. Not applied in Southeast Asia and inapplicable in the Persian Gulf, it came to acquire a meaning very different from what its architects had originally intended. Its implementation required strong presidential leadership; this was not to be. Watergate destroyed the Nixon presidency with extraordinary suddenness in 1973. By July of that year, the president had been reduced to pathetic proportions. A cipher, he was incapable of overturning the congressional decision to halt all American military operations in Indochina, and policy there unravelled. The threat to reintroduce American air and naval power in the event of a massive North Vietnamese violation of the Paris peace accords was now missing; so, too, was a sufficient amount of economic and military aid to the South Vietnamese. The South Vietnamese armed forces, having been constructed on the American model, were denied by Congress the continuing transfusions of logistical support indispensable to their effectiveness and morale. Whether the continued application of the Nixon Doctrine to Indochina would have preserved the independence of South Vietnam or merely permitted a "decent interval" before defeat we cannot know; the fall, when it came, was marked by severe errors of judgment on the part of President Thieu. But these errors of judgment were themselves conditioned by our previous actions; his failures do not excuse our own.

Exhibit 10—*Active U.S. Ground Forces, Selected Years, 1940–85*

	Army		Marine Corps		Total	
Year	Thousands of Men	Divisions	Thousands of Men	Divisions	Thousands of Men	Divisions
1940	264	8	28	0	292	8
1945	5,912	89	485	6	6,397	95
1950	591	10	75	2	666	12
1953	1,534	20	249	3	1,783	23
1960	873	14	171	3	1,044	17
1962	1,066	18	191	3	1,257	21
1964	972	16	190	3	1,162	19
1968	1,570	19	307	4	1,877	23
1972	811	13	198	3	1,009	16
1976	779	16	192	3	971	19
1980	774	16	189	3	963	19
1985	782	17	198	3	980	20

Source:—William P. Mako, *U.S. Ground Forces and the Defense of Central Europe* (Washington, D.C.: The Brookings Institution, 1983), 4; and *Budget of the United States Government Fiscal Year 1987*, 5–12.

If the Nixon Doctrine was not applied after early 1973 in Southeast Asia, it was inapplicable to the circumstances in the Persian Gulf, and only a bastardized version was applied there. The strategic dilemma in the Persian Gulf in the 1970s arose from the explosive growth of economic dependence on the Gulf oil producers, combined with the loss of political control. The Nixon Doctrine had implicitly assumed a situation in which a friendly state was threatened by external forces, but the primary threat to western access in the 1970s was posed by the oil-producing states themselves. The Soviet threat became more serious with each passing year; but the main problem throughout the decade arose from the hostility or unreliability of the indigenous powers.

There was not an infinite number of solutions to this dilemma. In fact, there were only two: one was the reassertion of political control through military power, the other a reduction of dependence through the decontrol of oil prices and the heavy taxation of energy consumption. But both options were foreclosed in the post-Watergate and post-Vietnam climate that existed at home. The former solution would have required ground forces with the capability of seizing quickly the principal oil fields and facilities on the southern shore of the Perisan Gulf. Neither the public nor the governing elites showed any disposition to contemplate this course of action when it was suggested by Robert W. Tucker in a January 1975 article in *Commentary*.[8] Still, given the apparently inescapable fact of oil dependence and the widely accepted assumption that it would grow in the future, it should have been a simple matter of prudence to direct the "half-war" forces stationed in the United States (and which ultimately formed the core foundation of the Rapid Deployment Force) to begin thinking about and making preparations for possible operations in the Gulf. But this was never done under either the Nixon or Ford administrations. And despite the 1977 recommendation of Presidential Directive-18, which called for the creation of a "rapid deployment force of several light divisions supported by sufficient air and sea lift to deal with Third World contingencies, particularly in Southwest Asia,"[9] the Carter administration began taking the need seriously only in the final year of its term, and then the RDF was directed against the Soviet Union and not the regional states. Having rejected the option of securing political control through military means, the United States nevertheless failed to embrace the obvious alternative of a reduction in oil dependence. As events have since made abundantly clear, this was an objective of policy achievable by means of decontrol and the heavy taxation of domestic energy consumption. Our allies took these measures; we were incapable of doing so. Instead, we subsidized the importation of energy through an "entitlements" scheme that was abandoned only in 1981.

The Carter Legacy

Under the Carter administration, the foundations of the Nixon Doctrine—reliance on economic and military aid and air and naval power—eroded still further. In its first two years in office, the Carter administration eliminated from the defense budget the two

great instruments of American air and naval power in the postwar
era—the long-range strategic bomber and the large deck aircraft
carrier. Both decisions were mistakes. The cancellation of the B–1
in 1977 reflected a fundamental misunderstanding of its importance
as both a strategic and conventional weapons carrier; worse, the
loss of this major strategic system would ultimately play a critical
role in giving birth, in the changed circumstance of 1979, to that
strange mutant of strategic theory, the MX missile. The loss of an
additional carrier in 1978—Carter vetoed the defense bill con-
taining it—was subsequently made up for in a later congressional
session, but the initial decision made little sense in light of the
expanded tasks for carrier power arising from the crisis in the
Persian Gulf. The Carter administration's attitude toward economic
and military aid also represented a sharp departure from the Nixon
Doctrine. It wished to turn over economic aid to the multilateral
lending agencies or otherwise to use it as an instrument to reform
other societies; it sought to cap military aid at $8.5 billion a year in
1978.[10]

If the Nixon Doctrine in its original meaning was thus repudiated
by the Carter administration, the other element of the legacy in
military policy bequeathed by the first Nixon administration was
preserved. By continuing the process of rapprochement with
China, the Carter administration abandoned once and for all the
notion of basing strategic doctrine for general purpose forces upon
the prospect of a large-scale conventional war with China in Asia.
The Nixon administration had in fact never abandoned this prospect in theory. Its one-and-one-half-war strategy called for maintaining "in peacetime general purpose forces adequate for
simultaneously meeting a major Communist attack in *either* Europe
or Asia, assisting allies against non-Chinese threats in Asia, and
contending with a contingency elsewhere."[11] In theory, what was
deemed unlikely was a simultaneous attack by Russia in Europe and
China in Asia; in practice, however, this was no less a "paper
exercise" than the two-and-one-half-war strategy had been, and the
Nixon Pentagon did not take it seriously. With the overall reduction
in force levels in the aftermath of Vietnam, preparations for Asian
contingencies were downplayed even further. The Ford and Carter
Pentagons came to focus almost exclusively on the exacting requirements of a European war with the Soviet Union, much more
demanding in the mid-to-late 1970s than they had been earlier by

virtue of the Soviet build-up in conventional forces. In keeping with this Eurocentric focus, and further impelled by its unhappiness with the character of the South Korean regime, the Carter administration also proposed the withdrawal of American ground forces from South Korea, an initiative it subsequently scuttled.

Thus the Carter administration remained faithful to one part of the legacy left by the first Nixon administration, and unfaithful to the other. The big war remained the keystone of force planning, but the Nixon Doctrine was all but abandoned. In its policy toward the big war, the Carter administration also introduced a significant change in approach from previous administrations. On the basis of his reassessment of Soviet military capabilities in the early 1960s, McNamara had assumed that the United States and its allies would obtain "thirty days' warning of enemy buildups, but owing to ambiguities in the signals and political hesitations about responding, will have only twenty-three days for their own mobilization and deployment." At the same time, he called for war reserve stocks to be based on the principle of stockpiling "enough combat consumables (excluding ships and aircraft) to maintain intense operations until production rates are adequate to supply combat needs—a period of about six months."[12] The Nixon administration had continued to assume a twenty-three-day period of warning, but had scaled back the requirements for war stocks to ninety days. Owing to the Vietnam War and the resupplying of Israel in 1973, however, war reserve stocks remained well short of these requirements. The Carter administration altered both standards. By the mid-1970s, the assumption of a twenty-three- (or thirty-) day warning time came increasingly to be questioned. Under the impetus of the Nunn-Bartlett report, which pointed to the extensive growth in the firepower of frontline Soviet divisions and warned of the danger of a "standing-start" attack, the Carter administration began to put increasing emphasis on our own frontline forces.[13] As part of the 1978 NATO Long-Term Defense Plan, the United States committed itself to having ten divisions in Europe ready to fight within ten days of a mobilization, and to fulfill this requirement began prepositioning heavy equipment in Europe (the POMCUS program) that would be matched up with troops airlifted to Europe upon mobilization. It also scaled back the requirements for assessing the adequacy of war reserve stocks from ninety to thirty days. This was done partly for budgetary reasons—the Brown

Pentagon faced an acute squeeze between modernization and sustainability—but the reassessment also reflected the judgment that a vigorous defense at the outset of the war was sufficient for the purposes of deterrence. In light of the budgetary restrictions that then prevailed, these decisions made the best of a bad situation. The Carter administration made egregious blunders in European policy, to be sure, the most infamous of which was Carter's decision to cancel procurement of the "neutron bomb" after encouraging Helmut Schmidt to walk the plank. The responsibility for this decision, however, lay wholly with the president himself and not with his civilian or military subordinates at the Pentagon.

The great errors of the Carter administration were not committed in the realm of strategic doctrine. Rather, they stemmed from the gap between doctrine and resources and the inability to come to terms with the inadequacies of the All Volunteer Force. As procurement schedules were scaled back year by year, it became increasingly apparent that the resources being devoted to the defense budget were wholly inadequate to satisfy the requirements of strategic doctrine. There was simply not enough money to go around. That Carter was forced to reverse his election pledge to reduce defense spending by 5 percent helped matters only slightly. The base from which these percentages were calculated was completely inadequate, an inadequacy that was in turn exacerbated by the administration's indifference to the debauchment of the currency.

This gap between strategic doctrine and defense resources had its most destructive consequences in the realm of manpower policy. Our forces became "hollow" in the late 1970s, in Army Chief of Staff Edward Meyer's phrase, not primarily because of a lack of modern equipment but because of the hemorrhage of experienced personnel from the services and the shortcomings of their recruits. The losses in the first category, particularly in the realm of noncommissioned officers, have yet to be fully made up under the Reagan administration. As for the second, it was discovered in 1980 that the numbers with which the manpower analysts had been working were mistaken. Recruits in the lowest classifications employed in army intelligence tests (categories 4 and 5) made up 44 percent of the accessions in 1979, rather than the 9 percent that had previously been estimated.[14] It was not a reflection of racism, as Secretary of the Army Clifford Alexander charged, to believe that this pattern if continued would gravely undermine the effectiveness of the military.

The Reagan Administration: Renewal and Decline

The great accomplishment in defense policy of the Reagan administration's first term was to overcome, at least for the moment, the two deficiencies bequeathed to it by its predecessor. By all accounts, the quality and morale of incoming recruits and experienced personnel in all the services improved sharply in the first half of the 1980s, in no small part due to the hefty pay increases and benefit packages the Reagan administration pushed through Congress in 1981 (incentives that were furthered, in turn, by recession in the civilian economy). Even with respect to the gap between doctrine and resources the outlook improved. The proliferation of strategic concepts under the Reagan administration—of which more later—in one sense widened the gap in the mid-1980s, despite the additional resources that were being devoted to the defense budget. In another and in the end more important sense, the gap was sharply narrowed. One reason for this was the decline in the strategic significance of the Persian Gulf. Another was that by the mid-1980s existing forces were no longer the hollow things they were at the beginning of the decade. The fundamental problem with American general purpose forces in the late 1970s did not consist of an insufficient number of ground divisions, tactical air wings, or even carrier battlegroups. Far more serious was that the Carter administration had badly underfunded the force structure that it had and had deprived the services of the resources they needed to retain an effective manpower base, modernize existing units, and keep them in fighting trim. By the mid-1980s those problems had greatly eased.[15]

In current dollars, both budget authority and outlays more than doubled under the Reagan administration, with outlays rising from $132.8 billion in 1980 to $265.8 billion in 1986. Spending on military investment rose much faster than that on force readiness, but the growth totals in both were impressive. Much effort went into raising the sustainability of American forces, as the Reagan administration abandoned the "short war" assumption of its predecessor and raised the requirement for war reserve stocks from thirty to ninety days. It also undertook a number of initiatives that would allow for a more rapid mobilization of the defense industrial base. Cumulative growth from 1981 to 1985 was $329.5 billion. The most common complaint against the administration was that it was "throwing money at defense." The charge had some merit, as we shall see. It should nevertheless not obscure the point that in many cases, as *The Economist* has observed, "money is just what the doctor ordered. Mr. Reagan took office at a time when a host of useful programmes had been developed and brought to the production stage. All that was needed was to start writing cheques."[16]

These virtues notwithstanding, the fact remains that the Reagan defense program is in serious trouble. The coherence of the Reagan defense plan depends on the maintenance of high levels of growth in defense spending, and this growth has become highly unlikely. Two problems are particularly serious. One is the growing gap between the procurement accounts and the funds required to maintain American forces in conditions of readiness. The bill is coming due for the weapons systems already authorized in the administration's first term. If the budget is frozen in real terms, this gap between procurement and readiness will become progressively more serious. To scale back weapons purchases across the board without cancelling any major items, on the other hand, will sharply drive up unit costs. This suggests, in turn, that some big items will have to be cut if the United States is to enjoy a balanced defense program in the future.[17]

The manpower dilemma faced by the administration is equally serious. By 1987, the size of the prime recruiting pool of males between seventeen and twenty-one will be 15 percent smaller than its 1978 level; by 1992, it will be 20 percent smaller. Given these demographic constraints, a political commitment to the All Volunteer Force, and a reasonably healthy economy—all of which the Reagan administration takes for granted—the manpower problem will almost certainly become worse.[18] If these constraints hold, the alternatives will be to lower substantially the standards for admission into the services or to admit a much larger proportion of women, or both. Neither alternative is acceptable. Lowering admission standards leads inevitably to pernicious results. Training manuals must be rewritten—as they were in the Army in the 1970s—to accommodate soldiers who cannot read above the sixth-grade level, and this leads therefore to the paradox of "dumb soldiers and smart weapons." The armed forces then acquire a social stigma that affects the willingness of more capable young men to join. The admission of more women into the armed forces is an equally unsatisfactory resolution of the "manpower" dilemma. The level of women in the services already reached—around 12 percent of the service population—is unprecedented by comparison with the experience of our own and other militaries. To pass further beyond this level would draw women much closer to combat units, from which they ought to be excluded.[19]

Reluctant to cancel any major weapons systems and unwilling to contemplate a reduction in manpower levels, the Reagan administration risks jeopardizing its principal accomplishments in defense policy. The failure to come to terms with these problems will inevitably sap the readiness of existing forces and may make them hollow again. To avoid this result, the investment-operations gap needs to be reduced, while pay advances at reasonable levels. These considerations, of course, do not tell us which procurement programs should be cut back and which should be preserved. Only strategic reflection can do that. In what follows, therefore, I examine the major strategic doctrines of the Reagan administration, and try to show why some of them are useful and necessary, and others not. This examination will enable us to see not only which areas of the defense budget should be cut back (and which supported). It will also reveal the principles by which American strategy itself might be transformed.

Air and Sea Power

In its first report to Congress (FY 1983), the Reagan administration held that the United States required "options for fighting on other fronts." Even if the Soviet Union "attacked at only one place, *we* might choose not to restrict ourselves to meeting aggression on its own immediate front." Weinberger warned against transposing "the defensive orientation of our peacetime strategy onto the strategy and tactics that would guide us in the event of war. A wartime strategy that confronts the enemy, were he to attack, with the risk of our counteroffensive against his vulnerable points strengthens deterrence and serves the defensive peacetime strategy."[20] This strategic concept—soon labeled "horizontal escalation"—came to be closely identified with the decision to build a six-hundred-ship navy centered around fifteen carrier battlegroups, though the concept was also relevant to the strategic role of long-range airpower.

The controversy aroused by horizontal escalation was in part simply an updating of the argument between Dulles and the Democrats in the 1950s over "massive retaliation" and "flexible response"—save that the Reagan administration hoped to do horizontally (i.e., with conventional forces) what the Eisenhower administration wanted to do vertically (i.e., with nuclear weapons). Both administrations spoke in almost identical terms of the value that the uncertainty of our response has in inducing caution in a potential aggressor. The debate is also familiar to students of naval strategy. One of the traditional buttresses of the case for naval forces is that they allow one to strike the enemy at will from positions of one's own choosing, and particularly at his extremities, where he is incapable of bringing to bear his main force in opposition.

The critics have succeeded in showing that many of the operational concepts with which horizontal escalation has become identified do not make a great deal of sense. Some military actions might tie up more American resources than Russian and thus not contribute to the ultimate strategic aim of our military effort. When Great Britain attempted a similar strategy in the eighteenth-century wars against France and in the twentieth-century wars against Germany, the results were often unfortunate.[21] Carrier strikes against the Soviet Union's northern fleet operating out of the Kola Peninsula would expose our battlegroups to a thick set of defenses, an engagement from which they might not emerge afloat. Such strikes may, in any case, be indistinguishable in practice from vertical escalation.[22] Nonnaval applications of the concept are also often suspect. The possibility of opening a front in Europe in response to a Soviet attack in the Persian Gulf sends cold shivers down the spines of our European allies, and is incompatible with the priority we ought to place on Europe's physical as opposed to economic security.

Still, the concept remains valid, even if many of the operations with which it has become identified are not. It is perfectly appropriate, for instance, to hold out to the Soviet Union the prospect that if it were to stage a massive attack in the Persian Gulf, the United

States might sweep Soviet shipping and naval forces from the high seas, and it was indeed precisely in the context of a possible Gulf contingency—our vulnerable extremity—that Secretary Weinberger raised the prospect of horizontal escalation in his *Fiscal Year 1983 Report*. It is equally appropriate to make clear to Cuba and Vietnam that if they make their naval bases available to Soviet use during a Soviet-American war, their territories will not be spared from American attack. The most serious danger raised by the concept of horizontal escalation is a dissipation of effort in pursuit of vague, unattainable, or indecisive objectives—which would be particularly serious if these were sought on the periphery instead of in the core. It is nevertheless justifiable to make it clear to the Soviet Union that a massive assault on western interests in a region like the Persian Gulf would represent a decision on their part to initiate a global war.

⋆   ⋆   ⋆

The debate over horizontal escalation was only one, and perhaps the least important, aspect of the controversy that raged in the early 1980s over the decision to expand the fleet to fifteen carrier battlegroups and six hundred ships. There were two main lines of attack on these decisions: continentalists argued that forward deployed ground and air forces were of far greater importance in deterring (or defending against) a Soviet attack along the Eurasian rimland, and they sharply questioned the administration's strategic priorities. As Edward Luttwak has recently noted,

At a time when the United States no longer has the shield of strategic nuclear superiority to suppress the invasion potential of the Soviet Army in Central Europe, Western Asia, and Korea, it is the land forces (ground and tactical air) that should have been strengthened to maintain the balance of deterrence that keeps the peace; yet in the Reagan buildup, the major effort has been to strengthen the naval forces.[23]

A second line of attack (subscribed to by a diverse array of continentalists, maritime strategists, and military reformers) questioned the Navy's whole scheme of operations, particularly its continued reliance on the large-deck nuclear-powered aircraft carrier.[24]

If we imagine a war in Central Europe with the Soviet Union (where the Soviets maintain their largest concentration of combat power), the continentalists have the better of the argument. Under these circumstances, the marginal advantages afforded by additional carrier battlegroups would almost certainly be outweighed by additional investments in ground and tactical air forces. This is so for several reasons:

—Heavy equipment can be (and is) prepositioned in Central Europe, to which troops can be ferried by air in ordinary civilian aircraft. All other manner of stocks can also be prepositioned and protected, with the result that retaining the use of the seas is not indispensable in the first month of a conflict.

—Over time, the Soviet Union faces serious disadvantages in prohibiting (or at least making very costly) western use of the seas, since its submarines must transit through narrow geographical choke points and are not well equipped for sustained operations. Over time, therefore, it is likely that a naval strategy making use of attack submarines, mined choke points, convoys, and land-based patrol aircraft could gradually win the control of the seas, even if a substantial number of aircraft carriers were lost in an initial Soviet salvo.

—Even if the carrier battlegroup were to survive against the coordinated conventional torpedo and cruise missile attacks the Soviet Navy is capable of launching against it in a surprise attack, its ability to survive a nuclear salvo is far more questionable. Because collateral damage would be minimized in a nuclear war at sea, the Navy has special vulnerabilities here that even extremely expensive escorts would have difficulty guarding against.

The continentalists therefore have the better of the argument if we imagine a Soviet-American war. The argument swings in favor of the Navy, however, if non-Soviet contingencies are considered, and these are far more likely than another conflict of the World War II variety. There is no real competitor with the large-deck aircraft carrier for the provision of sea-based fighter protection. The smaller carrier recommended by a number of critics (in classes ranging from 20,000 to 40,000 tons) might be more useful in contending with Soviet attack submarines, but it is no competitor with the large-deck carrier in protracted deployments to distant oceans and in dealing with threats to American interests from non-Soviet states. The better sea-keeping qualities of the large carriers allow the launching and recovery of aircraft in sea states that would either prohibit or make very dangerous recovery operations onto smaller ones—which would be an operational factor of critical significance if enemy land-based aircraft were capable of getting airborne. Effective fighter operations, moreover, require a variety of early warning, reconnaissance, electronic warfare, and tanker aircraft. The number of such aircraft for effective operations tends to be fixed, leaving less room for the fighter and attack aircraft that are at the heart of the carriers' defensive and offensive capabilities. [25]

It was, indeed, largely the emergence of the crisis in the Persian Gulf at the end of the 1970s that highlighted the need for additional carriers. In the 1970s, when the Navy's fleet of deployable aircraft carriers was reduced to twelve, it was normally able to maintain only four carriers in forward deployed positions (usually in the Mediterranean and Western Pacific). The necessity of maintaining at least one carrier on station in the Indian Ocean severely taxed this deployment schedule, and this was only accomplished by drawing down on the Sixth Fleet (in the Mediterranean) and the Seventh Fleet (in the Western Pacific). In the words of Thomas Hayward, chief of naval operations from 1978 to 1982, the United States had a one-and-a-half-ocean navy with responsibilities in three different oceans. This situation called for at least one additional carrier when the Reagan administration took office. [26]

These considerations in turn suggest that the questionable aspect of Secretary of the Navy John Lehman's shipbuilding plan was not the decision to ask for two additional Nimitz-class carriers in FY 1983, both of which were authorized by Congress, but rather the investments expected in future years for the surface vessels designed to protect the carrier. The real issue, in other words, revolves around the Navy's two surface escorts—the Ticonderoga-class cruiser (CG–47), and the Burke-class destroyer (DD–51), each of which has been designed primarily for operations with a carrier task force. It is these escorts that will make up, in future years, the largest part of the Navy's shipbuilding budget, and they are the most questionable outlays on strategic grounds. Both the cruiser and the destroyer are designed around the contingency of a world-wide naval conflict with the Soviet Union, and their enormous expense derives from the necessity of protecting the carrier against air- and submarine-launched Soviet cruise missiles. Against lesser opponents, air defense systems of the number and sophistication asked for by the Navy are not necessary. But if we postulate a Soviet-American contingency, it is very doubtful that these systems would justify their cost in comparison with air and ground forces. These considerations, in turn, suggest that there is a good case for scaling back the procurement of the two AEGIS escorts.[27]

★   ★   ★

The Reagan administration pursued a number of important initiatives supporting the role of airpower in national strategy. It sought to raise the number of active and reserve Air Force fighter wings from thirty-six to forty while simultaneously modernizing the force with new planes, missiles, and improved conventional munitions. It decided to procure a fleet of one hundred B–1B bombers, to replace aging B–52s. It also threw its support around the "deep strike" initiatives associated with the "Follow on Forces Attack" (FOFA) plan of General Bernard Rogers, supreme allied commander in Europe. The Rogers Plan and others like it, such as the Air Force's "Counterair Ninety," are for the most part merely variations on old strategies of interdiction and air base attack, and some of the initiatives involve the use of existing technologies and involve little risk. Others, however, are based on the assumption that the improved lethality of conventional munitions can be combined with the revolution in microelectronics to produce military effects comparable to those produced by nuclear weapons. Their supporters see in the emerging technologies ("E.T.") a veritable revolution in warfare.[28]

Whether the weapons systems and doctrinal concepts of the Air Force are sound is a topic that has stirred an enormous amount of debate in military circles in the 1980s, which I have examined at length elsewhere. The view taken here is that there is a great deal to be said on behalf of the Air Force's program to modernize its tactical air arm, and there are good reasons to exclude this part of the defense budget from the indiscriminate ax of the budget cutter. Perhaps the most important initiative in airpower is the procurement of a fleet of long-range bombers, together with aerial radars capable of identifying moving and stationary targets at long ranges, armed with precision–guided air-to-surface missiles, rockets, and bombs capable of strikes against critical choke points, air bases, ground forces, and economic targets. The precise mix of forces may safely be left to the discretion of the Air Force, but the purpose of this initiative requires political understanding and support.

The principal purpose of the initiative ought to be the creation of a global strategic reserve centered on airpower, and not on ground forces, which would constitute the cutting edge of our rapid deployment forces. Such a force would have a diversity of applications in the world, and this is so even if it is acknowledged that there are more cost-effective ways of hitting military targets along the inner German border or deeper into Eastern Europe. It would be valuable all along the Soviet periphery, but its utility is clearest in the Persian Gulf, where it could greatly ease the problems caused by uncertain basing commitments, allowing both for a nonnuclear interdiction campaign in the event of a Soviet invasion or for strikes against the military forces or oil facilities of a regional adversary. Such a force could also have maritime applications that complement the functions of naval power, thus allowing long-range air forces to participate in operations of horizontal escalation. Finally, it ought to have the capability of inflicting a great deal of punishment on the extensive armored forces maintained by a host of states in the Third World. It may be that, in most cases, airpower cannot achieve an "independent decision." But it can be added to the ground forces of allied states, and if used in sufficiently massive quantities (as it was for instance in 1972 in Vietnam), it could constitute a formidable instrument for the defeat, and deterrence, of aggression.[29]

"Three Wars," Ground Forces, and No-First-Use

In perhaps its most important new doctrine, the Reagan administration repudiated the one-and-a-half-war strategy adopted by the Nixon administration and insisted that conventional forces be capable of meeting the demands of a worldwide war including concurrent reinforcement of Europe, deployment to Southwest Asia and the Pacific and to support other areas. In one sense this requirement recalls the two-and-a-half-war strategy embraced by the Democratic administrations of the 1960s, although not wholly so. The Reagan administration, like its predecessors in the 1970s, did not take seriously the possibility of a concerted and simultaneous Soviet and Chinese attack. It did not take seriously the possibility of a Chinese attack at all. It did take seriously—in a way its predecessors in the 1970s did not—the assumption that a Soviet-American war would be a conflict of global proportions.[30]

The shift to a "three-war" strategy, as many critics have observed, reintroduced the old disparity between doctrine and force structure that had characterized the two-and-a-half-war strategy in the 1960s. In a widely publicized estimate, later confirmed by Under Secretary of Defense Fred Iklé, the Joint Chiefs of Staff held that $750 billion would have to be added to the $1.6 trillion projected in the administration's 1983–87 five-year plan to achieve such capabilities, a figure arrived at by estimating the cost of the additional seven Army and Marine divisions, seventeen Air Force wings, and nine carrier battlegroups such a strategy would require.[31] This objection, to be sure, is not decisive. The Reagan administration may answer, as Caspar Weinberger did, that the areas to be defended—Western Europe, the Persian Gulf, and South Korea—are all vital. The disjunction between strategy and resources, if it exists, does not for the administration constitute an argument for a retrenchment. On the contrary, it simply means that we are spending less than we should. It is thus not sufficient to point to the disjunction between the administration's three-war strategy and the resources it has devoted to the defense budget. The real objection lies elsewhere.

The true grounds of objection to the Reagan administration's approach are remarkably similar to those that Henry Kissinger raised fifteen years ago against the two-and-a-half-war strategy. Kissinger, it will be recalled, not only argued that a joint Soviet and Chinese attack was unlikely; he also questioned the assumption that, if it were to occur, it "could or should be met with ground forces." The same consideration applies today. A massive Soviet assault on Western Europe and the Persian Gulf, combined with a simultaneous attack by North Korea on the South, is extremely unlikely. But if it were to occur, "to pretend that we would confine our response to a conventional war in two [or three] widely separated areas would multiply our dangers."[32] In the Persian Gulf, the proper response under these circumstances would be to limit our own use of military power to air and naval forces and shipments of arms to those willing to carry on the resistance—of which there would be many. If these measures or the threat of horizontal escalation failed to stop a Soviet invasion toward the Gulf, we should resort to the use of tactical nuclear weapons against Soviet military forces in the region. At all events, the Soviet Union must under-stand that we will not allow them to occupy the oil fields of the Persian Gulf and that we will destroy, with nuclear weapons if necessary, those elements of their forces that attempt to do so.

The same considerations apply to the use of American ground forces in Korea, if a North Korean attack were to occur in conjunc-tion with a Soviet assault on Western Europe and the Persian Gulf. It is by no means apparent, to be sure, that the reinforcement of South Korea with American ground forces would be required to repel a North Korean invasion. The South Koreans maintain a sizeable army and extensive fortifications; their equipment is supe-rior to that of the north, a disparity that promises to widen with the growth of their economy; and the morale of their soldiers remains high. The conventional air and naval forces of the United States impose a further obstacle in the path of North Korean aggression, and although our ability to reinforce them would be limited under the "three-war" scenario, the forces that are already there would almost certainly be sufficient to gain aerial supremacy and to im-pose high attrition on North Korean military units. Both the un-likelihood of a North Korean attack simultaneous with a massive Soviet assault elsewhere, and the strength of the South Korean forces themselves, combine to make the assumption of reinforcing the South Koreans with American ground forces dubious.

Our solid expectations might be betrayed, of course: attacks in three theaters at once might take place, and the South Korean military might prove inadequate to its tasks. But if this were to happen, there is no sound reason to exclude the use of American nuclear weapons on a limited scale against North Korean military units. Such a use would carry few of the dangers of escalation that would be present in Europe and would in all likelihood reap sub-stantial military advantages. Atomic demolition mines can be rapidly placed in prechambered holes along the most likely axes of a North Korean advance. If these failed to stop an attack, massed North Korean units could be hit with low-yield nuclear weapons, as could the numerous hardened airbases the North Koreans have constructed in recent years. The objection that any such use of nuclear weapons would fail to meet the test of proportionality imposed by international law and moral reasoning is not per-suasive. This would be the case only if nuclear attacks were made against cities, which is a possibility that ought to be excluded.

The reasons for believing that these are credible threats I have already examined at length. The actual use of nuclear weapons is something that should be considered only as a last resort, but to preclude this option in the last resort is, in the end, consistent with neither our safety nor our interests. Despite the overweening objectives of the Reagan administration's strategic nuclear policy, it was decidedly reluctant to rely on these threats—perhaps because it has conceded so often to the Soviets a degree of "strategic superiority" that they do not in fact enjoy. It is this reluctance that drives the requirements of a three-war strategy.

Intervention and the Third World: The Contemporary Relevance of the Nixon Doctrine

In its view of the military forces necessary to satisfy the "half-war requirement," the Reagan administration has also been overly ambitious. In some respects it has returned to the Nixon Doctrine. In striking contrast to the Carter administration, it has had a clear appreciation of the utility of American air and naval power. At the same time, economic and military aid grew sharply in the first years of the administration. It was nevertheless unwilling to discriminate between the utility of ground forces and air and naval power in assessing requirements for the half war. In practice, the administration has been reluctant to commit American ground forces in the Third World, and indeed the recurring public exchanges between Secretary of State George Shultz and Secretary of Defense Caspar Weinberger over the use of force show that this reluctance is deeply embedded in the Reagan Pentagon. The six requirements that, in Weinberger's view, had to be satisfied before an intervention could be justified were so imposing as to preclude interventions in practice. Yet the administration has continued to prepare for large-scale interventions of American ground troops in the Third World. Its decision to convert two older infantry divisions to a new ten-thousand-man light infantry type and to add two others on the same model indicated that the interventionary capabilities foreclosed in theory were still required in practice. In addition, many outside analysts have argued that the chief deficiency of American ground forces has been their continuing focus on the "big war," to the exclusion of preparations for small wars. Thus Eliot Cohen: "Three examples of small wars one would imagine the United

States fighting in the next decade are: a war to preserve the independence of Honduras, Costa Rica, and Panama; a war to prevent Iranian disruption of Western and Japanese oil supplies; a war to preserve the independence of Thailand."[33]

The internal debate between Shultz and Weinberger has been very peculiar in one respect. Both sides appear to have assumed that "interventions" are all necessarily of the same character, that there is no qualitative difference between an air strike on a terrorist base and the commitment of American ground forces on a large scale to some Third World contingency. But there is every difference in the world between these two acts. Air strikes have been required to punish those responsible for terrorist acts against American civilians and diplomats abroad, and may yet be required again. These crimes should not go unavenged. But the use of ground forces is inconsistent with our basic interests, and it is not necessary in order to safeguard our position in the Third World.

If we see this issue as the Nixon administration did, we will be well on our way to resolving it in a satisfactory manner. By prescribing a line of division between ground forces on the one hand and air and naval power (and economic and military aid) on the other, Nixon and Kissinger split the difference between isolationists and interventionists in as sensible a fashion as it is possible to do. The Nixon Doctrine was not, to be sure, entirely novel. Its main lines were set down by Franklin Roosevelt, who viewed the United States as an "arsenal of democracy," with both special strengths and special weaknesses. Our economic and technological resources were, in Roosevelt's view, our primary strengths; our unwillingness to incur large casualties our principal weakness.[34] That continues to be the case today.

The Nixon Doctrine is not a formula that can be applied everywhere. It was never applied by Nixon and Kissinger to Europe, and wisely so. The fundamental interest we have in safeguarding the physical security of Europe makes ground forces indispensable, and their physical presence in Europe since 1951 has been part and parcel of the postwar order. It is therefore entirely proper that the majority of our ground forces—including those stationed in the United States—should have a primarily European orientation.[35] A bastardization of the doctrine was applied to the Persian Gulf in the 1970s, in circumstances in which it was clearly inappropriate. But circumstances have now changed profoundly in the Gulf, which gives it in the mid-1980s a relevance it did not enjoy a decade ago. It would also probably be unwise to apply the doctrine fully to South Korea. There, too, American ground forces have for a long time formed part of the balance of power, and it is probably not worth the trouble to remove the one remaining ground division. What can be eliminated without upsetting the balance on the Korean peninsula is a capability to reinforce with substantial ground forces. The same considerations that make the reinforcement of South Korea with ground forces an unwise commitment in a global war with the Soviet Union apply also to a North Korean attack that occurs by itself. Thirty-four thousand Americans died in the first Korean War; one hundred and three thousand were wounded. There is no reason to pay this price again; and no reason to renounce the declaration that if North Korea again attacks South Korea, it will be their forces and not ours on the firing line.

Elsewhere in the world, it is difficult to believe that ground forces are necessary to vindicate our interests. Whether we consider the Near East, Indochina, Africa, or Latin America, it seems apparent that an American ground force intervention either would be disproportionate to the interests at stake or would confer on our adversaries a strategic advantage we ought to be intent on denying them.

—In the Near East, the only interest that might justify the commitment of American ground forces is a threat to the security of Israel. But the Israelis have never requested this kind of an American commitment; and if the United States continues to support them and does not cut them off in the vain hope of currying favor in the Arab world, they will be perfectly capable of taking care of themselves.

—In Southeast Asia, North Vietnamese expansion has reached a natural limit with its conquest of Indochina, and if it were to press further onward against Thailand despite the opposition of China and the ASEAN states there would be plenty of indigenous manpower to draw on to frustrate such an enterprise.

—In Africa, western interventions are best undertaken by the Europeans, who have the forces and the experience to conduct them successfully. Analysts, to be sure, often cast their eyes south of the Sahara and wonder if the United States may one day lose access to the strategic minerals that lie under the African crust. But what

John Kenneth Galbraith said in 1970 of the Third World generally continues to hold true today for Africa:

Even by the crudest power calculations, military or economic, such nations have no vital relations to the economic or strategic position of the developed countries. They do supply raw materials. But even here the typical observation concerns not their power as sources of such supply but their weakness as competitive hewers of wood in the markets of the industrially advanced countries.[36]

Insofar as danger exists of cartels in strategic commodities, these dangers can be sharply mitigated by stockpiling, recycling, and other measures that require no use of military power. Stockpiles sufficient for the short-term crisis are, if sensibly managed, adequate for the long-term problem. For the commodities that we need to buy, they need to sell, and this is a consideration that will operate on any government that sits on top of them, whatever its ideological or racial coloration.[37]

—Latin America and the Caribbean basin represent the most plausible areas for an American ground force intervention, if only because the Reagan administration has entertained the ambitious objective of overthrowing the Sandinista government in Nicaragua. Whatever the merits of that objective,[38] it is revealing that the administration has consistently sought to do so through economic and military aid and not through the direct application of American military power. Neoconservative critics have argued that an agreement with Nicaragua along the lines of the Contadora Process would leave the United States powerless to contend with an emboldened revolutionary axis centered on Managua and Havana, but of all the arguments for *contra* aid, this is the least plausible. Cuba and Nicaragua are completely vulnerable to an American air and sea blockade; if the Cubans were to attempt to introduce large numbers of ground forces into Latin America, the proper response would be to cut off its air and sea links with the outside world, on the maintenance of which it is profoundly dependent. The same is true of the threat that Nicaragua might invade its neighbors to the north or south. American air and naval power could effectively isolate Nicaragua from outside assistance; American economic and military aid could then be funneled to its regional antagonists. Even with the cuts in the size of our active ground forces recommended below, the United States would still retain the capacity to undertake a substantial ground force intervention in Central America. Why we would want to is a more difficult matter to fathom.

Limited interventionary forces the United States still needs to maintain, for operations like the one in Grenada, if nothing else. The expansion of special forces undertaken by the Reagan administration, moreover, was entirely proper. Such forces are likely to be useful in the strange world populated by terrorists of all varieties that we may confront in the late 1980s and 1990s. What we do not require is the nine active divisions that are now maintained primarily for Third World interventions.

How American ground forces might be reduced is something that would have to be worked out in consultation with the Army, from whom most of the cuts should be taken. The objective should be the reduction in active Army and Marine forces of around 150,000 troops. The United States should honor its commitment to NATO to provide ten divisions within ten days of mobilization, while retaining a smaller strategic reserve for unforeseen contingencies (centered around a slightly reduced Marine Corps and Army divisions also committed to the reinforcement of NATO.) Our primary strategic reserve, however, would consist of our air and sea power, both conventional and nuclear. Army leaders and supporters will certainly object to the strategic risks entailed by such a plan of reductions. They ought more properly to see it as a great opportunity to recast the Army into a more elite force than it has usually been considered, one capable of enforcing rigorous standards on the officers and men who join it, one cast more on the British model than the continental design we have normally followed. Given manpower constraints, indeed, it is doubtful whether the attempt to maintain an Army of 780,000 men and women would result in a force more effective in war than one reduced in size. To assume that it would was the mistake of the 1970s: it yielded hollow forces. The quantity of personnel raised by a volunteer force, in other words, will inevitably have an inverse relation to quality—a consideration that would make advisable a reduction in numbers even in the absence of the strategic rationale for doing so presented here.

The reduction in requirements for interventionary capabilities would also allow for cuts in strategic mobility systems. Designed to carry heavy equipment like tanks, strategic airlifters are not necessary for the reinforcement of NATO, for such equipment can (and should) be prepositioned in Europe. And if we take a different view toward substantial ground force interventions in the Third World, it becomes apparent that there is no strategic justification for the sixty-six-million-ton-per-day requirement called for in the Air Force's congressionally mandated mobility study. Scaling back this inflated requirement would still leave the United States with sizeable and diverse strategic mobility assets (including a force of maritime prepositioning ships, eight fast sealift ships, a fleet of amphibious assault carriers, and a sizeable force of strategic airlifters), which are more than ample for unforeseen contingencies; and it would also allow for substantial savings in the defense budget.

★   ★   ★

"One must therefore be a fox to recognize traps, and a lion to frighten wolves. Those who wish to be only lions do not understand this."[39] Such was Machiavelli's advice to Lorenzo de' Medici. A similar thought was expressed—in a phrase worthy of the great and infamous Florentine—by Muhammad Ali, in description of his early boxing style: float like a butterfly, sting like a bee. Large and protracted commitments of American ground forces in the Third World violate both injunctions, for they afford the enemy the opportunity to strike us at our most vulnerable point. They are the strategic equivalent of the rope-a-dope.

In the concluding book of *On War*, Clausewitz observed that to gain a true understanding of strategy "one must keep the dominant characteristics of both belligerents in mind. Out of these characteristics a certain center of gravity develops, the hub of all power and movement, on which everything depends. That is the point at which all our energies should be directed."[40] Can economic and military aid, allied with air and naval power, successfully reach the center of gravity of our potential adversaries in the Third World? If we are moderate in our objectives, I believe that it can. We know in any case what our own center of gravity consists of. It rests on the value we place on the lives of our soldiers. We cannot bear their loss unless the interest is overwhelming and the cause is just. There is no more powerful civic sentiment in the American people than this concern for the fate of our soldiers. That sentiment, however, is not to be confused with an unwillingness to employ force at all. The deeper meaning of the new nationalism is to be found in the radical distinction the American people would continue to draw, in war, between our own suffering and that of others, a distinction that makes them averse not to the use of force as such, but only to force of a certain kind. A statecraft and strategy that fails to comport with these sentiments betrays a profound misunderstanding of the true outlook of the American people, and courts a certain—and deserved—repudiation.

Notes

1. For the Army's critique of this position, see Maxwell Taylor, *The Uncertain Trumpet* (New York, 1959). The pentomic divisions in the 1950s are examined in Major Robert A. Doughty, *The Evolution of US Army Doctrine, 1946–1976*, Leavenworth Paper No. 1, Combat Studies Institute, (Fort Leavenworth, Kansas, 1979).

2. As Karl Lautenschläger has noted in his excellent review, "Technology and the Evolution of Naval Warfare," *International Security* (Fall 1983), 3–51, the Navy sought to integrate nuclear weapons into its battlefleet throughout the 1950s, but only achieved "a complete suit of offensive and defensive nuclear weapons" in 1961, just in time for the Kennedy administration. The difficulty of effecting the shift from nuclear to conventional capabilities in U.S. tactical air forces is considered in Robert F Coulam, *Illusions of Choice* (Princeton, 1976). As Coulam notes, McNamara did not initially see the significance of the TFX in terms of the shift from nuclear to conventional missions, though the plane was initially designed for nuclear missions. Rather, he saw it in terms of the necessity of eliminating "waste and duplication," and hence insisted that the Navy procure it as well. The McNamara Pentagon did much better in forcing Navy procurements on the Air Force (e.g., the A–7 and F–4) than in forcing Air Force procurements on the Navy.

3. William Kaufmann's essay on *Planning Conventional Forces: 1950–1980* (Washington, D.C., 1982) is the best short introduction to general forces planning during the postwar period. See also the valuable discussion in Jeffrey Record, *Revising U.S. Military Strategy: Tailoring Means to Ends* (Washington, D.C., 1984).

4. The political implications of this doctrinal change, Kissinger writes, "were even more decisive. We had to give up the obsession with a Communist monolith. By linking Soviet and Chinese purposes we created presumptions that circumscribed the flexibility of our diplomacy and ran counter to the demonstrable antagonism between the two major Communist powers. The reorientation of our strategy signaled to the People's Republic of China"—well before the maturing of the opening to Peking—"that we saw its purposes as separable from the Soviet Union's, that our military policy did not see China as a principal threat." Henry Kissinger, *White House Years* (Boston, 1979), 221–22.

5. Ibid., 221.

6. Ibid., 224–25.

7. See Guenter Lewy, *America in Vietnam* (Oxford, 1978), 147; and William P.

Mako, *U.S. Ground Forces and the Defense of Central Europe* (Washington, D.C., 1983), 2.

8. Robert W. Tucker, "Oil: The Issue of American Intervention," *Commentary*, (January 1975), 21–31.

9. Huntington, "Defense Policy," 12; and Zbigniew Brzezinski, *Power and Principle: Memoirs of the National Security Advisor, 1977–1981* (New York, 1983), 177–78.

10. Reductions were then to be made thereafter from this level. On the "dubious numbers game" that was played with this limit, and on the Carter administration's arms policy as a whole, see Andrew J. Pierre, *The Global Politics of Arms Sales* (Princeton, 1982), 45–72. The relationship of the B–1 to the MX has an uncanny resemblance to the relationship between the "neutron bomb" and the Pershing II. The cancellations of the former paved the way for the latter in both cases; in nuclear policy, the Carter administration swung from defect to excess in the space of two short years. See, for example, Leon V. Sigal, *Nuclear Forces in Europe: Enduring Dilemmas, Present Prospects* (Washington, D.C., 1984), 55–58. The story of the carrier debate of the late 1970s is told in James Nathan and James Oliver, *The Future of U.S. Naval Power,* (Bloomington, 1979).

11. Kissinger, *White House Years,* 221.

12. Kaufmann, *Planning Conventional Forces,* 9–10.

13. *NATO and the New Soviet Threat,* Report of Senator Sam Nunn and Senator Dewey F. Bartlett to the Committee on Armed Services, U.S. Senate (Washington, D.C. 1977).

14. Martin Binkin, *America's Volunteer Military: Progress and Prospects* (Washington, D.C., 1984), 12.

15. Assertions to the contrary, such as those made in a report published by the House Appropriations Subcommittee on Defense in 1984 often confuse "readiness" with "sustainability" and measure the latter in relation to the high standards set by the Reagan administration itself and not in relation to what American forces could accomplish in 1980. In relation to the past, there has been clear improvement. In relation to the administration's own strategic standards—of which more later— serious deficiencies remain. See, for instance, the following articles by Richard Halloran in *The New York Times*: "U.S. Forces May Lack Resources for Sustained War, Officers Say," 14 May 1984; "Combat Readiness: Despite Administration Protestations, Evidence of Deficiencies is Growing," 25 July 1984; and "U.S. Troops Termed Able to Fight for 30 Days in Conventional War," 24 August 1984.

16. See "Rearming America," *The Economist,* 13 April 1985, 32; Richard Stubbing, "The Defense Program: Buildup or Binge?" *Foreign Affairs* (Spring 1985), 858; and *Budget of the United States Government: Fiscal Year 1987,* 6e–34.

17. See Asa A. Clark IV and Thomas W. Fagan, "Trends in Defense Budgeting: Mortgaging the Future," in Asa A. Clark et al., *The Defense Reform Debate: Issues and Analysis* (Baltimore, 1984); William W. Kaufmann, *The 1985 Defense Budget* (Washington, D.C., 1984); and Richard K. Betts, "Conventional Forces: What Price Readiness?" *Survival* (January/February 1983), 25–34.

18. See the discussion in Martin Binkin, *America's Volunteer Military,* 31–39, and in Martin Binkin, "Manpower," in George E. Hudson and Joseph Kruzel, *American Defense Annual: 1985–1986,* 138–44. Binkin argues that 50 percent of the qualified and available males will be required to fulfill the administration's manpower requirements during the 1984–88 period. From 1991–95, "the figure grows to 55 percent as the noninstitutionalized eighteen-year-old cohort drops to about 1.6 million."

Adding planned increases in Navy and Air Force manpower would require 60 percent of the qualified and available population in the early 1990s, and if the Army were to adopt the minimum standards now used by the Air Force, "the pool of qualified and available male youths would shrink by over 20 percent, and three out of every four would eventually have to enlist to meet projected military requirements in the early 1990s." Binkin, "Manpower," 140–41.

19. The reasons for this judgment are set forth in Eliot A. Cohen's excellent analysis of the historical and philosophical conundrums attending military service in Eliot A. Cohen, *Citizens and Soldiers: The Dilemmas of Military Service* (Ithaca, 1985), esp. 176–78; and Seth Cropsey, "Women in Combat?" *The Public Interest* (Fall 1980), 58–89. On expectations of comradery among men and women in combat, see the disturbing reflections of J. Glenn Gray in his classic work, *The Warriors: Reflections on Men in Battle* (New York, 1970), 59–97. Two other valuable examinations of the manpower problem are William J. Taylor et al., eds., *Defense Manpower Planning: Issues for the 1980s* (New York, 1981), and Brent Scowcroft, ed., *Military Service in the United States* (Englewood Cliffs, N.J., 1982).

20. See *Report of Secretary of Defense Caspar W. Weinberger to the Congress on the FY 1983 Budget. . . .* (Washington, D.C., 1982), 1:14–17.

21. See the analysis in Michael Howard, "The British Way in Warfare: A Reappraisal," in Howard, *The Causes of War and Other Essays* (Cambridge, Mass., 1983), 169–87. See also Russell F. Weigley, *The American Way of War: A History of United States Military Strategy and Policy* (Bloomington, 1973), esp. 318–334. I examine this issue in greater detail in "Maritime vs. Continental Strategy" (forthcoming).

22. Cf. Barry R. Posen, "Inadvertent Nuclear War? Escalation and NATO's Northern Flank," *International Security* (Fall 1982), 28–54. Cf. also Joshua M. Epstein, "Horizontal Escalation: Sour Notes of a Recurrent Theme," *International Security* (Winter 1983/84): 19–31.

23. Edward Luttwak, *The Pentagon and the Art of War* (New York, 1985), 260. See also Robert W. Komer, *Maritime Strategy or Coalition Defense?* (Cambridge, Mass., 1984).

24. See Gary Hart, "The U.S. Senate and the Future of the Navy," *International Security* (Spring 1978), 175–94; William Lind, "Is it Time to Sink the Surface Navy?" *Proceedings of the United States Naval Institute* (March 1978), 62–67; Admiral Stansfield Turner, "Thinking About the Future of the Navy," *Proceedings of the United States Naval Institute* (August 1980), 66–69; and Stansfield Turner (with George Thibault), "Preparing for the Unexpected: The Need for a New Military Strategy," *Foreign Affairs* (Fall 1982), 122–35; George W. S. Kuhn, "Department of Defense: Ending Defense Stagnation," in *Agenda '83,* ed. Richard N. Holwill (Washington, D.C., 1983); and William W. Kaufmann, "The Defense Budget," in *Setting National Priorities: the 1982 Budget,* ed. Joseph A. Pechman (Washington, D.C., 1981), 161. I consider this critique at length in *Reforming Defense.*

25. See Norman Friedman, *Carrier Air Power* (New York, 1981), and "The Falklands War: Lessons Learned and Mislearned," *Orbis* (Winter 1983), 907–40; and John Lehman, *Aircraft Carriers: The Real Choices,* Washington Paper no. 52. (Beverly Hills, 1978.) The political utility of the carrier is stressed in Barry M. Blechman and Steven S. Kaplan, *Force Without War* (Washington, D.C., 1977). The findings of this study are updated in Philip D. Zelikow, "Force Without War, 1975–82," in *Journal of Strategic Studies* (March 1984), 29–54.

26. On the Navy's deployment concepts and tempo of operations, see

Christopher C. Wright, "U.S. Naval Operations in 1982," in *Proceedings of the U.S. Naval Institute* (May 1983), 51, 54, and 57, an annual feature of the Naval Institute's *Naval Review Issue*. The Navy recently announced plans to reduce the time the carriers "sail in foreign waters in an effort to reduce the strain on the large crews and to save money." See Richard Halloran, "Navy Plans to Reduce Time Carriers Are Overseas," *The New York Times,* 30 April 1985.

27. On the new surface escorts, see Congressional Budget Office, *Naval Surface Combatants in the 1990s: Prospects and Possibilities* (Washington, D.C., 1981); Capt. Alva M. Bowen, USN (ret.), and Ronald O'Rourke, "DDG–51 and the Future Surface Navy," *Proceedings of the U.S. Naval Institute* (May 1985), 176–89; and Norman Friedman, "The Arleigh Burke—A New Brand of Destroyer," *International Defense Review* 3 (1985), 323–330. The decision to build two additional Nimitz-class carriers in FY 1983 has not settled the question of the number of carrier battlegroups that will be maintained in the fleet in the 1990s. The Navy will face a choice between reducing the number of surface escorts it desires or reducing the number of deployable carriers in the fleet. Budgetary and other constraints are reviewed in Howard W. Serig, Jr., "Stretching the Fleet into the 1990s," *Proceedings of the U.S. Naval Institute* (May 1984), 164–79.

28. On the modernization of U.S. tactical air forces, see the report of the Congressional Budget Office, *Tactical Combat Forces of the United States Air Force: Issues and Alternatives* (Washington, D.C., 1985). On the deep strike initiatives, see the report of the European Security Study, *Strengthening Conventional Deterrence in Europe: Proposals for the 1980s* (New York, 1983); Fred Wikner, "NATO's Conventional Defense Myopia," *The Wall Street Journal,* 24 July 1984, and Fred Wikner, "ET and Western Technology," *Armed Forces Journal International* (December 1984), 85–102. Instances of political support for the deep strike initiatives may be found in Sam Nunn, "Saving the Alliance," *The Washington Quarterly* (Summer 1982), esp. 22–23; and Manfred Woerner and Peter-Kurt Wurzbach, "NATO's New 'Conventional Option,'" *The Wall Street Journal,* 19 November 1982. See also "NATO: Reshaping the Alliance," *Aviation Week and Space Technology,* 21 May 1984. The literature critiquing the deep strike initiatives is already quite large. Among these, see particularly Josef Joffe, "Stability and Its Discontent: Should NATO Go Conventional," *The Washington Quarterly* (Fall 1984), esp. 142–44; Jeffrey Record, "NATO's Forward Defense and Striking Deep," *Armed Forces Journal International* (November 1983), 42–48; John J. Mearsheimer, "Nuclear Weapons and Deterrence in Europe," *International Security* (Winter 1984/85), 57–82; Matthew A. Evangelista, "Offense or Defense: A Tale of Two Commissions," *World Policy Journal* (Fall 1983), 45–69; and Phil Williams and William Wallace, "Emerging Technologies and European Security," *Survival* (March-April 1984), 70–78. I examine the issues raised by the critics in *Reforming Defense*.

29. The case for the long-range combat aircraft is made in Jacquelyn K. Davis and Robert L. Pfaltzgraff, Jr., *Power Projection and the Long-Range Combat Aircraft: Missions, Capabilities, and Alternative Designs* (Cambridge, Mass., 1981); and John Newhouse, "Yes to the B–1," *The Washington Post,* 9 July 1981. The B–1B's capabilities are described in James W. Canan, "The Magnificent B–1B," *Air Force Magazine* (November 1984), 58–65. See also the important essay by Gen. Curtis E. LeMay (ret.), "Non-Nuclear Bomber Forces," *Aviation Week and Space Technology,* 28 May 1984, 11. A thorough examination of the role of the long-range bomber in conventional operations is contained in Col. Thomas A. Keaney, *Strategic Bombers*

and Conventional Weapons: Airpower Options, National Security Affairs Monograph Series 84–4 (Washington D.C., 1984). Maritime applications are examined in Seymour J. Deitchman, "Turning Point for Tactical Naval Forces?" *Astronautics & Aeronautics* (November 1982), 22–33, and *Military Power and the Advance of Technology.*

30. Jeffrey Record first put the "three-war" appellation on the Reagan administration's approach, and it is a good shorthand description of the administration's view. (See "A Three-War Strategy?" *The Washington Post,* 22 March 1982.) It is doubtful whether the administration would accept the term. Weinberger noted in his FY 1983 *Report* that

the geographic distribution of our assets must be guided by the prospects for protecting our vital interests and winning the war. We cannot settle this question in advance by defining the risk we confront as 'one war' or a 'war and a half.' Moreover, the decision on how large our overall defense effort ought to be must be based on much broader and more fundamental judgments than some arbitrary and facile assumption about the number of 'wars,' or fronts, that we must be prepared for.

The administration's views are set out most clearly in its first defense report to Congress, *Report of Secretary of Defense Caspar W. Weinberger to the Congress on the FY 1983 Budget,* (Washington D.C., 1982). See also by Jeffrey Record, "Jousting with Unreality: Reagan's Military Strategy," *International Security* (Winter 1983/84), 3–18.

31. See George C. Wilson, "U.S. Defense Paper Cites Gap Between Rhetoric, Intentions," *The Washington Post,* 27 May 1982; and Richard Halloran, "New Weinberger Directive Refines Military Policy," *The New York Times,* 22 March 1983.

32. *White House Years,* 221.

33. Eliot A. Cohen, "Constraints on America's Conduct of Small Wars," *International Security* (Fall 1984), 155.

34. See Richard M. Leighton, "The American Arsenal Policy in World War II: A Retrospective View," in *Some Pathways in Twentieth Century History: Essays in Honor of Charles Reginald McGrane,* ed. Daniel R. Beaver (Detroit, 1969), 221–52; and Gaddis, *Strategies of Containment,* 4–9.

35. The fundamental difficulty with Jeffrey Record's strategic outlook is that he would apply the Nixon Doctrine to Europe, where it is inapplicable, and abandon it in relation to Third World interventions, where it continues to be of relevance. See, e.g., Jeffrey Record, "The Europeanization of NATO," *Air University Review* (November-December 1982). The same objection applies to the maritime strategists and global unilateralists who would withdraw American troops from Europe, so as to raise up a formidable capability for ground force interventions in the Third World.

36. John Kenneth Galbraith, "Plain Lessons of a Bad Decade," in *Beyond Containment: U.S. Foreign Policy in Transition,* ed. Robert W. Tucker and William Watts (Washington, D.C., 1973), 58.

37. See Robert B. Shepard, "South Africa: The Case for Disengagement," *The National Interest* (Winter 1985/86), 46–57.

38. See Robert W. Tucker, with commentary by Charles Krauthammer and Kenneth W. Thompson, *Intervention and the Reagan Doctrine,* Ethics and Foreign Policy Lecture Series, Council on Religion and Public Affairs (New York, 1985).

39. Machiavelli, *The Prince,* chap. 17.

40. Clausewitz, *On War,* p. 595.

Conclusion:
The Disjunction between Power and Commitment

I began this work by drawing attention to what Walter Lippmann called "the fundamental principle of a foreign policy." For Lippmann, that principle consisted of "bringing into balance, with a comfortable surplus of power in reserve, the nation's commitments and the nation's power. The constant preoccupation of the true statesman is to achieve and maintain this balance." An imbalance between power and commitment, whatever its precise characteristics, Lippmann identified as insolvent, and he noted that "without the controlling principle that the nation must maintain its objectives and its power in equilibrium, its purposes within its means and its means equal to its purposes, its commitments related to its resources and its resources adequate to its commitments, it is impossible to think at all about foreign affairs."[1]

Our policy is insolvent in the literal sense today. "No one would seriously suppose," Lippmann noted, "that he had a fiscal policy if he did not consider together expenditure and revenue, outgo and income, liabilities and assets."[2] Mr. Lippmann, alas, did not live to see the 1980s. It is the insolvency of policy reflected in the federal budget deficit—the failure "to pay for what we want, and to want only what we are willing to pay for"—that has been the most astonishing aspect of the Reagan administration's governing program. There are other features of the administration's program that should be called into question, such as its failure to harmonize energy policy and military strategy, the difficulty of achieving the administration's manpower objectives without a return to the draft, and the ambitions reflected in its strategic nuclear policy. But the need to restore solvency to the nation's fiscal accounts still represents the dominant problem that president and Congress must address.

The assumption of this work has been that reductions in the projected rate of growth of defense spending must form a part,

177

alongside increased taxes and reduced social spending, of any plan to bring solvency to our economic policy. The great objection to this course of action is that it will exacerbate the other elements of our strategic predicament. It was, of course, the imbalance between power and commitment that Lippmann identified with insolvency—the relationship between income and expenditure was for him simply a metaphor for this larger problem. The gravamen of the objection, therefore, is that by addressing the insolvency of our economic policy with reductions in the defense budget we shall aggravate the larger insolvency of our foreign policy and strategy, that in closing the gap between expenditure and revenue in this manner we shall widen the gap between military power and political commitment.

There are two common expressions of the nature of the disjunction between power and interest. Some locate it primarily in the neutralization of the deterrent capability of American nuclear forces and the persisting imbalance in conventional forces between the United States and the Soviet Union.[3] Others see it arising primarily from the inadequacy of American interventionary forces. The preoccupation with Europe, in Eliot Cohen's words, "occurs at the expense of strategic flexibility: forces designed for European warfare cannot be adequately prepared for other contingencies."[4] An impressive consensus appears to exist on behalf of both views. I believe this consensus to be mistaken. In both critiques, there has been an understandable yet ultimately pernicious tendency to depreciate our power and to exaggerate our interests. The power most often depreciated resides in our air and naval forces, both conventional and nuclear; the interests most often exaggerated lie in the Third World. Our tactical and strategic nuclear forces continue to offer us solid assurances of deterrence against a Soviet assault on the citadels of western strength, even under conditions of mutual vulnerability. By the same token, the interests we have in the Third World may be satisfied by means of the extension of economic and military aid, or the use or threatened use of air and naval power.

The exaggeration of interest and the depreciation of power are closely related phenomena. In strategy and warfare, there must be a continuous interaction between ends and means, for each is "fully comprehensible only in terms of the other."[5] Because of this relationship, the rule usually holds true in strategy that the more limited the interest, the less exacting the military capabilities one must raise up to secure it. In turn, this proposition reflects, as Bernard Brodie once noted,

the conception simply of reasonable price, and of its being applied to strategy and national policy—the idea that some ends or objectives are worth paying a good deal for and others are not. The latter includes ends that are no doubt desirable but which are worth attempting to achieve only if the price can *with confidence* be kept relatively low.[6]

The reciprocal relationship between interest and power (ends and means) is observable with respect to all the great problems of contemporary American strategy, and indeed the requirements of strategy in Europe, the Third World, and the Persian Gulf cannot be understood apart from this relationship:

—If the avowed objective of our policy toward the Soviet Union in Europe is not only to preserve the independence of Western Europe but also to bring about a retreat of Soviet power from Eastern Europe, as it was a generation ago, we have set a very large standard for policy. Such a policy requires military capabilities of so robust a character that the Soviet Union is intimidated—or even, *in extremis,* physically prevented—from reasserting its power over its satellites in Eastern Europe. This standard, moreover, condemns our policy toward the Soviet Union to a judgment of almost certain failure, for success can come about only by virtue of a sharp retreat of the Soviet strategic frontier. A more modest conception of the purposes of containment, on the other hand, does not require this kind of strategic superiority; and if our postwar European policy is seen in the light of this more moderate conception, it must be judged a success rather than a failure. Eastern Europe has not been liberated; but Western Europe remains free.

—If our objective in the Third World may be expressed largely in terms of the maintenance of the balance of power—that is, ensuring that the Soviet Union or the regional imperialists with which it is associated do not conquer and absorb vast tracts of the globe—then we may, with assurance of success, rely upon the energy such imperious enterprises unfailingly release in opposition to them, adding to it our economic and military aid and air and naval power. If, on the other hand, we see our interests in the Third World in the more ambitious terms suggested in John Kennedy's Inaugural Address, and if we come to believe that American ground forces are required to vindicate our interests in Central America, Africa, the Middle East, Southeast Asia, and Korea, then we will be condemned to a perpetual gap between interest and power. We will, moreover, have great difficulty in restoring the domestic consensus indispensable to any democratic statecraft, for it is highly unlikely that the American people will support a large and protracted commitment of ground forces to any of these areas.

—Perhaps the most striking instance of the relationship between power and commitment today is the effect that the reduction in dependence on Persian Gulf oil from twenty to ten million barrels a day has had on the need for and relevance of military power in dealing with contingencies in the Gulf. Compared with the situation that existed at the outset of the 1980s, this change has both lessened the need for ground forces and made our air and naval power more relevant to the vindication of our interests. A revival of Persian Gulf exports in the late 1980s and 1990s, on the other hand, would make it far more difficult to bring about any kind of disengagement from the region at all, with far-reaching effects on our military requirements and our diplomatic posture.

Because the United States is a global power with global responsibilities, the maintenance of a balance between power and commitment is a difficult thing to achieve over time. Much of the history of postwar American foreign policy, and indeed of American foreign policy generally,[7] may profitably be viewed in terms of our success or failure in maintaining an equilibrium between the two. From the early 1960s to the late 1970s, we swung from a policy that was insolvent because of an excess of political commitment to one that was insolvent because of an inadequacy of military power. In the former case, the vindication of our interests was seen to require not only the maintenance of the balance of power among states but also the preservation of a certain kind of internal order within states.[8] In the latter case, the proposition that military power is of limited utility—a sensible idea in some instances—was conceived to cover virtually all instances. To define our interests in the world in the manner of the 1960s was to create an imbalance between power and interest such that no increase in domestic resources was capable of overcoming it. But an imbalance was also created by the opposite error committed in the 1970s.

To overcome the imbalance between power and commitment

that had developed by the end of the 1970s, substantial increases in defense spending were required. The most serious weaknesses of the American military lay in the "hollowness" of conventional forces: experienced personnel were leaving the services in substantial numbers, recruits were sometimes incompetent, ships and aircraft and tanks were hobbled for a lack of spare parts. The Carter defense program, as the Reagan administration cogently argued when it came into office, had been severely underfunded. There was as a consequence a great deal to be said for the Reagan administration's across-the-board increases in the funding of general purpose forces. There also existed, at the level of strategic nuclear forces, a set of problems that had to be addressed: strategic modernization—though not on the scale that has in fact been pursued by the Reagan administration—was a necessity. Finally, the crisis in the Persian Gulf required a response. The emergence of that crisis in effect cancelled out the strategic advantages gained by the United States as a consequence of the Sino-Soviet rivalry. For this reason, retrenchment in East Asia did not pay the kind of strategic dividend in the 1970s that many observers had expected it would.

These three problems all reflected an underlying imbalance between power and interest; all three have substantially eased in the intervening period. There has been a remarkable improvement in the morale and readiness of our conventional forces; the critical vulnerabilities that existed at the end of the 1970s have been markedly eased. The strategic modernization conceived by the Carter administration and expanded upon by the Reagan administration, though some of it still remains on the drawing board, has also had a profound effect on perceptions of the underlying balance of power. The argument over the Reagan administration's strategic nuclear policy is whether it is trying to do too much. There appears to be no danger, to put it mildly, that it will do too little. Finally, the reduction of dependence on the oil of the Persian Gulf permits a measure of disengagement from that region, with strategic advantages for the United States that may yet approach those that resulted, a generation ago, from the Sino-Soviet split.

★   ★   ★

None of this is meant to deny that the crunch in defense spending, now fully upon us, will not pose special and imposing dilemmas for American strategy. If the retrenchment is undertaken across the board or in accordance with misguided strategic principles, we may yet find ourselves again in the perilous condition of the late 1970s. For this reason the reformation of American strategy requires not only a transformation in the internal budgetary priorities of the Defense Department but also a change in our thinking about the possible uses of American military power. We need a strategy that is at once less plural and more asymmetrical—that is, one that prunes the lavish growth of strategic concepts that arose under the Reagan administration and one that will allow us to set American strengths against adversary weaknesses. Abandoning the attempt to achieve a damage-limitation capability against the Soviet Union (while retaining first use), discarding the three-war requirement for ground forces, and rehabilitating the Nixon Doctrine would each satisfy both requirements.

With strategic nuclear policy no longer based on the dangerous quest to eliminate our vulnerability to the Soviet Union in a full-scale exchange of nuclear weapons (a strategy of annihilation or damage limitation), we would be free to revert to a strategy of attrition—that is, one that seeks deterrence through the anticipated exhaustion or shock of the enemy. The latter objective is far more modest than one based on the disarmament of enemy military forces; it is consistent with the defensive character of our statecraft; and it would allow us to focus our strategic nuclear planning on a criterion—survivable second-strike forces—far less ambitious (and costly) than the combination of counter-silo systems and strategic defenses championed by the Reagan administration.

The reversion to such a strategy—which closely resembles that which prevailed in the 1970s under successive American administrations—would not enable the United States to dispense with the threatened first use of nuclear weapons. That threat will remain of indispensable importance in the deterrence of a massive Soviet assault on western interests; only its maintenance would allow us to dispense with the three war requirement for ground forces championed by the Reagan administration—a requirement well beyond our resources. The reasons for thinking such a threat is credible even under conditions of mutual vulnerability rest not only on the successful experience of deterrence over the last generation but also, and more fundamentally, on the asymmetry of interest (and hence will) that a clash between the two great nuclear powers would involve. Recognizing the necessity of such a threat, to be sure, does not mean that we should abandon the attempt to defend against a Soviet conventional attack in Europe with conventional weapons: the United States should honor the commitment, made in the late 1970s, to have ten divisions and sixty fighter squadrons in Europe ready to fight within ten days of mobilization, and we should try to increase the staying power of these forces. But beyond this it would be inadvisable to go; and under some circumstances—such as a joint Soviet assault against Western Europe, the Persian Gulf, and South Korea—the threat of nuclear escalation will remain unavoidable. To pretend that we would confine our response to a conventional war in all these areas would multiply our dangers.

The rehabilitation of the Nixon Doctrine—with its reliance on American air and naval power and economic and military aid— would also allow for a retrenchment in defense spending. If we retain moderate security objectives in the developing world, seeking primarily to guard against overt aggression by hostile powers, then we may safely rely on the energy any attempted conquest would excite in the threatened peoples, offering our services, in the form of air and naval power and economic and military aid, while also making clear that the primary effort in the way of sacrifice and manpower must be made by those we are aiding. The introduction of American ground forces on a significant scale in virtually any Third World theater, on the other hand, seems certain to be a losing proposition, for such a commitment would afford the enemy the opportunity to strike us at our most vulnerable point—the value we place on the lives of our soldiers. Reductions in active ground forces would not only represent a reconciliation of interest and power more consistent with the disposition of the American people; it would also help reduce the dimensions of the impending manpower crisis—a crisis that would make advisable a reduction in numbers even in the absence of the strategic rationale for doing so presented here. And it would allow the United States to continue devoting substantial resources to areas of our force posture where we continue to enjoy substantial advantages—particularly our air and sea forces.

Especially important in this respect are the capabilities provided by the long-range conventionally armed bomber and the large-deck aircraft carrier. In combination they ought to constitute the main element of our rapid deployment forces. The former is relevant to both Soviet and non-Soviet contingencies; the latter has an operational flexibility and political significance that will continue to be of critical importance in securing our interests in the Third World. Not all aspects of the Navy's shipbuilding program deserve support, to be sure: the most vulnerable elements of it on strategic grounds are the expensive escorts now planned to protect the carrier. Against Third World states, air defense systems of the number and sophistication asked for by the Navy are not necessary. But if we assume a Soviet-American war, it is very doubtful if these systems would justify their cost in comparison with air and ground forces.

The strategy recommended here is thus partly continental, and partly maritime. We are still compelled to accept the primacy of a continental commitment in Europe, and thus a commitment to ground forces, because our objective is to hold territory (which only ground forces can do) and because Europe is still threatened by a potentially hegemonic power and lacks the internal capacity to develop military forces adequate to balance that threat. In the Third World, however, American interests are more limited, and our own power is less necessary in the maintenance of political equilibrium. Here we can afford a more disinterested stance, supporting the weak and opposing the strong, avoiding intervention where possible, while also having the capability of rapidly concentrating our air and sea forces—and our prodigious material weight—against those who mistakenly believe they can undertake overt aggression with impunity.

These changes in national strategy are particularly relevant to the Persian Gulf, the extra-European theater that placed the most demanding requirements on American military forces in the late 1970s and early 1980s. If we are prudent in our energy policy, the military and diplomatic advantages that ensued from the collapse of Persian Gulf oil exports can be extended well into the future, and in a fashion that would do much to overcome our fiscal predicament at home. Nor is this all. The transformation of American strategy in the Persian Gulf would also greatly ease some of the disputes over allied burden sharing that flared up again in the 1980s. The most inequitable feature of the transatlantic (and transpacific) division of labor in the recent past lay in the responsibilities that the United States assumed in the Persian Gulf. The contraction of such responsibilities—rather than the withdrawal of American forces from Europe—ought to be the principal means by which we restore equity in the late 1980s.

These changes would allow us not only to restore solvency to our financial accounts but also to ensure a balance between military power and political commitment. They will not persuade everyone. Those analysts who find the threatened first use of nuclear weapons to have lost all credibility will tell us that such changes would widen the gap between power and interest ever further. And those who cast their eyes about the Third World and count the number of tanks in the possession of powers such as Libya, North Korea, Iraq, Iran, Cuba, Nicaragua, Syria, and North Vietnam will insist that our military capabilities would fall far short of our political commitments. But the analysis that finds the first use of nuclear weapons to have lost all credibility is not persuasive; and the requirement for large ground forces in dealing with the aforementioned list of bad characters is contrary to both the interest of the United States and the disposition of the American people.

★   ★   ★

Whether a disjunction exists today between power and commitment ultimately rests on the view we take of the Soviet Union—on the nature of its intentions toward the West and the rationality (or irrationality) of its elite. If, despite the formidable obstacles we have erected in its path, the Soviet leadership nevertheless undertakes a massive assault against the lineaments of our strength, then we surely are not spending enough on our military forces. Yet the prospect of such an assault is in fact exceedingly remote. The United States now has a long history of dealing with the Russians as an adversary—around forty years worth—and in that time the Russian method has always consisted of a series of small moves and not a single great move. It has been a style of expansion basically at odds with that displayed by Hitler in the 1930s. Arms shipments, propaganda, disinformation, subversion, assassination—these are well-documented Soviet methods. But they all reflect the Soviet proclivity for the indirect approach and an aversion to a direct assault on the citadels of western power. The ruthlessness with which the Soviets have used force in the postwar era, most recently in Afghanistan, should not be confused with recklessness. The Soviets have never used force in the postwar era in circumstances where they thought that western counterintervention was remotely possible. Happily, they do not like the grandstand play, the single stroke that solves all problems in a fortnight (or half an hour). People will find it strange and even perverse to say so, but the truth is that we are fortunate in having an adversary that is of this character. We know from the history of the twentieth century that our fate could have been much worse.

We know also from the history of the twentieth century—indeed, of great power conflict generally—that nuclear weapons might have appeared on the scene at a moment when international politics were bedeviled by some intractable problem that deeply engaged the vital interests of the Great Powers of the day. On this score, too, we have cause to be thankful. For there is nothing comparable today to the kind of standing grievance represented by Slavic nationalism in 1914 or by the Polish corridor in 1939; the two superpowers are not locked in a knot "beyond the ingenuity of man to untie" and that can be broken only by war. Throughout the rimlands of Eurasia, the United States has a settled antagonism with the Soviet Union, but in neither East Asia nor the Persian Gulf nor Europe do there exist conflicts of vital interest comparable to those that produced the two great wars of this century. The spheres of vital interest are, for the most part, readily recognizable, the lines beyond which neither side may pass are clearly drawn. In the hands of a competent statecraft, the clarity of the division can mitigate the operation of the "security dilemma"—that is, the tendency observable in all great power competitions for the fears of one side to have a reinforcing effect on the fears of the other. It can also make of the maxim "to live and let live" a clearly understood and easily observable ethic.

If there is thus every prospect of securing the core, American prospects on the periphery and in the contest for the Third World are not as poor as many have supposed. The rules by which the Great Game is played do not inherently favor the Russians. The United States did poorly at this competition in the 1970s because we ceased to believe that it made any difference and found it rather unseemly in any case, thus shunning the tools that were available to us. That perception was not wholly wrong: the stakes frequently are not all that great; the game is often unseemly. The former fact allows the West to accept a few retreats, so long as the retreats do not gain self-reinforcing momentum (as they did in the late 1970s) and are made up over time by advances elsewhere. The Soviet Union, in truth, has little to offer Third World peoples; if the South succeeds in raising itself from its squalor and misery it will do so through association with the West and in no other way—a truth far more widely appreciated in the Third World in the middle of the 1980s than it was a decade ago.

The prospects for preserving the American position are therefore good. The core is safe; and our position on the periphery can be safeguarded if interest and self-respect so dictate. Only with regard to the nuclear rivalry do we have real grounds for pessimism. The danger lies not in the condition of mutual vulnerability: over the past generation, this condition has reinforced the prudential calculations by which each side found safety in avoiding any great challenges to the vital interests of the other. The future danger, if it comes, will arise from the attempt to transcend this condition. In the form in which this transcendence is sought by the Left, it invites aggression; in the form sought by the Right, it invites a spiral of fears in which each side draws the conclusion that the true intentions of the other are malignant and murderous. Only if we reject both these visions can we find the basis for a durable order, no less solid for being constructed out of the very ambitions and fears that might otherwise produce war.

Notes

1. Walter Lippmann, *U.S. Foreign Policy: Shield of the Republic* (Boston, 1943), 7–8.

2. Ibid., 7–8.

3. See, for example, James R. Schlesinger, 'The Handwriting on the Wall May be a Forgery," *Armed Forces Journal International* (March 1982), 28–77; Edward N. Luttwak, *The Pentagon and the Art of War* (New York, 1985), 256; Jacquelyn K. Davis and Robert L. Pfaltzgraff, Jr., *The Atlantic Alliance and U.S. Global Strategy* (Cambridge, Mass., 1983), 42; Sam Nunn, "The Need to Reshape Military Strategy," in *Nuclear Arms: Ethics, Strategy, Politics,* ed. R. James Woolsey (San Francisco, 1984), 240–242. This view is shared all along the political spectrum, even by traditional isolationists such as Earl Ravenal: "It isn't dim-witted generals and grasping defense contractors (the stuff of current mythology) that are driving up the price of our forces and weapons. It is determined, capable adversaries and the requisites of modern combat." Ravenal, *The FY 1985 Defense Budget* (Washington, D.C. 1984), 11.

4. "When Policy Outstrips Power," *The Public Interest* (Spring 1984), 14. For a similar view of the "strategy-forces mismatch," see Jeffrey Record, *Revising U.S.*

Military Strategy: Tailoring Means to Ends (Washington, D.C., 1984); and Philip Gold, "What the Reserves Can—and Can't—Do," *The Public Interest* (Spring 1984), 47–61.

5. Michael Howard, *Clausewitz* (Oxford, 1983), 34.

6. Bernard Brodie, *War and Politics* (New York, 1973), 159.

7. This was, of course, the prism through which Lippmann, in *U.S. Foreign Policy: Shield of the Republic,* surveyed the whole of American diplomatic history.

8. See Robert W. Tucker, *Nation or Empire: The Debate Over American Foreign Policy* (Baltimore, 1968).

Select Bibliography

Adelman, Kenneth. "Toward a Defense Strategy." *The New York Times,* 10 March 1985.
———. "Arms Control With and Without Agreements." *Foreign Affairs* 63, no. 2 (Winter 1984–85): 240–63.
Albright, David E. "On Eastern Europe: Security Implications for the USSR." *Parameters* 14, no. 2 (Summer 1984): 24–36.
Allison, Graham T., Albert Carnesale, and Joseph Nye, Jr. *Hawks, Doves, and Owls: An Agenda for Avoiding Nuclear War.* New York: Norton, 1985.
Aron, Raymond. *Clausewitz: Philosopher of War.* Translated by Christine Booker and Norman Stone. Englewood Cliffs, N.J.: Prentice-Hall, 1985.
———. "Is Isolationism Possible?" *Commentary* 57, no. 4 (April 1974): 41–46.
———. *Peace and War: A Theory of International Relations.* New York: Praeger, 1967.
Art, Robert J. "Fixing Atlantic Bridges." *Foreign Policy,* no. 46 (Spring 1982): 67–85.

Bailey, Major J. B. A. "The Case for Pre-Placed Field Defenses." *International Defense Review* 7 (1984): 887–92.
Bakhash, Shaul. *The Politics of Oil and Revolution in Iran.* Washington, D.C.: The Brookings Institution, 1982.
Ball, Desmond. *Targeting for Strategic Deterrence.* Adelphi Paper no. 185. London: International Institute of Strategic Studies, 1983.
Barzini, Luigi. *The Europeans.* New York: Simon and Schuster, 1983.
Beaufre, André. *Deterrence and Strategy.* London: Faber and Faber, 1965.
Bell, Daniel. "The End of American Exceptionalism." *The American Commonwealth—1976.* Edited by Irving Kristol and Nathan Glazer. New York: Basic Books, 1976.
———. *The Cultural Contradictions of Capitalism.* New York: Basic Books, 1976.
Betts, Richard K. "Conventional Deterrence: Predictive Uncertainty and Policy Confidence." *World Politics* 35, no. 2 (January 1985): 153–79.
———. "Conventional Forces: What Price Readiness?" *Survival* 25, no. 1 (January–February 1983): 25–34.

―――. *Surprise Attack: Lessons for Defense Planning.* Washington, D.C.: The Brookings Institution, 1982.
Binkin, Martin. *America's Volunteer Military: Progress and Prospects.* Washington, D.C.: The Brookings Institution, 1984.
Blechman, Barry M., ed. *Rethinking the U.S. Strategic Posture.* Cambridge, Mass.: Ballinger, 1982.
Blechman, Barry M., and Steven S. Kaplan. *Force Without War: U.S. Armed Forces as a Political Instrument.* Washington, D.C.: The Brookings Institution, 1978.
Blechman, Barry M., and Edward N. Luttwak, eds. *International Security Yearbook 1984/85.* Boulder, Colo.: Westview Press, 1985.
Bowen, Alva M., and Ronald O'Rourke, "DDG-51 and the Future Surface Navy." *Proceedings of the U.S. Naval Institute* 111, no. 5 (May 1985): 176–89.
Bracken, Paul. "The NATO Defense Problem." *Orbis* 27, no. 1 (Spring 1983): 83–105.
Brennan, Donald. "When the SALT Hit the Fan." *National Review,* 23 June 1972.
Brodie, Bernard. *Escalation and the Nuclear Option.* Princeton: Princeton University Press, 1966.
―――. *Strategy in the Missile Age.* Princeton: Princeton University Press, 1959.
―――. *War and Politics.* New York: Macmillan, 1973.
Brown, Harold. "Is SDI Technically Feasible?" *Foreign Affairs: America and the World 1985* 64, no. 3: 435–54.
―――. "Reagan's Risky Approach." *The New York Times,* 10 March 1985.
―――. "The Strategic Defense Initiative: Defensive Systems and the Strategic Debate." *Survival* 27, no. 2 (March–April 1985): 55–64.
―――. *Thinking About National Security: Defense and Foreign Policy in a Dangerous World.* Boulder, Colo.: Westview Press, 1983.
Brown, Neville. "The Changing Face of Non-Nuclear War." *Survival* 24, no. 5 (September–October 1982): 211–19.
Brzezinski, Zbigniew. *Power and Principle: Memoirs of the National Security Advisor.* New York: Farrar, Straus, and Giroux, 1983.
Budget of the United States Government, Fiscal Year 1984. Washington, D.C.: Government Printing Office, 1983.
Bull, Hedley. "European Self-Reliance and the Reform of NATO." *Foreign Affairs* 61, no. 4 (Spring 1983): 874–92.
Bundy, McGeorge, George F. Kennan, Robert S. McNamara, and Gerald Smith. "Nuclear Weapons and the Atlantic Alliance." *Foreign Affairs* 60, no. 4 (Spring 1982): 753–68.
Burt, Richard. "The Relevance of Arms Control in the 1980s." *Daedalus* 110, no. 1 (Winter 1981): 159–78.
Butterfield, Herbert. "The Tragic Element in Modern International Conflict." In Herbert Butterfield, *History and Human Relations.* London: Collins, 1951.

Canby, Steven. "General Purpose Forces." *International Security Review* 5, no. 3 (Fall 1980): 319–40.

————. "Military Reform and the Art of War." *Survival* 25, no. 3 (May–June 1983): 120–27.

————. "Territorial Defence in Central Europe." *Armed Forces and Society* 7, no. 1 (Fall 1980): 51–67.

Carter, Ashton B., and David N. Schwartz, eds. *Ballistic Missile Defense.* Washington, D.C.: The Brookings Institution, 1984.

Chace, James. *Solvency: The Price of Survival.* New York: Random House, 1981.

Chubin, Shahram. "The Iran-Iraq War and Persian Gulf Security." *International Defense Review* 6 (1984): 705–12.

Clark, Asa A. et al. *The Defense Reform Debate: Issues and Analysis.* Baltimore: Johns Hopkins University Press, 1984.

Clausewitz, Carl von. *On War.* Edited and translated by Michael Howard and Peter Paret. Princeton: Princeton University Press, 1976.

Cockburn, Andrew. *The Threat: Inside the Soviet Military Machine.* Rev. ed. New York: Vintage Books, 1984.

Cohen, Eliot A. *Citizens and Soldiers: The Dilemmas of Military Service.* Ithaca: Cornell University Press, 1985.

————. "Constraints on America's Conduct of Small Wars." *International Security* 9, no. 2 (Fall 1984): 151–81.

————. "The Long Term Crisis of the Alliance." *Foreign Affairs* 61, no. 2 (Winter 1982/83): 325–43.

————. "When Policy Outstrips Power." *The Public Interest,* no. 75 (Spring 1984): 3–19.

Congressional Budget Office. *Naval Surface Combatants in the 1990s: Prospects and Possibilities.* Washington, D.C.: GPO, 1981.

————. *Tactical Combat Forces of the United States Air Force: Issues and Alternatives.* Washington, D.C.: GPO, 1985.

Cordesman, Anthony. *The Gulf and the Search for Strategic Stability.* Boulder, Colo.: Westview Press, 1984.

————. "The NATO Central Region and the Balance of Uncertainty." *Armed Forces Journal International* 120, no. 12 (July 1983): 18–58.

————. "The 'Oil Glut' and the Strategic Importance of the Gulf States." *Armed Forces Journal International* 121, no. 3 (October 1983): 30–47.

Coulam, Robert F. *Illusions of Choice: The F-111 and the Problem of Weapons Acquisition Reform.* Princeton: Princeton University Press, 1977.

Cropsey, Seth. "Women in Combat?" *The Public Interest,* no. 61 (Fall 1980): 58–89.

Danziger, Raphael. "The Persian Gulf Tanker War." *U.S. Naval Institute Proceedings* 111, no. 5 (May 1985): 160–67.

Davis, Jacquelyn K., and Robert L. Pfaltzgraff. *Power Projection and the Long Range Combat Aircraft: Missions, Capabilities and Alternative Designs.* Cambridge, Mass.: Institute for Foreign Policy Analysis, 1981.

————. *The Atlantic Alliance and U.S. Global Strategy.* Cambridge, Mass.: Institute for Foreign Policy Analysis, 1983.

Davis, Lynn Etheridge. *Limited Nuclear Options: Deterrence and the New American Doctrine.* Adelphi Paper no. 121. London: International Institute of Strategic Studies, 1976.

Deitchman, Seymour J. "Turning Point for Tactical Naval Forces?" *Astronautics & Aeronautics* 20, no. 11 (November 1982): 22–33.

———. *Military Power and the Advance of Technology: General Purpose Military Forces for the 1980s and Beyond.* Rev. ed. Boulder, Colo.: Westview Press, 1983.

Deporte, A. W. *Europe Between the Superpowers: The Enduring Balance.* New Haven: Yale University Press, 1979.

Dicker, R. J. L. "RDF Sealift Programs: The Long-term Maritime Prepositioning Force Takes Shape." *International Defense Review* 7 (1983): 956–958.

Doughty, Major Robert A. *The Evolution of US Army Doctrine, 1946–1976.* Leavenworth Paper no. 1. Combat Studies Institute. Fort Leavenworth, Kansas: US Army Command and General Staff College, 1979.

Draper, Theodore. "How Not to Think About Nuclear War." *New York Review of Books* (15 July 1982).

———. "Nuclear Temptations." *New York Review of Books* (19 January 1984).

Dunn, Keith A. "Limits Upon Soviet Military Power." *Journal of the Royal United Services Institute* 124, no. 4 (December 1979): 38–45.

Earle, Edward Mead, ed., with the collaboration of Gordon A. Craig and Felix Gilbert. *Makers of Modern Strategy: Military Thought from Machiavelli to Hitler.* Princeton: Princeton University Press, 1943.

The Economist. "Curing that American Deficit," 15 December 1984.

———. "Labour and the Bomb," 2 April 1983.

———. "OPEC: Grimace and Bear It," 10 December 1983.

———. "The Power Savers," 26 December 1981.

———. "Rapid Deployment Force: Will Europe help America help Europe?" 11 December 1982.

———. "Rearming America." 13 April 1985.

———. "Thank You, Sam." 8 December 1984.

Enthoven, Alain, and Wayne K. Smith. *How Much is Enough?* New York: Harper and Row, 1971.

Epstein, Joshua M. "Horizontal Escalation: Sour Notes of a Recurrent Theme." *International Security* 8, no. 3 (Winter 1983–84): 19–31.

———. "On Conventional Deterrence in Europe: Questions of Soviet Confidence." *Orbis* 26, no. 1 (Spring 1982): 71–86.

———. *Measuring Military Power: The Soviet Air Threat to Europe.* Princeton: Princeton University Press, 1984.

———. "Soviet Vulnerabilities in Iran and the RDF Deterrent." *International Security* 6, no. 2 (Fall 1981): 126–58.

Etzold, Thomas, and John Lewis Gaddis, eds. *Containment: Documents on American Policy and Strategy.* New York: Columbia University Press, 1978.

European Security Study, *Strengthening Conventional Deterrence in Europe: Proposals for the 1980s.* New York: St. Martin's Press, 1983.

Evangelista, Matthew A. "Offense or Defense: A Tale of Two Commissions." *World Policy Journal* 1, no. 1 (Fall 1983): 45–69.

Franssen, Herman T. et al. *World Energy Supply and International Security.* Cambridge, Mass.: Institute for Foreign Policy Analysis, 1983.

Freedman, Lawrence. "Britain: The First Ex-Nuclear Power?" *International Security* 6, no. 2 (Fall 1981): 80–104.

———. *The Evolution of Nuclear Strategy.* New York: St. Martin's Press, 1981.

Friedman, Norman. "The Arleigh Burke—A New Brand of Destroyer." *International Defense Review* 3 (1985): 323–30.

———. *Carrier Air Power.* New York: Rutledge Press, 1981.

———. The Falklands War: Lessons Learned and Mislearned." *Orbis* 26, no. 4 (Winter 1983): 907–40.

Gaddis, John Lewis. "The Rise, Fall, and Future of Detente." *Foreign Affairs* 62, no. 2 (Winter 1983–84): 354–77.

———. *Strategies of Containment: A Critical Appraisal of Postwar American National Security Policy.* New York: Oxford University Press, 1982.

Garnham, David. "Extending Deterrence with German Nuclear Weapons." *International Security* 10, no. 1 (Summer 1985): 96–110.

Gilbert, Felix. *To the Farewell Address: Ideas of Early American Foreign Policy.* Princeton: Princeton University Press, 1961.

Gilpin, Robert. *War and Change in World Politics.* Cambridge: Cambridge University Press, 1981.

Gold, Philip. "What the Reserves Can—and Can't—Do." *The Public Interest,* no. 75 (Spring 1984): 47–61.

Golden, James R. *NATO Burden Sharing: Risks and Opportunities.* The Washington Papers, no. 96. New York: Praeger, 1983.

Gordon, Michael. "The Rapid Deployment Force—Too Large, Too Small or Just Right for its Task?" *The National Journal,* 13 March 1982.

Gray, Colin. *Strategy and the MX.* Washington, D.C.: The Heritage Foundation, 1980.

———. "War Fighting For Deterrence." *Journal of Strategic Studies* 7, no. 1 (March 1984): 5–28.

Gray, J. Glenn. *The Warriors: Reflections on Men in Battle.* New York: Harper and Row, 1970.

Grosser, Alfred. *The Western Alliance: European American Relations Since 1945.* New York: Vintage Books, 1982.

Haffa, Robert P., Jr. *The Half War: Planning U.S. Rapid Deployment Forces to Meet a Limited Contingency, 1960–1983.* Boulder, Colo.: Westview Press, 1984.

Halloran, Richard. "Poised for the Persian Gulf." *The New York Times Magazine,* 1 April 1984.

Hamilton, Andrew. "Redressing the Conventional Balance: NATO's Reserve Military Manpower." *International Security* 10, no. 1 (Summer 1985): 111–136.

Hanning, Lt. Col. Norbert. "The Defense of Central Europe with Conventional Weapons." *International Defense Review* 11 (1981): 1439–1443.

194   SELECT BIBLIOGRAPHY

Hanson, Donald W. "Is Soviet Strategic Doctrine Superior?" *International Security* 7, no. 3 (Winter 1982–83): 61–83.

Hassner, Pierre. "France, Deterrence, and Europe: Rationalizing the Irrational." *International Defense Review* 2 (1984): 133–42.

Heller, Mark, ed. *The Middle East Military Balance.* Tel Aviv, Israel: Jaffee Center for Strategic Studies, 1983, 1984.

———. "Turmoil in the Gulf." *The New Republic,* 23 April 1984.

Herspring, Dale R., and Ivan Volgyes. "Political Reliability in the Eastern European Warsaw Pact Armies." *Armed Forces and Society* 6, no. 2 (Winter 1980): 270–96.

Hinsley, F. H. "The Development of the European States System Since the Eighteenth Century." *Transactions of the Royal Historical Society* (1963): 70–81.

———. *Power and the Pursuit of Peace: Theory and Practice in the History of Relations Between States.* Cambridge: Cambridge University Press, 1967.

Hoffman, Fred S. "The SDI in U.S. Nuclear Strategy." *International Security* 10, no. 1 (Summer 1985): 13–24.

Hollingsworth, Lt. Gen. James F. "The Light Division." *Armed Forces Journal International* 121, no. 3 (October 1983): 84–90.

Hollingsworth, Lt. Gen. James F., and Maj. Gen. Allan T. Wood. "The Light Armored Corps—A Strategic Necessity." *Armed Forces Journal International* 117, no. 7 (January 1980): 20–24.

Holloway, David. "Military Power and Political Purpose in Soviet Policy." *Daedalus* 109, no. 4 (Fall 1980): 13–30.

Holloway, David, and Jane M. O. Sharp, eds. *The Warsaw Pact: Alliance in Transition?* Ithaca: Cornell University Press, 1984.

Howard, Michael. *The Causes of War and Other Essays* Cambridge, Mass.: Harvard University Press, 1983.

———. *The Classical Strategists.* London: International Institute of Strategic Studies, 1968.

———. *Clausewitz.* Oxford: Oxford University Press, 1983.

———. *The Continental Commitment: The Dilemma of British Defence Policy in the Era of the Two World Wars.* London: Temple Smith, 1972.

———. "NATO and the Year of Europe." *Survival* 16, no. 1 (January–February 1974): 21–27.

———. "Reassurance and Deterrence." *Foreign Affairs* 61, no. 2 (Winter 1982–83): 309–24.

Hudson, George E., and Joseph Kruzel. *American Defense Annual 1985–1986.* Lexington, Mass.: Lexington Books, 1985.

Huntington, Samuel P. "Broadening the Strategic Focus: Comments on Michael Howard's Paper." *Defence and Consensus: The Domestic Aspects of Western Security, Part III.* Adelphi Paper no. 184. London: International Institute of Strategic Studies, 1983.

———. *The Common Defense: Strategic Programs in National Politics.* New York: Columbia University Press, 1961.

———. "Conventional Deterrence and Conventional Retaliation in Europe." *International Security* 61, no. 2 (Winter 1983–84): 32–56.

————. "The Defense Policy of the Reagan Administration." An unpublished paper presented at the Woodrow Wilson School of Public and International Affairs, 23 October 1982.

————. "Defense Organization and Military Strategy." *The Public Interest,* no. 75 (Spring 1984): 20–46.

————. *The Soldier and the State: The Theory and Politics of Civil-Military Relations.* Cambridge, Mass.: Harvard University Press, 1957.

Huntington, Samuel P., ed. *The Strategic Imperative: New Policies for American Security.* Cambridge, Mass.: Ballinger, 1982.

Iklé, Fred, "Can Nuclear Deterrence Last Out the Century?" *Foreign Affairs* 51, no. 2 (January 1973): 267–85.

————. "NATO"'s 'First Nuclear Use': A Deepening Trap?" *Strategic Review* 8 No. 1 (Winter 1980): 18–23.

————. "Nuclear Strategy: Can There Be a Happy Ending? *Foreign Affairs* 63, no. 4 (Spring 1985): 810–26.

International Energy Agency. *World Energy Outlook.* Paris: OECD, 1982.

Jastrow, Robert. "Star Wars & the Scientists: Robert Jastrow & Critics." *Commentary* (March 1985), 4–22.

————. "The War Against 'Star Wars.'" *Commentary* (December 1984), 19–25.

Jervis, Robert. *The Illogic of American Nuclear Strategy.* Ithaca: Cornell University Press, 1984.

Joffe, Josef. "The Dreams and the Power: Europe in the Age of Yalta." *Naval War College Review* 36, no. 5 (September–October 1983): 49–60.

————. "Europe's American Pacifier." *Foreign Policy,* no. 54 (Spring 1984): 64–82.

————. "Stability and Its Discontent: Should NATO Go Conventional?" *The Washington Quarterly* 7, no. 4 (Fall 1984): 136–47.

Johnson, A. Ross, Robert W. Dean, and Alexander Alexiev. "The Armies of the Warsaw Pact Northern Tier." *Survival* 23, no. 4 (July–August 1981): 174–82.

Kaplan, Morton A. *A Rationale for NATO.* Washington, D.C.: American Enterprise Institute, 1973.

Karber, Phillip A. "The Strategy: In Defense of Forward Defense." *Armed Forces Journal International* 121, no. 10 (May 1984): 27–50.

Kaufmann, William W. "The Defense Budget." In *Setting National Priorities: the 1982 Budget,* Joseph A. Pechman, ed. Washington, D.C.: The Brookings Institution, 1981.

————. *The Fiscal Year 1986 Defense Budget.* Washington, D.C.: The Brookings Institution, 1985.

————. *The McNamara Strategy.* New York: Harper and Row, 1964.

————. *Planning Conventional Forces: 1950–1980.* Washington, D.C.: The Brookings Institution, 1982.

Kaufmann, William, ed. *Military Policy and National Security.* Princeton: Princeton University Press, 1956.

Keaney, Col. Thomas A. *Strategic Bombers and Conventional Weapons: Airpower Options*. National Security Affairs Monograph, series 84–4. Washington, D.C.: National Defense University, 1984.

Keeny, Spurgeon M., Jr., and Wolfgang K. H. Panofsky. "MAD Versus NUTS: The Mutual Hostage Relationship of the Superpowers." *Foreign Affairs* 60, no. 2 (Winter 1981–82): 287–304.

Kennan, George F. *American Diplomacy, 1900–1950*. Chicago: University of Chicago Press, 1951.

———. *Memoirs 1925–1950*. Boston: Little, Brown, 1967.

Kennedy, Paul M. *The Rise and Fall of British Naval Mastery*. New York: Scribners, 1976.

———. *Strategy and Diplomacy: 1870–1945*. London: Fontana, 1984.

Kissinger, Henry A. "Limited War: Conventional or Nuclear? A Reappraisal." *Daedalus* 89, no. 4 (Fall 1960): 800–17.

———. "A Plan to Reshape NATO." *Time*, 5 March 1984.

———. *White House Years*. Boston: Little, Brown, 1979.

———. *A World Restored: Metternich, Castlereagh, and the Problems of Peace, 1812–1822*. Boston: Houghton Mifflin Co., 1957.

Komer, Robert W. *Maritime Strategy or Coalition Defense?* Cambridge, Mass.: Abt Books, 1984.

———. "Maritime Strategy vs. Coalition Defense." *Foreign Affairs* 60, no. 5 (Summer 1982): 1124–44.

———. "The Rejuvenation of the Seventh Army." *Armed Forces Journal International* 120, no. 10 (May 1983): 54–59.

Krauss, Melvyn. "Prompting Europe to Better Defend Itself." *The Wall Street Journal*, 15 March 1984.

Krauthammer, Charles. "On Nuclear Morality." *Commentary* 76, no. 4 (October 1983): 48–52.

Kristol, Irving. "What's Wrong with NATO?" *The New York Times Magazine*, 25 September 1983.

Kuhn, George W. S. "Department of Defense: Ending Defense Stagnation." *Agenda '83*, Richard N. Holwill, ed. Washington, D.C.: The Heritage Foundation, 1983.

Lacqueur, Walter. "Poland and the Crisis of the Alliance." *The Wall Street Journal*, 5 January 1982.

Lambeth, Benjamin S. *On Threshholds in Soviet Military Thought*. Santa Monica: The Rand Corporation, 1983.

———. *Risk and Uncertainty in Soviet Deliberations About War*. Santa Monica: The Rand Corporation, 1981.

———. *Soviet Strategic Conduct and the Prospects for Stability*. Santa Monica: The Rand Corporation, 1980.

Lambeth, Benjamin S. and Kevin N. Lewis. *Economic Targeting in Modern Warfare*. Santa Monica: The Rand Corporation, 1982.

Lautenschläger, Karl. "Technology and the Evolution of Naval Warfare." *International Security* 8, no. 2 (Fall 1983): 3–51.

Leebaert, Derek, ed. *Soviet Military Thinking*. London: Allen and Unwin, 1981.

Lehman, John. *Aircraft Carriers: The Real Choices.* Washington Paper no. 52. Beverly Hills, Calif.: Sage Publications, 1978.

Lehrman, Lewis, and Gregory A. Fossedal. "How to Decide About Strategic Defense." *National Review,* 31 January 1986, 32–37.

Leighton, Richard M. "The American Arsenal Policy in World War II: A Retrospective View." *Some Pathways in Twentieth Century History: Essays in Honor of Charles Reginald McGrane,* Daniel R. Beaver, ed. Detroit: Wayne State University Press, 1969.

Lellouche, Pierre. *L'Avenir de la Guerre.* Paris: Mazarine, 1985.

―――. "Europe and Her Defense," *Foreign Affairs* 59, no. 4 (Spring 1981): 813–34.

LeMay, Gen. Curtis E. "Non-Nuclear Bomber Forces." *Aviation Week and Space Technology,* 28 May 1984.

Levine, R. et al. *A Survey of NATO Defense Concepts.* Santa Monica: The Rand Corporation, 1982.

Levy, Walter. "Oil and the Decline of the West." *Foreign Affairs* 58, no. 5 (Summer 1980): 999–1015.

―――. "The Years that the Locust Hath Eaten: Oil Policy and OPEC Development Prospects." *Foreign Affairs* 57, no. 2 (Winter 1978–79): 287–305.

Lewy, Guenter. *America in Vietnam.* Oxford: Oxford University Press, 1978.

Liddell Hart, Sir Basil H. *Strategy: The Indirect Approach.* New York: Praeger, 1954.

Lieber, Robert J. "Energy Policy and National Security: Invisible Hand or Guiding Hand?" In Kenneth A. Oye et al., *Eagle Defiant: United States Foreign Policy in the 1980s.* Boston: Little, Brown, 1983.

Lincoln, Abraham. *The Political Thought of Abraham Lincoln,* Richard N. Current, ed. Indianapolis: Bobbs-Merrill, 1967.

Lind, William S. "Is it Time to Sink the Surface Navy?" *Proceedings of the United States Naval Institute* 106, no. 8 (August 1980): 62–67.

Lippmann, Walter. *The Cold War: A Study in U.S. Foreign Policy.* New York: Harper and Row, 1947.

―――. *U.S. Foreign Policy: Shield of the Republic.* Boston: Little, Brown, 1943.

Long, Franklin A. et al. *Weapons in Space.* New York: W. W. Norton, 1986.

Lueck, Thomas J. "Coping with an Oil Cutoff: Persian Gulf's Role Lessened." *New York Times,* 29 February 1984.

Lunn, Simon. *Burden Sharing in NATO.* Chatham House Paper no. 18. London: Routledge and Kegan Paul, 1983.

Luttwak, Edward N. "The American Style of War and the Military Balance." *Survival* 21, no. 2 (March–April 1979): 55–58.

―――. "How Not to Think About Nuclear War." *Commentary* 74, no. 2 (August 1982): 21–28.

―――. *The Grand Strategy of the Soviet Union.* New York: St. Martin's Press, 1983.

―――. *The Pentagon and the Art of War.* New York: Simon and Schuster/Institute for Contemporary Studies, 1984.

Machiavelli, Niccolò. *The Prince and the Discourses*, Max Lerner, ed. New York: Random House Modern Library, 1950.

McNamara, Robert. "The Military Role of Nuclear Weapons: Perceptions and Misperceptions." *Foreign Affairs* 62, no. 1 (Fall 1983): 59–80.

McNaugher, Thomas L. *Arms and Oil: U.S. Military Strategy and the Persian Gulf.* Washington, D.C.: The Brookings Institution, 1985.

Magaziner, Ira, and Robert Reich. *Minding America's Business: The Decline and Rise of the American Economy.* New York: Vintage Books, 1982.

Mako, William P. *U.S. Ground Forces and the Defense of Central Europe.* Washington, D.C.: The Brookings Institution, 1983.

Mandelbaum, Michael. "The Luck of the President." *Foreign Affairs: America and the World 1985* 64, no. 3 (1986): 393–412.

———. *The Nuclear Future.* Ithaca: Cornell University Press, 1983.

———. *The Nuclear Question: The United States and Nuclear Weapons, 1946–1976* (Cambridge: Cambridge University Press, 1979).

Mandelbaum, Michael, ed. *American Military Policy.* New York: Holmes & Meier, forthcoming.

Martin, Laurence. "Changes in American Strategic Doctrine: An Initial Interpretation." *Survival* 16, no. 4 (July–August 1974): 158–64.

———. "Limited Options in European Strategic Thought." In J. Holst and U. Nerlich, eds., *Beyond Nuclear Deterrence.* New York: Crane, Russak, 1977.

Martin, Laurence, ed., *Strategic Thought in the Nuclear Age.* Baltimore: Johns Hopkins University Press, 1979.

Maurer, John H., and Gordon H. McCormick. "Surprise Attack and Conventional Defense in Europe." *Orbis* 27, no. 1 (Spring 1983): 107–26.

Mearsheimer, John J. *Conventional Deterrence.* Ithaca: Cornell University Press, 1983.

———. "Nuclear Weapons and Deterrence in Europe." *International Security* 9, no. 3 (Winter 1984–85): 19–46.

Mossavar-Rahmani, Bijan. "The OPEC Multiplier." *Foreign Policy,* no. 52 (Fall 1983): 136–48.

Myers, Kenneth A. *NATO: The Next Thirty Years.* Boulder, Colo.: Westview Press, 1979.

Nathan, James, and James Oliver. *The Future of U.S. Naval Power.* Bloomington: Indiana University Press, 1979.

Newhouse, John. "The Diplomatic Round: Europe and Star Wars." *The New Yorker,* 22 July 1985.

Nitze, Paul. "The Objectives of Arms Control." *Survival* 27, no. 3 (May–June 1985): 98–107.

Nunn, Sam. "Saving the Alliance." *The Washington Quarterly* 5, no. 3 (Summer 1982): 19–29.

———. "The Need to Reshape Military Strategy." In *Nuclear Arms: Ethics, Strategy, Politics,* R. James Woolsey, ed. San Francisco: Institute for Contemporary Studies, 1984.

Nunn, Sam, and Dewey F Bartlett. *NATO and the New Soviet Threat.* U.S.

Senate, Committee on Armed Services, 95th Congress, 1st Session. Washington, D.C.: GPO, 1977.

Odell, Peter. "An Alternative View of the Outlook for the International Oil Market." *Petroleum Economist* (October 1983): 392–94.
————. *Oil and World Power.* 7th ed. New York: Penguin Books, 1983.
Odell, Peter R., and Kenneth E. Rosing. *The Future of Oil: A Simulation Study of the Inter-relationships of Resources, Reserves, and Use, 1980–2080.* New York: Nichols, 1980.
O'Malley, General Jerome F. *Armed Forces Journal International* 122, no. 6 (January 1985): 71–79.
Osgood, Robert E. *Limited War: The Challenge to American Strategy.* Chicago: Chicago University Press, 1957.

The Pastoral Letter of the U.S. Bishops on War and Peace. "The Challenge of Peace: God's Promise and Our Response." *Origins* 13, no. 1 (19 May 1983).
Peterson, Phillip A., and John G. Hines. "The Conventional Offensive in Soviet Theater Strategy." *Orbis* 27, no. 3 (Fall 1983): 695–739.
Philipp, Udo. "NATO Strategy Under Discussion in Bonn." *International Defense Review* 9 (1980).
Pierre, Andrew J. *The Global Politics of Arms Sales.* Princeton: Princeton University Press, 1982.
Pierre, Andrew J., ed. *Nuclear Weapons in Europe.* New York: Council on Foreign Relations, 1984.
Pipes, Richard. "Why the Soviet Union Thinks It Could Fight and Win a Nuclear War." *Commentary* (July 1977): 21–34.
Posen, Barry R. "Inadvertent Nuclear War? Escalation and NATO's Northern Flank." *International Security* 7, no. 2 (Fall 1982): 28–54.
————. "Measuring the European Conventional Balance: Coping with Uncertainty." *International Security* 9, no. 3 (Winter 1984–85): 47–88.
Posen, Barry R. and Stephen Van Evera. "Defense Policy and the Reagan Administration: Departure from Containment." *International Security* 8, no. 1 (Summer 1983): 3–45.

Quandt, William. *Saudi Arabia's Oil Policy.* Washington, D.C.: The Brookings Institution, 1982.

Radway, Laurence. "Let Europe Be Europe." *World Policy Journal* 1, no. 1 (Fall 1983): 23–43.
Ravenal, Earl. "The Case for Withdrawal of Our Forces." *The New York Times Magazine,* 6 March 1982.
————. "Counterforce and Alliance: The Ultimate Connection." *International Security* 6, no. 4 (Spring 1982): 26–34.
————. "Europe Without America." *Foreign Affairs* 63, no. 5 (Summer 1985): 1020–35.
————. *The Fiscal Year 1985 Defense Budget.* Washington, D.C.: The Cato Institute, 1984.

Record, Jeffrey. "The Europeanization of NATO: A Restructured Commitment for the 1980s." *Air University Review* 33, no. 6 (September–October 1982): 23–28.

———. *Force Reductions in Europe: Starting Over.* Cambridge, Mass.: Institute for Foreign Policy Analysis, 1980.

———. "Jousting With Unreality: Reagan's Military Strategy." *International Security* 8, no. 3 (Winter 1983–84): 3–18.

———. "NATO's Forward Defense and Striking Deep." *Armed Forces Journal International* 121, no. 4 (November 1983): 42–48.

———. *The Rapid Deployment Force and U.S. Military Intervention in the Persian Gulf.* 2nd ed. Cambridge, Mass.: Institute for Foreign Policy Analysis, 1983.

———. *Revising U.S. Military Strategy: Tailoring Means to Ends.* Washington, D.C.: Pergamon-Brassey's, 1984.

———. "A Three War Strategy." *The Washington Post,* 22 March 1982.

Record, Jeffrey, and Robert Hanks. *U.S. Strategy at the Crossroads: Two Views.* Cambridge, Mass.: Institute for Foreign Policy Analysis, 1982.

Reich, Robert. *The Next American Frontier.* New York: Times Books, 1983.

Reichart, John F., and Steven R. Sturm. *American Defense Policy.* 5th ed. Baltimore: Johns Hopkins University Press, 1982.

Report of Secretary of Defense Harold Brown to the Congress on the FY 1982 Budget. . . . Washington, D.C.: GPO, 1981.

Report of Secretary of Defense Caspar W. Weinberger to the Congress on the FY 1983 Budget. . . . Washington, D.C.: GPO, 1982.

Roberts, Adam. *Nation in Arms: The Theory and Practice of Territorial Defense.* New York, 1976).

Rowen, Henry S. "Potholes on the Road to Geneva." *The Wall Street Journal,* 17 December 1984.

Rustow, Dankwart A. *Oil and Turmoil: America Faces OPEC and the Middle East.* New York: W. W. Norton, 1982.

———. "Realignments in the Middle East." *Foreign Affairs: America and the World, 1984* 63, no. 3 (1985): 581–601.

Sagan, Carl. "Nuclear War and the Climatic Catastrophe." *Foreign Affairs* 62, no. 2 (Winter 1983–84): 257–92.

Schelling, Thomas C. "What Went Wrong With Arms Control? *Foreign Affairs* 64, no. 3 (Winter 1985–86): 219–33.

Schemmer, Benjamin F. "Soviet Technological Parity in Europe Undermines NATO's Flexible Response Strategy." *Armed Forces Journal International* 122, no. 10 (May 1984).

Schilling, Warner R. "U.S. Strategic Nuclear Concepts in the 1970s: The Search for Sufficiently Equivalent Countervailing Parity." *International Security* 6, no. 2 (Fall 1981): 49–79.

Schilling, Warner et al., eds. *Strategy, Politics, and Defense Budgets.* New York: Columbia University Press, 1962.

Schlesinger, James R. "The Eagle and the Bear." *Foreign Affairs* 63, no. 5 (Summer 1985): 937–61.

———. "The Handwriting on the Wall May be a Forgery." *Armed Forces Journal International* 119, no. 9 (March 1982): 28–77.

————. "Reagan's Budgetary Dunkirk." *The Washington Post,* 9 September 1981.

————. "Rhetoric and Realities in the Star Wars Debate." *International Security* 10, no. 1 (Summer 1985): 3–12.

Schmidt, Helmut. *Defense or Retaliation?* New York: Praeger, 1962.

Schroeder, Paul W. *The Axis Alliance and Japanese-American Relations, 1941.* Ithaca: Cornell University Press, 1958.

————. "World War I as a Galloping Gertie: A Reply to Joachim Remak." *Journal of Modern History* 44, no. 3 (September 1972): 319–45.

Scowcroft, Brent, ed. *Military Service in the United States.* Englewood Cliffs, N.J.: Prentice-Hall, 1982.

Seib, Gerald F. "Persian Gulf Declines as a Vital Highway for Mideastern Oil." *The Wall Street Journal,* 24 January 1986.

Seigious II, George M., and Jonathan Paul Yates. "Europe's Nuclear Superpowers." *Foreign Policy,* no. 55 (Summer 1984): 40–53.

Serig, Howard W., Jr. "Stretching the Fleet into the 1990s." *Proceedings of the U.S. Naval Institute* 110, no. 5 (May 1984): 164–79.

Shepard, Robert B. "South Africa: The Case for Disengagement." *The National Interest,* no. 2 (Winter 1985–86): 46–57.

Shishko, Robert. *The European Conventional Balance of Power: A Primer.* Santa Monica: The Rand Corporation, 1981.

Sigal, Leon V. *Nuclear Forces in Europe: Enduring Dilemmas, Present Prospects.* Washington, D.C.: The Brookings Institution, 1984.

Singer, S. Fred. "An End to OPEC: Bet on the Market." *Foreign Policy,* no. 45 (Winter 1981–82): 115–21.

————. "Saudi Arabia's Oil Crisis." *Policy Review,* no. 21 (Summer 1982): 87–100.

Slocombe, Walter. "The Countervailing Strategy." *International Security* 5, no. 4 (Spring 1981): 18–27.

Snyder, Jack L. *The Soviet Strategic Culture: Implications for Limited Nuclear Options.* Santa Monica: The Rand Corporation, 1977.

Steinbruner, John D. "Arms Control: Crisis or Compromise." *Foreign Affairs* 63, no. 5 (Summer 1985): 1036–49.

Steinbruner, John D., and Leon V. Sigal, eds. *Alliance Security: NATO and the No-First-Use Question.* Washington, D.C.: The Brookings Institution, 1983.

Stobaugh, Robert, and Daniel Yergin, eds. *Energy Future: Report of the Energy Project at the Harvard Business School.* New York: Ballantine Books, 1980; 3rd ed., New York, Vintage Books, 1983.

Stockman, David A. *The Triumph of Politics: Why the Reagan Revolution Failed.* New York: Harper and Row, 1986.

Taft, Robert, Jr. *White Paper on Defense, 1978 Edition: A Modern Military Strategy for the United States.* The 1978 edition published in cooperation with Senator Gary Hart, prepared with the assistance of Mr. William S. Lind. Washington, D.C., 1978, mimeographed.

Talbott, Strobe. *Deadly Gambits.* New York: Alfred A. Knopf, 1984.

Taylor, Maxwell. *The Uncertain Trumpet.* New York: Harper and Row, 1959.

Taylor, William J., et al. *Defense Manpower Planning: Issues for the 1980s.* New York: Pergamon Press, 1981.

Thurow, Lester. "The Moral Equivalent of Defeat." *Foreign Policy,* no. 42 (Spring 1981): 114–24.

Tillson, J. C. F. "The Forward Defense of Europe." *Military Review* 61, no. 5 (May 1981): 66–76.

Tucker, F. Stanley. "Focus on Pipeline Developments." *Petroleum Economist* (August 1982): 313–15.

Tucker, Robert W., *Nation or Empire: The Debate Over American Foreign Policy.* Baltimore: Johns Hopkins University Press, 1968.

————. *A New Isolationism: Threat or Promise?* Washington, D.C.: Potomoc Associates, 1972.

————. "The Nuclear Debate." *Foreign Affairs* 63, no. 1 (Fall 1984): 1–32.

————. *The Nuclear Debate: Deterrence and the Lapse of Faith.* New York: Holmes & Meier, 1985.

————. "Oil: The Issue of American Intervention." *Commentary* 59, no. 1 (January 1975): 21–31.

————. *The Purposes of American Power: An Essay on National Security.* New York: Praeger, 1981. A Lehrman Institute Book.

Tucker, Robert W., and William Watts, eds. *Beyond Containment: U.S. Foreign Policy in Transition.* Washington, D.C., Potomac Associates, 1973.

Tucker, Robert W., and Linda Wrigley, eds. *The Atlantic Alliance and Its Critics.* New York: Praeger, 1982.

Tucker, Robert W., with commentary by Charles Krauthammer and Kenneth W. Thompson. *Intervention and the Reagan Doctrine.* Ethics and Foreign Policy Lecture Series. New York: Council on Religion and International Affairs, 1985.

Turner, Stansfield. "Thinking About the Future of the Navy." *Proceedings of the United States Naval Institute* 106, no. 8 (August 1980): 66–69.

Turner, Stansfield, and George Thibault. "Preparing for the Unexpected: The Need for a New Military Strategy." *Foreign Affairs* 61, no. 1 (Fall 1982): 122–35.

Tussing, Arlon R. "An OPEC Obituary." *The Public Interest,* no. 70 (Winter 1983): 3–21.

Vigor, P. H. "Doubts and Difficulties Confronting a Would Be Soviet Attacker." *Journal of the Royal United Services Institute* 125, no. 2 (June, 1980): 32–38.

Weigley, Russell F. *The American Way of War: A History of United States Military Strategy and Policy.* Bloomington: Indiana University Press, 1973.

Weiseltier, Leon. *Nuclear War, Nuclear Peace.* New York: Holt, Rinehart and Winston, 1983. A New Republic Book.

Wight, Martin. *Power Politics.* Hedley Bull and Carsten Holbraad, eds. New York: Holmes & Meier, 1979.

Williams, Phil, and William Wallace. "Emerging Technologies and European Security." *Survival* 26, no. 2 (March–April 1984): 70–78.

Wohlstetter, Albert. "Between an Unfree World and None." *Foreign Affairs* 63, no. 5 (Summer 1985): 962–94.

————. "Meeting the Threat in the Persian Gulf." *Survey* 25, no. 2 (Spring 1980): 128–88.

The World Bank. *The Energy Transition in Developing Countries.* Washington, D.C., The World Bank, 1983.

Wright, Christopher C. "U.S. Naval Operations in 1983." *Proceedings of the U.S. Naval Institute* 109, no. 5 (May 1983): 51–57.

Wright, Moorhead, ed. *The Theory and Practice of the Balance of Power: 1486–1914.* Totowa, N.J.: Rowman and Littlefield, 1975.

Yergin, Daniel, and Martin Hillenbrand, eds. *Global Insecurity: A Strategy for Energy and Economic Renewal.* Boston: Houghton Mifflin, 1982.

Zelikow, Philip D., "Force Without War, 1975–82," *Journal of Strategic Studies*, 7, no. 1 (March 1984): 29–54.

Index

ABM treaty, 1972, 128, 140
Adelman, M. A., 107
Afghanistan, 17–18, 28
Africa, 168–69
Air forces, U.S.: and Carter
administration, 151–52; force
structure of, 145–46, 155, 162,
183; and horizontal escalation,
157–59, 162–63; in Korea, 165;
long-range, 163, 164, 167–68;
and NATO, 45, 84n; and Nixon
Doctrine, 148–49, 166–70, 183;
in rapidly deployable forces, 87,
163, 183; relevance of, in Persian
Gulf, 92, 95–99, 102–5; in Third
World, 166–71, 178–80, 183–84;
use of, in Vietnam, 148
Alexander, Clifford, 154
Ali, Muhammad, 171
Amin, Hafizullah, 86
Annihilation, strategy of, 49–51,
119–20, 130–34; Soviet strategy
and, 123; vs. strategy of
attrition, 4, 142n, 182. See also
Strategy, U.S.
Arms control, 137–40
Army, U.S., 14–16, 57, 87; force
structure of, 145–47, 149;
manpower problems of, 16, 154–
55, 156–57, 170, 173–74n, 181,
183; reform of, 170. See also
Ground Forces, U.S.
Aron Raymond, 1, 63
Assured destruction, 119–22

Attrition, strategy of, 56, 66, 119–
22, 130; vs. strategy of
annihilation, 4, 142, 182. See also
Annihilation, strategy of

Balance of power: anatomy of, in
Europe, 47–58, 62–64; and crisis
stability, 132–34; and divide et
impera, 105; in 1970s, 14–26, 56,
154, 180–81; under Reagan, 26–
29, 155, 180–81
Beaufre, André, 63
Bellum justum, 130, 132
Brezhnev, Leonid, 134
Brodie, Bernard, 77, 122, 179
Brown, Harold, 16, 120–21
Burden-sharing, U.S. and Europe,
33–37, 45–56, 58–73, 82–84n,
182–83; and Persian Gulf, 96–98,
109–11, 184–85
Butterfield, Herbert, 124

Canby, Steven, 67, 69, 71
Carter administration, 14–16, 26,
151–55; and All Volunteer Force,
16, 154; cancellation of B-1, 152;
and Carter Doctrine, 46; gap
between doctrine and resources
under, 154–55n, 181; and Nixon
Doctrine, 149, 151–53; response
to crisis in Persian Gulf, 87–88
CENTCOM, 87, 88; and ground
forces in Iran, 95–97. See also